LOS ANGELES

Gil Reavill
Photography by Mark Wexler

GW00726722

Hong Kong

Distribution in the United Kingdom, Ireland, Europe and certain Commonwealth countries by Hodder & Stoughton, Mill Road, Dunton Green, Sevenoaks, Kent TW13 2YA.

British Library Cataloguing-in-Publication Data.
A catalogue record for this book is available from the British Library

Editors: Jamie Jensen, Kit Duane
Series Editor: Kit Duane
Designers: David Hurst, Christopher Burt
Map Designer: Bob Race

Acknowledgements

The author would like to thank the Academy of Motion Picture Arts and Sciences, especially the staff of the Margaret Herrick Library; the staff at the Hollywood Studio Museum, Hollywood Heritage, and the Los Angeles Conservancy; the Frances Goldwyn Regional Branch Library; Forrest Ackerman for his generous help in reviewing the manuscript; Al Goldstein; Manny Neuhaus; Betty Hughes of Universal; Shirley Krims of Warner Brothers; Jeri at Barbara Trister Public Relations; Eric Saks and Nikki; Rich Procter; Jo and Seth Miller; Christopher Burt, Jamie Jensen and Kit Duane at Compass American; and especially Peter Zimmerman for advice and support.

Photographer Mark Wexler wishes to thank Gary Sherwin of the L.A. Convention and Visitors Bureau; Ana Martinez Holler of the Hollywood Chamber of Commerce; J.C. Backings; Beverly Hills Motor Accessories; and College for Cats.

Additional photography supplied courtesy of: Academy of Motion Picture Arts and Sciences 17, 34, 44, 47, 86, 87, 90, 96, 97, 134, 143, 152, 157, 174, 201, 206, 250; L.A. County Natural History Museum 33, 36, 37, 41, 43, 50, 51, 153, 198, 235; Wiltern Theatre, Inc. 200; J. Paul Getty Museum 159, 239; Richard Wyatt 196; Museum of Contemporary Art 193

We also wish to thank A.P. Watt Ltd. on behalf of the Trustees of the Wodehouse Estate for permission to print the P.G. Wodehouse letter on p.101.

Production House: Twin Age Limited, Hong Kong
Printed in Hong Kong

To Sandy and Pamela, who opened the door.
To Jean, who walked through it with me.
And to Maud, who kicked out the jambs.

C O N T E N T S

Literary Excerpts

Sidebars

Maps

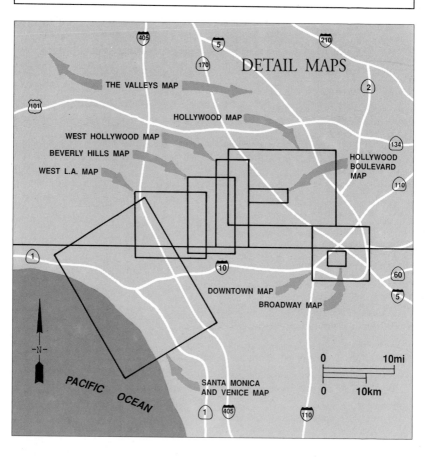

L.A. FACTS

BASICS

	CITY OF LOS ANGELES	LOS ANGELES COUNTY
Year incorporated	1850	1850
Population 1980	2,968,528	7,477,238
Population 1990	3,485,398	8,863,164
Area	467.4 sq mi (1,210 sq km)	4,070 sq mi (10,480 sq km)
Population density (per sq mi)	6,380	2,160

ETHNIC COMPOSITION

	CITY OF LOS ANGELES		LOS ANGELES COUNTY	
white	1,841,200	(50%)	5,035,100	(56%)
black	487,700	(14%)	1,000,000	(11%)
American Indian	16,400	(0.5%)	45,500	(0.5%)
Asian	341,900	(10%)	954,500	(11%)
other*	798,200	(22.5%)	1,828,100	(21.5%)
Hispanic	1,392,400	(40%)	3,351,200	(38%)

THREE L.A. CITIES

	BURBANK		COMPTON		BEVERLY HILLS	
Population	93,600		90,500		31,900	
white	77,300	(82%)	9,600	(11%)	29,200	(91%)
black	1,600	(2%)	49,600	(55%)	500	(2%)
Asian	6,300	(7%)	1,700	(2%)	1,700	(5%)
other*	8,400	(9%)	29,600	(33%)	500	(2%)
Registered voters	19,098	(D)	33,000	(D)	11,300	(D)
	20,800	(R)	1,500	(R)	5,100	(R)
Income per capita	$14,500		$7,000		$36,000	

EARTHQUAKES

Faults: San Andreas Fault 33 mi (50 km) west of downtown L.A.

Last major earthquake: Sylmar Earthquake, February 9, 1971; 6.0 on the Richter scale.

L.A. FILM INDUSTRY

60,000 people employed in movie business provides $4 billion per year to local economy

California has two-thirds of U.S. film starts

L.A. TOURISM

86,000 people employed in tourism industry; provides $5.5 billion to local economy

L.A. SPORTS TEAMS

Football: L.A. Raiders, L.A. Rams
Basketball: L.A. Lakers, L.A. Clippers
Baseball: L.A. Dodgers, California Angels

OTHER FACTS

19 TV stations
88 radio stations
822 hospitals and clinics
11 universities and colleges
1,642 public schools
800 private schools

* "others" declined to indicate race or did not belong to above categories

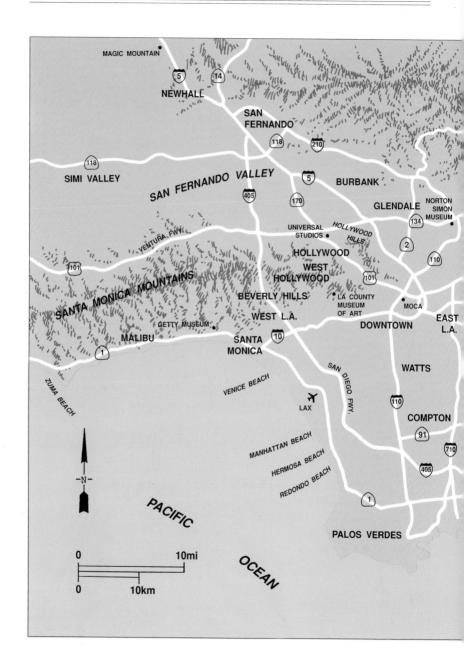

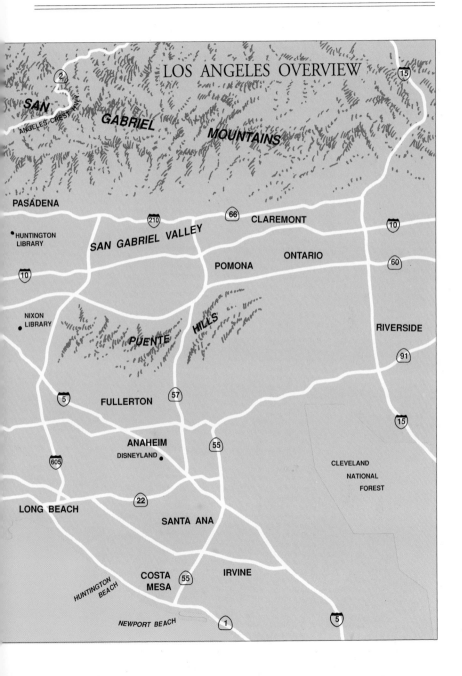

LOS ANGELES OVERVIEW

AUTHOR'S PREFACE

"Hollywood is a town that has to be seen to be disbelieved."
—Walter Winchell

THE DECISION TO APPROACH LOS ANGELES through the lens of Hollywood was easy to make. L.A. and the movies grew up together, and beyond the easy cliché of "Movieland U.S.A." lies a central truth about the place. In the eyes of much of the world, at least, L.A. *is* Hollywood, and vice versa.

But maybe the eyes of the world have been deceived. As soon as I embarked upon the research for this book, I began to have doubts. Could it be done? Could I deliver a guide to Los Angeles that was complete and plenary by focusing on one aspect of the city's famously varied existence? Granted, that single aspect—Hollywood and filmmaking—was L.A.'s most famous facet. But wouldn't I be missing something if I concentrated on the part and not the whole?

What I found during my labors was that in a very real way, Hollywood enlarges and encompasses the vast and variegated city it represents. Every major attraction of Los Angeles, every stop along the tourist trail as well as every undiscovered corner, has been touched by the movies. You go to a heretofore innocuous bank building on Hollywood Boulevard, look up, and suddenly you realize you're looking at Superman's *Daily Planet* launch pad. You go to the Natural History Museum, and you find yourself in the middle of a setting used in *Bonfire of the Vanities*. Even an innocent viaduct of the L.A. River has echoes of hot rods from *Grease*, cyborgs from *The Terminator*, or visions of giant ants from *Them!*

You cannot go anywhere in the sprawling behemoth called "Greater Los Angeles" without encountering some spoor of Hollywood, some shred of filmmaking past or present. By focusing in on the movies, I found I was making some sort of sense out of the impossible, out of what Henry James would have called the "baggy monster" of Los Angeles.

The principle of synecdoche takes the part to symbolize the whole, but the relationship between moviemaking and Los Angeles goes beyond that. Because of Hollywood, because of the movies, Los Angeles has taken on a larger-than-life glow in the minds of visitors to the city—even in the minds of Angelenos

"Sometimes I feel like I left the rainbow back at MGM. And it really wasn't a rainbow at all—just a Hollywood backdrop that some indifferent stagehands had painted." —Judy Garland

themselves. The magic of storytelling—which all the magic of Hollywood is —has elevated L.A. into the world of myth.

I found that when I used the movies to talk about Los Angeles, I was using myth to talk about reality. That's a pretty good way to approach almost anything. Because by investigating the myths of a place (and L.A. has more of them than practically anywhere, thanks to Hollywood), you brush beyond the clutter and background static of the facts to get at the soul of a place.

Los Angeles is a city of myths. I hope this guide uses that idea to good effect, presenting a Los Angeles that is vibrant, entertaining, surprising, and unique.

"I like every damned thing about the place. Palms and brown hills and boulevards and geraniums six feet tall and flowers running riot everywhere and the grand roads and the golfing and the picture people and even the work, grinding as it is. I like it! Why the hell shouldn't I?"

—Katharine Hepburn

Daryl Hannah and her nieces at play.

JOHN WAYNE AIRPORT

I N T R O D U C T I O N
L. A.   T H R O U G H   T H E   M O V I E S

WHEN I FIRST MOVED TO L.A., I WAS TOLD the Hollywood bungalow I stayed in was once the home of Simone Simon, the tempestuous French star of *Cat People* and *The Devil and Daniel Webster.*. She was whispered to be the illegitimate child of William Randolph Hearst and Marion Davies, educated in France and brought to America only after she reached her independence.

Simone Simon. (Academy of Motion Picture Arts and Sciences)

It was also rumored that Simone had a smoldering Gallic sexuality, and that she gave golden keys to all her lovers—keys to the very house in which I was then living. I was especially captivated by this part of the tale, enough so that I found myself poking around the garden of the place, hoping to turn up one of Simone's stray gold keys.

I never found one, and I later found out that the story, like a lot of Hollywood rumors, had about as much truth to it as a truly dry martini has vermouth. But that's just how Hollywood is. Made out of rumors, as if you'd take away the stone and adobe and lumber and plaster-and-lathe with which the town is built and all you'd have left would be swirling, echoing, extremely talkative ghosts. Rumors are the fund on which myth draws, and you would expect a town that's rich in one to be rich in the other.

The difficulty about a guide to Los Angeles, and Hollywood, is that "Hollywood" suffers from a split personality. I'll let Robert Redford explain:

> *H*ollywood is two things. It's a state of mind, and it's a particular location in Los Angeles. Hollywood as a location is pretty grim. I mean, there is really nothing there. And it's certainly nothing to write home about. Probably hasn't been since the early twenties. But as a state of mind it certainly does exist, even more strongly than an actual location. It's the movie business, but the movie business is where you go. If you're in New York making *Mean Streets,* that's where it is. It's definitely a state of mind. As far as being decadent—there is a Babylon quality about it, but that's what it's supposed to be. It's the end of the rainbow, the melting pot, the edge of the continent.

Now Bob, ensconced up in Utah, has a vested interest in saying, "Hollywood is where you want it to be." The thing to remember is this dual nature of Hollywood, the hybrid beast that is part flesh, part smoke. And don't go mistaking one Hollywood for the other.

This book, like almost all books about Hollywood and the movies, is a sorting out of rumor and myth, fact and fallacy. Some writers come down more on the side of the P.R. agent than the research librarian—I've tried not to be one of those. But I hold in reverence the deeper truth embedded in the rumor, the shred of basic human reality encapsulated by the lie. The word "myth," as Joseph Campbell points out, can mean "lie" as well as "all-encompassing truth."

Besides, it is a Sisyphean labor, in this crucible of illusion called Hollywood, to really nail down who did what to whom and where they did it. In their introduction to *Naked Hollywood,* journalist Mel Harris and the immortal voyeur-photographer Weegee stated the quandary well: "The word corroborated by the picture must impart to the book that rare quality of presenting facts as they are—simply, honestly and objectively. We regret that it has failed."

"Facts as they are"—not a bullish commodity in the land of the press agent. It's almost as if Hollywood, the dream factory, is a little afraid of waking truth. When a 1991 BBC documentary, also called *Naked Hollywood,* gave a warts-and-all portrait of several of the industry's most powerful men, at least two of them—*Top Gun* team Don Simpson and Jerry Bruckheimer—managed to have a segment suppressed.

> *"Hollywood is a dreary industrial town controlled by hoodlums of enormous wealth, the ethical sense of a pack of jackals, and taste so degraded that it befouled everything it touched."*
> —*S.J. Perelman*

But a certain chariness with the truth is a characteristic I guess Hollywood shares with many other parts of the world. But people in other parts of the world don't make their living dressing up the truth, burnishing it, gilding it, and making it sing. Movies are, after all, based on illusion in a strictly physical sense, since it is a trick of the eye (technically called "persistence of vision") that makes still images snapping past us at 24-frames-per-second seem to move and take on life. Does all the Hollywood froufrou obscure reality or, through the supremely human endeavor of storytelling, furnish us with a higher one?

A lot is riding on the answer. California has almost two-thirds of the film starts in the nation, with the industry employing over 60,000 people in greater Los Angeles. Filmmaking generates over $4 billion annually for the area economy, money which is recycled and regenerated until it at least partially powers the great economic dynamo of Southern California. In the world marketplace, America may be perceived as fading as a manufacturing giant, but it remains unchallenged in the field of dreams: 55 percent of total global movie revenues, 55 percent of total video and an astounding 75 percent of total global television revenues are generated by the Los Angeles-based American entertainment industry.

So the gold keys are more often than not truly golden, and they've been proliferating around Hollywood since 1913, when Cecil B. De Mille shot *The Squaw Man* in an old barn at Selma and Vine. Selma and Vine is the site of a bank and (inevitably) a parking lot now, but De Mille's barn itself has had a peripatetic history. It was moved to the Paramount lot on Melrose in 1927, used as a library, gym and *Bonanza* set, then trucked to a lot across the street from the Hollywood Bowl in 1979, for its transformation into a movie museum. Hollywood is a moveable feast.

Which may be a good thing, because Hollywood—the city, not the myth—is a bit seedy and decayed today. A massive refurbishing effort has only partially turned the town around. The myth has moved on, leaving the streets haunted and depressing, like a faded silent-movie queen on a bad day. This is a truth that all natives of the place will recognize: Hollywood is no longer Hollywood. The film industry long ago decamped for Burbank and Culver City, with a more radical diaspora continuing to Florida, the Carolinas or even Europe. If anything, the corner of Hollywood and Vine is now simply a place to stand in order to be stripped of your illusions—and possibly your wallet.

Other times it seems as if Hollywood and Los Angeles and the movie industry are all synonymous. Anecdotes abound to illustrate just how much Los Angeles is a company town, but here are three:

- The actor and monologist Spalding Gray was once given a grant to do a performance piece, a series of interviews with people off the street, at the Mark Taper Forum in Los Angeles. The only stipulation was that the interviewees could be in no way involved in the film business. Gray said he had a hard time finding people.

- A local television station once sent out a mini-cam team to pose a simple question to random passersby: "How is your screenplay going?" "How did you know?" was the inevitable reply. Check-out girls, muscle boys, salespeople, and truck drivers all gushed at how close they were to signing the big deal.

- A letter-to-the-editor in the *Los Angeles Times* related the following: A woman is walking down Wilshire in a group of about ten pedestrians (already the story is slightly novel, given the notorious lack of sidewalk traffic in the city). Suddenly, a disembodied voice shouts out, "Rolling!" The pedestrians all immediately stop dead in their tracks. A minute, two minutes go by, with the street scene a frozen tableau. Then the word "Cut!" is heard, and the pedestrians automatically continue on their way.

One reason researching this book was such a dream is that everyone, but everyone, has Hollywood stories, and they're all dying to impart them. Many times, I would simply mention to a stranger what type of book I was writing and it would be like popping a quarter into a slot: the stories would pour out.

But of course these are simply more of the layered illusions of a city famous for them. There are millions of people in Los Angeles who couldn't care less about the pictures, who don't go to them, don't think about them, don't associate them with their personal lives. There are many L.A.s, just as there are many incarnations of all great cities, and some of the most interesting don't have anything to do with Hollywood. The great, dense harbor neighborhoods of San Pedro and Wilmington, for example, where "points up front" and "negative pick-up deals" seem a million miles away.

But these other L.A.s don't have the publicists Hollywood has. For better or worse, Hollywood, Los Angeles, and the movies are wedded in the public mind, along with impossible, mythic equations of glamor, heroism, and triumph over the twin evils of death and time.

The draw has proved irresistible: millions of visitors every year come to Los Angeles to see the places and people associated with the motion picture industry. Many are simply movie fans, playing out a lifelong dream to track the paths of their gods. Others come to Los Angeles not absolutely rabid to see the cement footprints in front of the Chinese Theater, but they wind up seeing them anyway. They're in town on business, say, or to visit Aunt Dorothy, and while they are here they think they'll take in what the town has to offer. One of them may have only the most general interest in movies. Another might have a specific passion, to the point where he'll plough straight past the bungalow where Marilyn Monroe breathed her last to reach the famed "piano staircase" of Laurel and Hardy.

ON SAM GOLDWYN

When he was making *Guys and Dolls*, Sam insisted that Frank Loesser, who'd written the Broadway show, be in residence while the picture was being shot. Frank was a definite night-person. He really couldn't adjust to the regular Goldwyn 9:00 A.M. to 6:00 P.M. routine. And Sam couldn't understand why if *he* put in such a day, Loesser could not.

Anyway, Frank would arrive at the studio around ten, check in, grab the trade papers, and head directly for the Formosa Restaurant, right across the street, and there he would warm himself up with a therapeutic breakfast—a couple of martinis and some ham and eggs. Only then would he be able to cope with Sam and all of his energy. (Goldwyn was then in his early seventies.)

Well, one bright morning Frank arrived. He grabbed his trades and ducked out on the sidewalk, and he ran into me. "C'mon, quick, let's get over to the Formosa," he muttered. "If Sam sees me out here, I'm finished."

We started out across the street to the Formosa. Sam's office looks out on the street, and then I heard his voice, calling out behind us, "Frankie! Frankie!"

"Ignore him," muttered Loesser, and dragged me toward the restaurant.

"Frankie!" persisted Goldwyn. We'd almost gotten to the Formosa doorway, when Sam changed his tune.

"Money, *money!*" he called.

Which broke us both up. "How can you turn *that* down?" groaned Loesser, and he went back to Sam, who was beaming triumphantly from his office window.

—David Golding, Sam Goldwyn's longtime press agent, quoted in *The Wit and Wisdom of Hollywood,* edited by Max Wilk, 1971

Oscar statue stands guard. "Hollywood is a carnival town where there are no concessions."
—Wilson Mizner

I tried to organize this book to answer these varying needs. I encourage you to read the first chapter, on the history of Los Angeles and Hollywood, if only because, like the history of the area itself, it's short and influences all that comes after. But it's not really necessary, especially if what you're really interested in is watching movies or television programs in the process of being made—all that, including Universal Studios, the second biggest draw in L.A. (after Disneyland), is covered under "Attractions and Tours," where you can find out how to have a hands-on (or at least an eyes-on) experience of the motion picture and television industry.

Gertrude Stein's famous mot about Oakland, "there is no there there," is true in reverse for Los Angeles. The city at times seems to be nothing but a vast conglomeration of "theres," and visitors and natives alike can get overwhelmed, lost in the low-density broth. To help you find your way, the bulk of the book is broken down according to geographical areas, and each chapter contains narrative tours of most of what may be of most interest to the visitor. These geographical areas are, like the city itself, vast, and I've suggested strategies to cut down on back-tracking, gas-wasting and rush-hour aggravation. I've also tried to lift out those specific sites which are important to the "myth of Hollywood," which means the book partakes, at least on some level, in the exuberant vulgarity of "the tour of star homes," as well as rounding up all the usual suspects on the tourist trail.

Mostly, it's a book about the pictures. How the movie business descended upon a specific turf and breathed into it a transformation that was half magic, half hype. How first television and then video threatened and transformed mainstream moviemaking. How the attack of the killer B-movies began on the fringes of the industry and was absorbed into its core. All these events have left traces, vestiges, landmarks which draw the film tourist and furnish footnotes for the Hollywood historian.

Through it all, I've kept my eyes peeled for the gold keys to Hollywood, those bits and pieces of the puzzle which somehow lend life to the final portrait. There seems something human, indeed something heroic, in the urge to fantasize, and I wanted this book to communicate some of that. In the end, I can only say with Weegee, "I'm sorry that it has failed."

You will be able to use this book simply as a guide to Los Angeles. Beyond that, I hope you will use it to track the real, secret, vital transformation of Hollywood, the one which made the town into a mecca to begin with. That transformation is not from then to now, not desert to orange grove to metropolis. The real myth of

Hollywood is the breathtaking, vertiginous leap from gawky hopeful to starlet to star, from Esther Blodgett to Vicki Lester, Norma Jean to Marilyn, from Margarita Carmen Dolores Cansino to Hayworth, from Hollywoodland (a housing development) to Hollywood (a state of mind). From rumor, in other words, to myth.

Poor Simone Simon got so fed up with the Hollywood mythmaking machine —which presented her to the public as a moody, mercurial Gaul who walked panthers as pets—that she gave up and went back to France. She had a solid career on stage and in French film before settling down and marrying a baron, a Rothschild from the Austrian branch of the family.

But I remember her well. That's why it was somehow magical that I landed in her old house, up under the "D" in the Hollywood sign, because she was always one of my favorites, for her steamy, evocative appearances in *Cat People* and *Curse of the Cat People*. So, gold keys as love tokens or gold keys as banal gifts, pantherish temptress or French actress just trying to make a living, she remains as we'd all like to remain, outside of time, frozen for eternity, or at least for as long as film stock lasts.

(following pages) Mann's Chinese Theatre is one of L.A.'s de rigueur attractions.

O R I E N T A T I O N

LOS ANGELES IS A PATCHWORK COMMUNITY, grown by accretion and annexation into a sprawling, 450-square-mile (1,165-sq-km) city of 3.5 million people. Add in the total metropolitan area, which includes various distinct cities, such as Beverly Hills and Santa Monica, trapped within the L.A. sprawl, as well as a host of satellite 'burbs, and you are in the largest (in terms of area) urban matrix on earth —over 1,000 square miles (2,500 sq km) in total, with a population approaching ten million.

How to come to terms with this? For such a large expanse, Los Angeles is fairly easy to understand. This is because there are several immediately apparent, and (earthquakes notwithstanding) stationary geographical features, to help you keep your bearings. Wherever you are in L.A., there will be a comforting, looming landform or expanse of ocean against which to orient yourself.

The **Pacific Ocean** is one, giving a convenient western edge to the sprawl. The **Santa Monica Mountains**, which run west to east, are another: if you are in Hollywood, Beverly Hills, or West L.A. the hills will always be to the north. In the Valleys, the collective name for the vast expanse of northern suburbs, the **San Gabriel Mountains** furnish the same kind of unvarying orientation point. To the south, the escarpment of Palos Verdes marks both the sea and the direction.

■ MAJOR AREAS OF LOS ANGELES

Hollywood is known as the center of the movie industry, but it is not the center of Los Angeles. It sits at the base of the **Hollywood Hills,** part of the Santa Monica Mountains which separate the Los Angeles basin from the suburban San Fernando Valley. **West Hollywood,** a recently incorporated city-unto-itself, is located, as its name implies, just west of Hollywood. The next city along, **Beverly Hills,** is perhaps the best known of L.A.'s constituent cities, and marks the beginning of wealthy **West L.A.,** which includes the enclaves of Bel-Air, Westwood, and Century City, as well as a long strip of seafront communities, centered upon Santa Monica and Venice and stretching north to Malibu

At the center of L.A.'s vast sprawl is **downtown,** the historic area first settled by the colonial Spanish now home to the city's corporate elite, whose towering skyscrapers are visible from all over the basin. In **South-Central L.A.,** some of the most poverty-stricken ghettos in the U.S. fill the gap between downtown and the harbor areas around **Long Beach.**

Overlying all this is the vast grid of L.A. **freeways.** Built mostly between the 1930s and 1960s, they are overcrowded but otherwise remarkable people-movers. Without them L.A. would be an undefined, heterogeneous mass; with them, for better or worse, L.A. is the prototypic modern city. For tips on how to negotiate this sometimes bewildering maze, see "Getting Around L.A." in "PRACTICAL INFORMATION" at the end of this book.

THE FREEWAY

*I*n the first hot month of the fall after the summer she left Carter (the summer Carter left her, the summer Carter stopped living in the house in Beverly Hills), Maria drove the freeway. She dressed every morning with a greater sense of purpose than she had felt in some time, a cotton skirt, a jersey, sandals she could kick off when she wanted the touch of the accelerator, and she dressed very fast, running a brush through her hair once or twice and tying it back with a ribbon, for it was essential (to pause was to throw herself into unspeakable peril) that she be on the freeway by ten o'clock. Not somewhere on Hollywood Boulevard, not on her way to the freeway, but actually on the freeway. If she was not she lost the day's rhythm, its precariously imposed momentum. Once she was on the freeway and had maneuvered her way to a fast lane she turned on the radio at high volume and she drove. She drove the San Diego to the Harbor, the Harbor up to the Hollywood, the Hollywood to the Golden State, the Santa Monica, the Santa Ana, the Pasadena, the Ventura. She drove it as a riverman runs a river, every day more attuned to its currents, its deceptions, and just as a riverman feels the pull of the rapids in the lull between sleeping and waking, so Maria lay in the still of Beverly Hills and saw the great signs soar overhead at seventy miles an hour, *Normandie ¼ Vermont ¾ Harbor Fwy 1.* Again and again she returned to an intricate stretch just south of the interchange where successful passage from the Hollywood on to the Harbor required a diagonal move across four lanes of traffic. On the afternoon she finally did it without once braking or once losing the beat on the radio she was exhilarated, and that night slept dreamlessly.

—Joan Didion, *Play It As it Lays,* 1970

A HISTORY OF LOS ANGELES
T H R O U G H   T H E   M O V I E S

THIS IS A GAME OF "LET'S PRETEND." LET'S PRETEND that the only way California schoolteachers had to teach area history was through the use of mainstream Hollywood films. Further, let's pretend that one can actually learn something about real events through such films—always a dangerous proposition, given Hollywood's penchant for mythmaking. I've chosen a dozen movies to illustrate the history of Los Angeles. Some I've used to illustrate broad themes more than specific periods, and some of them are useful only in the degree they show what *not* to believe about a certain period.

■ PRE-TITLE SEQUENCE

Those who follow trends will be pleased to know California has been on the cutting edge of things for millions of years, at least in a geologic sense. The state forms the blade of a continental massif, forced into slow, grinding, inexorable movement against another plate moving in from the Pacific. This tectonic movement is the source of both the San Andreas Fault, 33 miles (50 km) from downtown, and the area's periodic "seismic adjustments," better known as earthquakes.

Given its reputation for histrionics eons later, it shouldn't come as much of a surprise that the area we now know as Los Angeles was born from successive upheavals and recessions of the earth's crust, aided and abetted by a series of spectacular volcanic eruptions.

Los Angeles rose from the sea 160 million years ago, was lost to the shallows once again, and burst forth at last as the result of massive igneous extrusions. The contours of present-day Los Angeles are of relatively recent origin. Six million years ago, Glendale could have been a shore resort. Palos Verdes, now a sentinel on the coast, would have been an island in the Catalina chain. In the Pliocene and the Miocene, carboniferous deposits were laid down that would result in the La Brea tar pits, the doom of countless prehistoric mammals. The same period saw the formation of Signal Hill and other oil fields, dependence on which may yet prove the doom of a more modern era life-form.

Claude Bell designed and built the dinosaurs at a truck stop off Interstate 10.

Geology gives up geography. What finally came of all this slow-motion roiling is a curiously insular country, blocked off from the rest of the continent by natural barriers. To the east, a huge inter-montane desert, the Mojave forms one barrier, while to the north, smaller ripples of the earth's crust run from the sea west to east, forming another. The ocean itself, of course, also represented a natural barrier, but one which would prove the first permeable to the European explorer.

Geographically, the Los Angeles basin is a huge natural-born amphitheater, as if, as D.H. Lawrence noted, "it has turned its back on the world, and looks into the void Pacific." In satellite photos, the area resembles a bulging, mottled happy-face: the long east-west scoop of the San Fernando Valley the forehead, the Santa Monica Mountains the brow, Los Angeles proper the face, its freeway smile bearded by Long Beach and the harbor.

The location work for Southern California was some of the most spectacular on earth, but it happened over such an extended period that it wouldn't make a very good movie. For that, we need human players, and in the full span of geologic time, they were a very late arrival on the scene. Late, but in another sense early, since the first people of California were some of the first human inhabitants of the "New World." Los Angeles Man, whose skeleton was discovered in 1936, is at 7,000 years, among the oldest of human remains found in North America.

■ FIRST INHABITANTS

The first full-length feature film made in Hollywood, *The Squaw Man,* takes as its subject Native Americans, the first permanent residents of Hollywood. Illusion and truth diverge radically in Hollywood right from the start, and the Indians of *The Squaw Man,* Cecil B. De Mille's miscegenist drama, shot in 1913 but released in 1914, are a little bit different. They are Indians of the mythical Hollywood tribe, different from the Native Americans who lived on the semi-arid flats of the Los Angeles basin, and different from the Indians of Wyoming, where the film was largely set. Shot in the favored backlot of early Hollywood, Bronson Canyon (then called Brush Canyon), *The Squaw Man* established early on the tradition of riding roughshod over Native American reality.

The ancestors of the California Indian picked their way across the Bering Strait and spread south, arriving in California some eight millennia ago. Of the tribal groups who eventually settled in the area, the most closely identified with Los

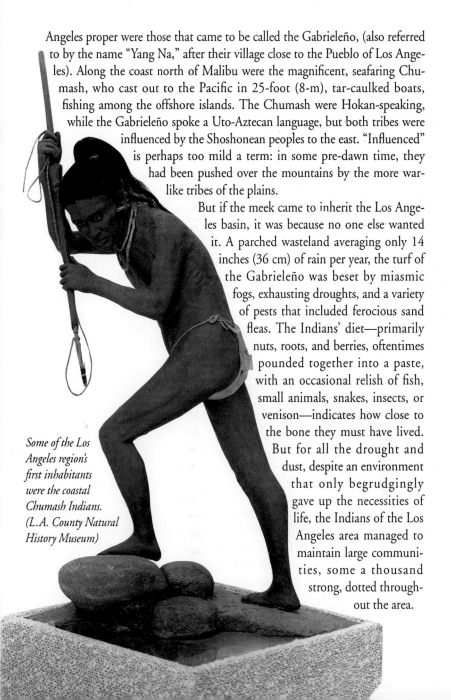

Angeles proper were those that came to be called the Gabrieleño, (also referred to by the name "Yang Na," after their village close to the Pueblo of Los Angeles). Along the coast north of Malibu were the magnificent, seafaring Chumash, who cast out to the Pacific in 25-foot (8-m), tar-caulked boats, fishing among the offshore islands. The Chumash were Hokan-speaking, while the Gabrieleño spoke a Uto-Aztecan language, but both tribes were influenced by the Shoshonean peoples to the east. "Influenced" is perhaps too mild a term: in some pre-dawn time, they had been pushed over the mountains by the more war-like tribes of the plains.

But if the meek came to inherit the Los Angeles basin, it was because no one else wanted it. A parched wasteland averaging only 14 inches (36 cm) of rain per year, the turf of the Gabrieleño was beset by miasmic fogs, exhausting droughts, and a variety of pests that included ferocious sand fleas. The Indians' diet—primarily nuts, roots, and berries, oftentimes pounded together into a paste, with an occasional relish of fish, small animals, snakes, insects, or venison—indicates how close to the bone they must have lived. But for all the drought and dust, despite an environment that only begrudgingly gave up the necessities of life, the Indians of the Los Angeles area managed to maintain large communities, some a thousand strong, dotted throughout the area.

Some of the Los Angeles region's first inhabitants were the coastal Chumash Indians. (L.A. County Natural History Museum)

The Squaw Man, made some three thousand years after the Gabrieleños settled in Los Angeles and a little over three centuries after the arrival of the European, sees none of the subtleties of Native American culture. It was a Western, and as such concerned itself with the adventures of Western Civilization (or the lack of it) in the American West.

Western Civilization is represented in *The Squaw Man* by Captain James Wynnegate (Dustin Farnum), an Englishman who decamps for Wyoming after being wrongly blamed in an embezzlement scheme involving his cousin, the Earl of Kerhill. Upon arrival he has a nasty run-in with Cash Hawkins, a cattle rustler, and saves the Indian maiden Nat-U-Ritch (we-kid-u-not) from the villain's clutches. The maiden, played by Red Wing, returns the favor by nursing the English aristocrat back to health after a sickness.

Wynnegate and Nat-U-Ritch marry and have a son, Hal (Baby Derue). Nat-U-Ritch kills Hawkins, and then kills herself when the sheriff closes in. Wynnegate is retrieved from Wyoming by the woman-he-left-behind, Lady Diana, who has come to tell him that after the death of his evil cousin he is now the Earl of

In 1914, The Squaw Man *was the first feature film produced in the L.A. area. (Academy of Motion Picture Arts and Sciences)*

Kerhill. The odd trio—Lady Diana, Wynnegate, and Hal—leave the New World for the Old, sadder and wiser.

As gaudy melodrama goes, this is great stuff. *The Squaw Man* was quite successful, launching De Mille's directorial career even though he didn't actually direct it (leaving that chore to the more accomplished Oscar C. Apfel), and proving producer Sam Goldwyn's first success. Today, it would seem only a charming curio, except for the fact that the Indians of *The Squaw Man,* rude parodies though they were, were at least accorded the dignity of central roles. Red Wing, as Nat-U-Ritch, has none of the Tonto-sidekick quality that would later become the only way Hollywood would draw an unthreatening Indian.

■ MISSION COLONIAL

Hernando Cortez is said to have named California after a fictional island of the Amazons in a popular fifteenth-century Spanish novel, Garci Ordoñez de Montalvo's *Las Sergas de Esplandián,* "The Exploits of Esplandian." But Cortez never made it to what is now the state of California. It was Juan Rodriguez Cabrillo (more correctly, in his native Portuguese, Joao Cabrilho) who is credited with becoming, in 1542, the first European to set eyes upon what was to be Los Angeles. Gazing landward from the bay at either San Pedro or Santa Monica, Cabrillo struck what in today's smog-locked times seems an ominous note: he called the place *Bahia de los Fumos* ("Bay of the Smokes"), because the brown haze of the Indian fires lay over the landscape. One of the fires no doubt came from the Gabrieleño settlement of Yang Na, on the banks of what would come to be called the Los Angeles River.

Such was the tentative nature of the nascent colonial effort that it was quite some time before Europeans returned to Yang Na. By the mid-eighteenth century, Spain's grip on the New World was threatened by the rumblings of the Russian bear, which was sending down fur traders from Siberia, and by the expansionist English. Baja (lower) California and Alta (upper) California made up New Spain's northernmost flank, and had to be secured. The Iberian plan was to establish a chain of missions and *presidios* (forts), linked by *El Camino Real,* the King's Road, thus solidifying Spain's claim to the area.

In 1769, the Spanish governor of the Californias, Gaspar de Portola, led an exploratory party overland from the south. The Spanish group's diarist, Father

MISSIONS OF LOS ANGELES

Franciscan missions, established in the late eighteenth century under the guidance of Father Junipero Serra, represented the first European presence in California. After a relatively brief heyday, the California missions experienced a long period of decline and neglect. Most of the original 21 have been restored or recreated, and stand today as fascinating touchstones from a time long past.

Two of these missions, San Gabriel Arcangel and San Fernando Rey de España, are located on the outskirts of Los Angeles. There are many myths and historical embroideries which surround the missions, not the least of which is the story that the San Gabriel Mission Indians were subdued by art. According to legend, Father Serra and his *conquistador* escorts were met with native opposition upon their arrival at what was to become San Gabriel. Mission lore says the padres held forth a painting, "Our Lady of Sorrows," which struck the Indian warriors with awe. In a religious miracle, or a simple case of culture shock, they laid down their weapons.

The San Gabriel Mission, founded in 1771, is well worth a visit even though the interiors are closed, since it represents a fine example of the early Spanish Colonial architecture. The church has been restored on the same site as the original, which was constructed by native labor beginning in 1791. The buttressed walls originally supported a magnificent vaulted roof, but the Franciscan architects did not take into account the site's seismic instability, and the roof was almost immediately damaged by an earthquake. The original bell tower also fell to a quake, and in the early 1800s

Mission San Gabriel. (L.A. County Natural History Museum)

the mission was rebuilt with three arched windows and a simple cross.

The impressive cemetery at San Gabriel is perhaps a less comforting symbol of another facet of the California missions—their devastating impact on the indigenous people. The combination of exposure to alien microbes and forced communal living in close quarters was disastrous: over 6,000 natives are buried here, mute testimony of the ravages of disease brought from Europe.

Compared to the San Gabriel Mission, the San Fernando Mission is a much more low-slung affair. Named for King Ferdinand III of Spain, it was sited on the northern slopes of the San Fernando Valley by Father Fermin Lasuén, who succeeded Serra as *presidente* of the mission system. It too was destroyed by earthquakes and restored, and then the restoration was leveled also, in the huge Sylmar quake of 1971. The building here today is a meticulous, reinforced concrete recreation of the original.

The museum and exhibits, in a low palazzo near the church, give a good idea of the lifestyle of the mission fathers, monks, and soldiers, even if they do slight the negative impact the Franciscans had on the local inhabitants. The grounds of the San Fernando Mission, with their graceful gardens, impressive central fountain (copied from an original in Cordova) and magnificent adobe buildings, were also a favorite backdrop of film director D.W. Griffith.

The San Gabriel Mission is located at 537 W. Mission Drive, in the town of San Gabriel, (818) 282-5191. The San Fernando Mission is located at 15151 San Fernando Mission Boulevard in the northern San Fernando Valley, (818) 361-0186. Both missions are open daily 9:30 A.M. to 5 P.M., but last entry is at 4:15 P.M.

Mission San Fernando. (L.A. County Natural History Museum)

Juan Crespi, described their arrival in what's now Los Angeles: "We entered a very spacious valley, well-grown with cottonwoods and alders, among which ran a beautiful river. . . . As soon as we arrived, about eight heathens from a good village (Yang Na) came to visit us; they live in this delightful place among the trees on the river." A sign of things to come: Crespi also noted three earthquakes during his one-night stay. Portola and company went on to found Mission San Gabriel Arcangel, some eight miles (12 km) to the northwest, in 1771. But the Spanish kept the riverside site in mind. A decade later, in 1781, Governor Felipe de Neve sent a group of 44 *vecinos pobladores*, "town settlers" or colonists, back to Yang Na to establish a village.

They were a mixed group, the *pobladores*. Half were children, and in keeping with most of the early history of Los Angeles, several races were represented, with the majority being of mixed Afro-Spanish-Indian descent. They arrived on September 4, 1781, and called their town *El Pueblo de Nuestra Señora la Reina de los Angeles del Río Porciúncula*, after the saint (Our Lady of the Angels of Porciuncula) who had celebrated her jubilee the day before.

While Los Angeles itself was never a mission town, it was the string of 21 missions the Spaniards placed throughout southern and central California that set the tone for the whole of the Spanish colonial period, embracing the next 40 years. Each mission, attached to a military *presidio*, took as its raison d'être the conversion to Christianity of any Native American unfortunate enough to fall within the grasp of the Franciscan monks, headed by Father Junipero Serra.

Serra himself may have had the loftiest of intentions, as did many in his order, but the results for the Native Americans were near genocidal. Syphilis, measles, and other diseases imported from Europe, exacerbated by the fact that "missionized" Indians were forced to live indoors in unsanitary conditions, felled them in droves.

The mission system was a peonage arrangement by which the fathers saved the Indians from Hell and the Indians saved the fathers from hard labor. By the time the missions were secularized under Mexican rule, a whole people had been virtually wiped out. "The brute upshot of missionization," wrote A.L. Kroeber, "in spite of its kindly flavor and humanitarian roots, was only one thing: death."

Curiously, however, through the lens of history, the mission period took on a roseate hue for nineteenth-century Californians. The dialectic was clear: Americans, wrenching California from the grip of the Mexicans, reached back to the Spanish colonial period as a simpler, more civilized time. The Spanish were

European whites who had had a beneficial effect on the Indians. The missions were pastoral outposts of gardens, vineyards, and wheatfields, the white man's first toehold in California.

The great romanticizer of the missions was Helen Hunt Jackson, a woman who, like Father Serra, had the best intentions regarding the Indians. Jackson, an independent writer and activist from Boston, had been hired by the Department of the Interior in 1883 to produce a report on the living conditions of the few mission Indians then left. She did so (with Abbot Kinney, tobacco heir and founder of the beach resort of Venice), but decided what people really needed to get them thinking about the Indians was a big, gripping, three-hanky novel. She would write for the mission Indians the equivalent of *Uncle Tom's Cabin*.

Jackson published *Ramona* in 1884, and it immediately became a sensation. Far from portraying the plight of the Indian as it was, *Ramona* spun a treacle glaze over the whole mission period. It effectively established the missions as archetypes of an earlier, more romantic time. Although the lives of the mestizo Ramona Ortegna and her Indian lover, Alessandro Assis, end in tragedy, Jackson removes their agony to an unreal, romantic plane. Instead of *Uncle Tom's Cabin*, she wrote *Gone With the Wind*. In fact, if there is anything similar to the *Ramona* phenomenon, it is the way in which Margaret Mitchell's epic Southern novel inflamed the imagination of a whole nation, shaping attitudes, biases, and prejudices about the past. On a smaller scale, *Ramona* did for California what *Gone With the Wind* later did for the South.

Both books got the full Hollywood treatment. If *Ramona,* the book, mythologizes the mission period, *Ramona,* the movie, goes one step better and puts a Tinseltown spin on the basic story, abridging, softening, and trivializing the events portrayed until they lose any semblance of truth. Once again, an illusion of the past is preferred to the past itself.

Although the role was originally promised to Rita Hayworth (then Rita Cansino), Ramona is played by a bewigged and somewhat brittle Loretta Young. Raised to think of herself as Spanish, Ramona's brooding Indian side is ignited by Alessandro (Don Ameche), with whom she elopes to a life of hardship and pain. In an excruciating paroxysm of sentiment, their daughter dies after being refused treatment by the mission doctors. Alessandro goes mad and is shot by a cowboy. Ramona and her second daughter are rescued by a rich Spanish rancher, heir to the ranch she grew up on, and the trio endures the fate of a conventional happy ending.

■ RANCHO CALIFORNIA

In the decades before and after Mexican independence in 1822, life in California was not much affected by the upheavals of its rulers. A different flag was raised in the plaza of the Pueblo of Los Angeles when the Mexican representatives arrived, a peaceful transition of power. On the whole, life continued in a slow pastoral parade, as the Southern California countryside became checkerboarded with vast cattle-grazing tracts called *ranchos*.

Almost all cities of the greater Los Angeles area trace their beginnings to *rancho* land. One *poblador* expelled from the Pueblo, Luis Quintero, had a grand-daughter who would inherit Rancho Rodeo de las Aguas ("Meeting of the Waters"), which eventually wound up as Beverly Hills. Rancho San José became the city of Pomona; Whittier was born of the Rancho Paso de Bartolo Viejo; parts of the Malibu *rancho* and the Rancho San Vicente y Santa Mónica make up the modern beachside city of Santa Monica.

In the early 1800s, Los Angeles began to take on the flavor of what it was to remain for much of the century: a cow town. Life on the *ranchos* was tied closely to the rhythms of cattle-raising, with horsemanship prized above all. Tough and ornery longhorn cattle were used not so much for their meat, which was meager and stringy, but for their hides and tallow. The California *ranchos* were self-consciously Spanish (rather than Mexican) in flavor, and it was a point of honor to identify oneself as a "Californio," of the old Spanish families, rather than associate oneself with the new regime.

Despite the encroachment of foreign (chiefly Russian, French, English, and American) influences—the trapper Jedediah Smith made the first overland approach to Los Angeles in 1826—Southern California remained a backward, largely agricultural department of troubled, faraway realms. In 1835, Los Angeles was declared a *ciudad* (city) and made the capital of Alta California, but the Mexican governors continued to prefer the more civilized refinements of Monterey. A year later a census revealed 2,228 souls populating the rowdy, anarchic cow town, including only 230 women, 15 of whom were listed as leading the *mala vida,* "bad life."

It was the world of the *rancho*, with its grand traditions and conflicting loyalties, incipient intrigue and portentous future, that was used as the setting for the swashbuckling romance-and-rapier adventure, *The Mark of Zorro*. Once again, Hollywood goes a long way to portray romance rather than reality, myth rather

"Los Rancheros" by Carlos Nebel. (L.A. County Natural History Museum)

than substance, but the result is so full of light-hearted energy that to quibble over historical details seems petty.

Called *The Californian* until the eve of its release, *The Mark of Zorro* was more than a remake of the 1920 Douglas Fairbanks silent classic (which back then had effectively recharged that actor's career). Director Rouben Mamoulian gave the 1940 *Zorro* a local flavor and adventuresome snap that set the tone for swashbucklers for decades to come.

Set in the waning years of the Spanish colonial empire, the film goes at least some distance to explain why the Spanish were thrown out of Mexico. Diego de Vega (Tyrone Power), a Californian being schooled in duelling, drinking, and haberdashery in Madrid, is summoned home. Saying goodbye, he tells his friends to " . . . think of me in a land of gentle missions, happy peons, sleepy *caballeros,* and everlasting boredom."

Arriving in Los Angeles, he finds his family, *rancho,* and village in the grip of a cruel Spanish *alcalde* (mayor), Don Luis Quintero (evidently screenwriter John

Taintor Foote picked a name at random from history, since "Luis Quintero" was one of the *pobladores* who helped found Los Angeles). Playing the fop by day, Diego disguises himself as the avenger, Zorro, by night, his bravery winning the affections of Lolita (Linda Darnell). With a wit as sharp as his blade, Diego/Zorro deposes the *alcalde* and lives happily ever after with Lolita. He even articulates a version of the American dream: "We'll follow the customs of California . . . . We must marry and raise fat children and watch our vineyards grow."

■ CALIFORNIA AS THE PROMISED LAND

By the mid-nineteenth century, the writing was on the wall in California, and it was not written in Spanish. Unrest at home made it impossible for the Mexican government to consolidate its northern province, and the annexation of Texas by the United States in 1845 foreshadowed California's future. A year later the Mexican governor Pio Pico saw the wave of the future coming, encapsulating his feelings in a famous quote:

> *H*ordes of Yankee emigrants . . . are cultivating farms, establishing vineyards, sawing up lumber, building workshops and doing a thousand things which seem natural to them, but which Californians neglect or despise. What then are we to do? Shall we remain supine, while those daring strangers are overrunning our fertile plains, and gradually outnumbering and displacing us? Shall these incursions go unchecked, until we shall become strangers in our own land?

Two of those daring strangers, Capt. John C. Frémont and Comdr. Robert F. Stockton, engineered the taking of Los Angeles for the United States on April 13, 1846. The Army had to return the next January to put down a rebellion, but from that time forth Los Angeles was an American city, a "gambling, drinking, whoring" city, known for its high murder rate. Just how close to anarchy Los Angeles lived was demonstrated on October 26, 1871, the night of a race-riot which left 19 innocent Chinese dead, and Chinatown looted and burned.

Homicidal and prosperous: the voracious appetites of the gold rushers in the northern part of the state assured a market for Southern California beef, which at one time fetched $435 a head. The *ranchos* boomed as never before. Boomed, and then went bust. A disastrous drought in the 1860s, combined with a changing

Mexican Governor Pio Pico. (L.A. County Natural History Museum)

market and killing confusion over Spanish land titles (fostered by American courts), doomed the *rancho* way of life. Cattle gave way to sheep, as the Civil War created a need for California wool, dyed blue or gray as the occasion demanded.

Later, sheep gave way to wheat, and then to citrus, pears, apples and grapes, truck and grain farms, and the California agricultural miracle took off. Los Angeles became the number one farming county in America, a position it would not relinquish until urban development gobbled up farmlands in the mid-twentieth century. When the railroads linked Los Angeles to the world—to San Francisco in 1871, to the East via the Southern Pacific in 1876 and via the Santa Fe in 1885—all the ingredients were there for a boom.

And boom Los Angeles did, an astonishing, century-long growth spurt that still has not abated. The decades of the 1880s and the 1920s were particularly red-hot —from 1880 to 1890, Los Angeles saw her population increase almost five-fold, and many of her social institutions, newspapers, art and cultural organizations, and civic clubs date from this amazing period.

A common thread runs through this period of Los Angeles history, a thread which stitches up the whole fabric: boosterism. Los Angeles is a created city, and to create something so large and successful you need to spark the imaginations of men—you need mythology. Southern California became an upper-case entity, as a particularly potent form of civic moonshine was distilled. Southern California was sun, land, health. Railroad trains bearing promotional exhibits toured the country, touting the area as earthly paradise.

The boosters of Los Angeles were men like Harrison Gray Otis of the *Los Angeles Times,* Jerome Madden and Charles Nordhoff of the Southern Pacific railroad's publicity office, Henry E. Huntington of Pacific Electric, Lorin Blodget (who invented the study of "climatology" so he could shill L.A.'s sunshine), and the greatest booster of them all, Charles Fletcher Lummis of *Land of Sunshine* and *Out West* magazines. They created a myth of Southern California that surpassed Chicago's "city of broad shoulders" and New York's beacon for immigrants. The booster credo: "Big is Good, Bigger is Better, Biggest is Best."

W.C. Fields's great, gag-filled comedy, *It's a Gift,* perfectly captures the effect all this mythology-making had on the ordinary Joe. Fields, as Harold Bissonnette, buys a Los Angeles orange grove through the mail. Throughout the movie, undergoing a succession of hilarious setbacks and detours, he pursues his dream like the Grail. At the core of the movie's rambunctious, episodic story there remains the basic human urge for a small plot of land, the Edenic dream which Los Angeles boosters played upon mercilessly.

In It's a Gift, *W.C. Fields pursues his dream of owning a Los Angeles orange grove.*
(Academy of Motion Picture Arts and Sciences)

Throughout the decades around the turn of the century they became cliché figures, these Midwestern transplants to Los Angeles. They were from Iowa, Indiana, Missouri ("Pikers" from Pike County), and they were more wealthy than most immigrants, modern-day Grail-seekers. In the 1870s, they came as tourists (a word coined in Southern California), but in the 1880s and for every decade after, they came to stay.

By all accounts, Los Angeles has no business being situated where it is. It has no natural harbor, no water supply, nothing but sunshine. Morris Markey was moved to exclaim, when he saw Los Angeles in 1938, that "here, alone of all the cities of America, there was no plausible answer to the question, 'Why did a town spring up here and why has it grown so big?'" Markey was wrong: there is a reason. Los Angeles had the best P.R. of any city in history.

"I like it out here very much, but it's goddamned far away from everything. It really is like Bridgeport with palm trees, only Bridgeport is greener." —Preston Sturges

■ RISE OF HOLLYWOOD

In the beginning, Hollywood transformed itself in typical Los Angeles fashion. It went from farm to subdivision to town to city in the years from 1887 to 1903, the year it incorporated, with a population of 700. Horace and Daeida Wilcox, owners of the original 200-acre fig and apricot ranch, named the place Hollywood, after the summer home of a woman from Chicago whom Mrs. Wilcox met on the cross-country train. At the turn of the century Hollywood was famous for its grapes, having the greatest concentration of vineyards in the state. It was a sleepy, well-starched, unpaved little community, its Protestant seemliness contrasting with the rowdier precincts of Los Angeles, eight miles (12 km) southeast.

If anything, it was Los Angeles which was keyed into the motion picture craze sweeping the country. In 1902, the city boasted the first auditorium in the country used exclusively as a cinema, the Electric Theater, downtown. Early moviemakers came to the area not only for the sunlight but because it was far away from the East Coast's gangs of roving "patent thugs," hired by Thomas Edison's Kinetoscope Company to enforce its patent on filmmaking equipment. Ironically, Edison, an early bugaboo of Hollywood, is awarded his star on the Hollywood Walk of Fame.

The first feature footage shot in Los Angeles is generally believed to be part of *The Count of Monte Cristo* that Francis Boggs shot from a downtown rooftop in 1907. In 1909, *The Heart of a Racing Tout*, also shot by Boggs for pioneering producer William Selig at a "studio" set up in a Chinese laundry downtown, became the first feature made wholly in Los Angeles (as opposed to Hollywood). Earlier shorts from the area had been more prosaic: one title was "The Pigeon Farm at Los Angeles."

Hollywood resisted the movies, associating them with sin and lower-class wildness. "No dogs or actors," read the sign at the Hollywood Hotel causing Gloria Swanson to grouse, "We didn't even get top billing!" When the moviemakers did come to Hollywood, the town's rampant Puritanism was at least partially to blame. Because the Blondeau Tavern on Sunset and Gower had been closed by local prohibitionists, the Nestor Film Company, late of New Jersey, had a ready-made place to set up shop when it moved west in 1911.

Two years later saw Cecil B. De Mille producing Hollywood's first feature, *The Squaw Man*, in a barn at Vine and Selma. The story has it that De Mille was heading west like a lot of early filmmakers, destined for Flagstaff, Arizona. But when he got off the train there, he didn't like the landscape (it didn't look "Western" enough!), so he continued on to the end of the line: Los Angeles. Over the next few years, Hollywood, the sleepy little conservative community, woke up and found itself HOLLYWOOD, movie capital of the world.

"The business of dreams," as Nathanael West called the film industry, settled into town with a vengeance. Jesse Lasky, Adolph Zukor, Samuel Goldwyn (born Samuel Goldfish), Carl Laemmle, Harry Cohn, the brothers Harry, Albert, Sam, and Jack Warner, Louis B. Mayer—the great studio moguls of Hollywood's first wave were, to a man, Jewish. They were all looking for a low-capital industry that the country's WASP establishment didn't have sewn up. They took over film-making.

By 1924, when Los Angeles moved ahead of San Francisco as the most populous city in the state, the motion picture weekly payroll had ballooned to $1,500,000. With a new style of dream, a new style of dreamer hit Hollywood, movie tourists seeking such star-hallowed sites as Douglas Fairbanks's and Mary Pickford's Pickfair in Beverly Hills, Bar-

"This is a business where people wish you well only if they know you are terminally ill." —former studio head Ned Tanen. Still from A Star is Born. *(Academy of Motion Picture Arts and Sciences)*

bara La Marr's mansion in Whitley Heights, Jack Holt's lodge in Laurel Canyon, William S. Hart's Sunset Boulevard abode, and the sensational Garden of Allah, playground-bungalow-hotel of the sultry Russian actress, Nazimova.

The 1937 version of *A Star Is Born,* written by Dorothy Parker for Warner Brothers, brings to life the incipient excitement of Hollywood and the "business of dreams." The original is more successful at this than either the later more musical 1954 version, with Judy Garland and James Mason, or the bloated star vehicle it became for Barbra Streisand in 1976.

Based on the earlier *What Price Hollywood?*, and one of Technicolor's first great successes, the original *A Star is Born* gives us Janet Gaynor as the waitress-caterer transformed into a star, and Fredric March as her star-Svengali husband headed the other way. One of the delights of the film is the glimpses we get of early Hollywood hot spots, including the Hollywood Bowl, the Trocadero Cafe, and Coconut Grove.

■ GREAT DEPRESSION

Which came first, the paradise or the myth? In so many ways, Los Angeles was blessed with such plenitude that it seemed naturally to justify any hyperbole flung its way. The city's rich petroleum deposits were first developed around the turn of the century by men and women like Edward L. Doheny and one-time piano teacher Emma Summers. The Signal Hill field, near Long Beach, eventually proved to be the most productive concentration of wells on earth.

But there was a dark side to all of this bounty. Union-busting "open shop" policies, made possible by the abundance of cheap labor, kept costs down and allowed Los Angeles to surpass San Francisco as the manufacturing nexus of the state. On October 1, 1910, the anti-union *Los Angeles Times* had its printing plant blown up, very nearly with its publisher, Harry Chandler, inside.

It seemed every element of the myth of sunny Southern California had a shadow dogging its reality. The "health rush" brought hordes of ill and afflicted emigrants seeking the area's revivifying air and sun. But boosterism was no cure for tuberculosis, and the sickly succumbed in droves when the miracle didn't happen. The health rush, ironically enough, gave Los Angeles a cemetery culture second to none.

For the city's burgeoning Hispanic, black, and Asian population, the California dream seemed always to be the restricted property of someone else. And not all the city's business ventures had the Midas touch: in October 1929, a group of businessmen inaugurated the Los Angeles Stock Exchange just days before the markets crashed.

But perhaps the saddest chapter in the California dream is the Dust Bowl migrations of the Great Depression, chronicled by screenwriter Nunnally Johnson's and director John Ford's eloquent cinematic treatment of John Steinbeck's novel *The Grapes of Wrath*. Thousands of displaced farmers from the drought-stricken

Great Plains trudged westward to the Golden State, in a tragic replay of the earlier (and better-financed) Midwestern emigrations. The boosters' promise turned out to be an illusion for the "Oakies," who endured harsh treatment and soul-numbing poverty in the land of plenty. In truth, the excess labor pool thus formed in the Los Angeles area did not get absorbed until the rise of the aircraft and munition industries during World War II.

The saga of the Joads and their California trek gives a tragic spin to Los Angeles's mythmaking. When the family, led by Tom Joad (Henry Fonda) finally struggles to California, they look over the endless orange groves as if they had finally seen the promised land. But their experience there—except for the relative idyll of a public works camp—proves the promise to be a false one.

■ GROWTH AND GREED

Having dreamt the dream of Southern California, the boosters went about making it a reality. Los Angeles had no deep-water harbor, so they built one, a process which pitted San Pedro against Santa Monica, big money against big money. The city had to have water, so the boosters supplied it, whole rivers being diverted and channeled into the mouths and gardens and factories of the thirsty metropolis.

Once again, the sunny daydream of Southern California had an all too human underside. The same boosters who extolled the virtues of Los Angeles sometimes enriched themselves by unsavory means. The process was brilliantly simple: the boosters would purchase parched cropland at dirt-cheap prices, cajole voters into passing bond initiatives to bring water and other city services to it, and then reap the benefits when the land shot up in price.

The San Fernando Valley was a case study of this type of genteel land-swindle in action. At the turn of the century, the Valley was a huge—and quite dusty—ranching district across the Santa Monica Mountains from Los Angeles proper. A group of backers, newspaper publisher Harrison Gray Otis and Harry Chandler, his son-in-law, among them, bought up huge chunks of the Valley, and the *Los Angeles Times* promoted the massive engineering project needed to bring it water.

Superintendent and chief engineer of the municipal water department, William Mulholland, diverted the water of a whole region—the Owens Valley northeast of Los Angeles—into a 233-mile system of aqueducts and reservoirs. On November 5, 1913, the first results gushed into a San Fernando reservoir. "There it is," the laconic Mulholland told the assembled crowd of 40,000, "Take it." Otis and Chandler certainly did, promoting the annexation of the 168 square miles of the San Fernando Valley into the city in 1915, a development historian Kevin Starr identifies as the local equivalent of the Louisiana Purchase.

Chinatown, the great Jack Nicholson–Roman Polanski detective film, takes these events, transposes them to 1937, and lends them both specific human drama and an apocalyptic sense of evil. Although such shady land dealings were typical of Southern California since the time of the Spanish land-title cases, *Chinatown* puts a human face on what would otherwise be stale political headlines ("Titanic Project to Give City a River," read the *Times*).

The movie does seem to slight the suffering of the swindled farmers themselves, hundreds of miles away from Los Angeles. (Mary Austin who lived in the Owens Valley and later became one of California's greatest expatriate writers, testified to the tragedy of the once-fertile farmland being sucked to dust by the water needs of a faraway city.) All told, however, *Chinatown* once again demonstrates that there is another side to the sunshine-and-roses myth of Southern California.

■ CAR CULTURE

In the full light of history, we can finally put a name to the person responsible for Los Angeles's first automobile. He is J. Philip Erie, and on May 30, 1897, he drove his wife and some friends in a "motor wagon" he had built with S. D. Sturgis in a Fifth Street shop. By 1915, the city had over 55,000 automobiles. Other forms of

"There it is. Take it."—William Mulholland at the opening of the L.A. Aqueduct, 1913. (L.A. County Natural History Museum)

transportation blossomed in Los Angeles, also—the world's first air show was held there in 1910—but to an overwhelming (and sometimes unbearable) degree, Southern California culture is car culture.

However difficult it is to imagine modern Los Angeles without the car, there was a time when it managed very well. Even though by late 1800s downtown Los Angeles had become so congested that officials were enforcing a half-hour "parking" limit on horses hitched curbside, wide streets and seemingly limitless amounts of space in which to expand gave the city an open, uncrowded feel.

While Los Angeles was tripling in population in the first decade of the modern century, Henry E. Huntington was building it the greatest mass-transit system in the world. His Pacific Electric Railway eventually boasted over 1,000 miles (1,600 km) of track, with street trolleys attaining the then unheard-of speeds of 40–50 miles per hour (64–80 kph). The interurban ("Red Car") lines connected such far-flung communities as Pasadena and Long Beach with downtown, while the local ("Yellow Car") lines made shorter runs for a nickel fare.

The world's first air show, the Dominguez Air Meet, was held in 1910 near today's L.A. airport. (L.A. County Natural History Museum)

"God set a limit to man's locomotive ambition in the construction of his body. . . .

. . . Man immediately proceeded to discover the means of over-riding the limit."—Mahatma Gandhi

Popular mythology has it that the big auto companies bought the Red Car in order to dismantle it, hoping to promote car consumption. Although this did happen in other communities, the truth is Angelenos did not need much urging to adopt the car as their basic mode of transport. Declining ridership, among other factors, killed the Red Car, which made its last run in 1961.

The automobile's reign really revved up the middle of this century, when the great freeways began to connect (and slice through) the city and its suburbs. The first freeway was called the Arroyo Seco Parkway, now known as the Pasadena Freeway. Inaugurated December 30, 1940, it connected Pasadena with downtown. Los Angeles saw the first gas station in 1912, and the first parking meter in 1949. It also witnessed the first instance of automobile pollution bad enough to need a new word for it: "smog," which came into general use during the mid-forties. September 8, 1943, was called "Black Wednesday," so dense was the soup descended upon the city.

Today, area transportation officials are implementing some of the most stringent anti-pollution statutes ever attempted. Most of these are aimed at cars, but some outlaw seemingly innocuous things like the lighter fluid used in backyard barbecues. Mass transit lines will once again link Long Beach and San Fernando to downtown. The freeways of the next century may actually be silent, host to hordes of quieter, pokier—but cleaner—electric cars.

Who Framed Roger Rabbit?, for all its animated razzle-dazzle, has at the center of its plot the dismantling of the old Red Car system and the coming of the freeways. Judge Doom of Cloverleaf Oil imagines it: "Eight lanes of shimmering cement, running from here to Pasadena, smooth, safe, fast. Traffic jams will be a thing of the past." In other parts of the country, that line might have raised a chuckle, but in Los Angeles theaters, audiences howled in derision.

■ POST-WAR NOIR

If the rest of America slipped into a coma in the fifties, in California the sleep was troubled. On the surface, Southern California presented a stunning realization of the American dream. The area resisted the recessions of the late forties and early fifties, seeming once again to lead a charmed life. Yet another population influx occurred, this one rivaling two previous boom decades, the 1880s and the 1920s, in intensity.

But beneath the sunny, immune, airbrushed surface, the conflicts of human life bubbled away, like the tar in the La Brea pits. The year 1947 saw the great witch-hunts of McCarthyism and the House Un-American Activities Committee, which eventually resulted in the tragedy of the Hollywood blacklist.

The films of the post-war era tend to be careful vehicles of sanitized vision—the "officially approved" version of white, middle-class respectability, where even the married couples slept in twin beds and Hays-code-approved good triumphed over evil. Director-writer Billy Wilder and screenwriter Raymond Chandler, working from a novel by James M. Cain, stripped away this veneer and came up with the great post-war *film noir* thriller, *Double Indemnity*.

In the movie, the Dietrichsons seem the perfect L.A. couple: he a Los Feliz oilman, she an elegant sophisticate living in a beautiful, well-appointed California home. But when Walter Neff (Fred MacMurray) of the All-Risk Insurance Company steps into their life, the brittle portrait begins to crack. Phyllis Dietrichson (Barbara Stanwyck) plots with Neff to kill her husband. In a dizzying shuffle of passions, Neff falls in love with Lola, the Dietrichson daughter. Murder breaks out like a plague. The movie is perhaps the perfect symbol of the staid and starched and overly repressed fifties, when an insurance man comes to lead a double life as a killer.

■ CALIFORNIA DREAMIN'

In a sense, California had been waiting a long time for the sixties to happen. There was a loopy side to Southern California almost from the start, an aspect of it that people came to joke about as "the land of fruits and nuts." Utopian dreamers, religious cultists, and lifestyle faddists seemed to be attracted to the area like bees to nectar.

There are quite a few reasons for this. The scores of invalids who flocked to the area were natural prey for faith-healers and marginal medical practitioners. In philosophy, religion, and politics, the new land was a *tabula rasa*, offering itself to be scribbled upon by whatever self-appointed expert had the temerity to do so. If the East Coast was still somewhat under the sway of Old World thought and practices, California seemed to have slipped the leash entirely. The new age (soon to become capitalized, like Southern California itself) demanded a new man, and many messiahs set about forming him.

William Money ("Bishop Money"), Katherine Tingley ("The Purple Mother"), and Albert Powell Warrington, who established Krotona, the "place of promise" right in the middle of Hollywood, were early theosophy cultists. Aimee Semple McPherson, the Jim and Tammy Bakker of her day all rolled into one, gained a massive following in the twenties with a form of Christian showmanship that was a sign of things to come. In 1926, she endured a sexual scandal that was, alas, also a sign of things to come.

The Mankind United cult was based on communiques from short men with metal heads who lived in the center of the earth. The I AM cult was supposed to shower its followers with gold, jewels, and treasure. A man named Otto Ranisch changed his name to Otoman Bar-Azusht Ra'nish to found the cult of Maz-daz-lan. Nor were all cults religion-based. Technocracy, the Utopian Society, and the EPIC movement were among the political groups born in Los Angeles in the first half of this century, none weirder than the Ham and Eggs Movement, which held out the promise of "$30-Every-Thursday" as a slogan for its followers. The passion of Angelenos for non-traditional social and religious movements seems to have abated only marginally in modern times. Even today, the Scientology cult owns a large section of downtown Hollywood, carrying forward the Krotona heritage.

"It's a mining camp in lotus land." —F. Scott Fitzgerald

Every day's a carnival on the Venice boardwalk.

It was the sea change of the sixties which seemed to forever fix Southern California as the place where social revolutions were welcomed and carried forward. San Francisco may have shouldered the brunt of the Summer of Love, but Los Angeles was right there too.

Strange days indeed. Only a little of this is directly reflected in the action of *Shampoo*, Warren Beatty's portrait of California culture on the eve of the 1968 presidential elections, but the film still warrants a vote as the archetypical look at sixties L.A. Beatty stars as a dithering, love-struck hairdresser, who tucks his blowdryer into his belt as if it were a six-shooter. Julie Christie is equally harebrained (hairbrained?) as a rich man's mistress at the dawn of the sexual revolution. All told, the personal upheavals of the film paint the portrait of a heady, amusing but finally confused decade. An ironic historical note: the Beatty character is loosely based on Jon Peters, who went from Beverly Hills hairdresser to being Barbra Streisand's producer-boyfriend, finally to become, for a while at least, the head of Columbia Pictures.

■ THE ETHNIC MAJORITY

The ethnic history of Los Angeles is one freighted with success and promise, weighted down with frustration and anger. Los Angeles reached a milestone in the 1970s, when whites became a minority for the first time since the 1800s (by the year 2000, they are expected to make up a only third of the population). But the area's political and social transformation have not entirely kept step with the demographic changes: though the city has had a black mayor, Tom Bradley, for the past two decades, it wasn't until 1991 that the first Hispanic took a seat on the Los Angeles County Board of Supervisors.

The city's burgeoning Hispanic population lends Los Angeles a large part of its flavor. Three million Hispanics, making up 35 percent of the area's people, hail from divergent backgrounds. Mexico contributes the major share, while Central and South American nations augment a vibrant, growing community. For example, Los Angeles is the second-largest Guatemalan city in the world, and the second-largest Salvadorean, too.

Olvera Street and the area surrounding the Spanish Pueblo of Los Angeles is the Hispanic focus of the city. The Queen of Angels church on the Old Plaza, built by the Spanish missionaries, has fought a long-running battle with U.S. immigration authorities, against whose officers it has declared itself a sanctuary for illegal aliens. Hispanic artists and musicians from all over the world journey to Los Angeles as a cultural center, and community murals, like those Willie Herron painted in the early 1970s, continue a pictorial tradition that has spread all over the city.

Hollywood, as if recently awakening to the Hispanic presence (and the Hispanic market), produced a spate of films at the end of the last decade which seek to frame the ethnic experience in Los Angeles in cinematic terms. Actually, the Hispanic has a long history in Hollywood, but one which sought to mask rather than feature ethnicity. The career of Rita Hayworth, born Margarita Cansino, is a case in point: in order to make her appear more WASPish, she had two years of painful electrolysis to have her hairline raised, and then had her eyebrows plucked, her hair dyed and her name changed.

Recent films bring the Hispanic in Southern California to center stage. Luis Valdez's *La Bamba*, about the teenage fifties rocker Ritchie Valens (born Richard Valenzuela), shows a whole culture striving to get ahead. About the title song, screenwriter-director Valdez said, "It's about ascending, moving higher and forward," and he could be talking about the Hispanic experience as a whole. *Stand and Deliver*, a semi-documentary about the East L.A. teacher Jaime Escalante (Edward James Olmos), carries this theme to more heroic heights, while *Colors*, the Dennis Hopper drama about warring gangs, shows a darker, more violent side of L.A.'s *barrios*. The 1990 hit *Boyz N the Hood* combined the two themes into one package, tracing the coming-of-age of a group of friends in the predominantly black neighborhoods of South-Central L.A.

■ CONTEMPORARY L.A.

Again and again, 1984, when the Olympic Games were held in Los Angeles, is pointed to as a watershed year for the city's image. Southern California played gracious host to the world, and some of the town's public institutions got a much needed facelift—Los Angeles International Airport, for example, was refurbished. More than a new coat of paint, however, the Olympic summer allowed Los Angeles to take stock of itself.

There had always been a slight tone of defensiveness on the part of Angelenos, especially vis-à-vis New York City. The East Coast was worldly, sophisticated, intellectual, while Los Angeles was trendy, superficial, body-obsessed. Frank Lloyd

Wright's sneer about the area still stung: "It is as if you tipped the United States up, so all the commonplace people slid down there to Southern California."

There was a coming of age in the mid-eighties that rejected this view. The festival of arts held during the Olympiad proved the city resources in this area were second to none. The Mark Taper Forum led a regional theater revival, and the burgeoning "off-Broadway" scene at Hollywood and Vine was so vibrant that the locals didn't mind the explicit comparison to the Great White Way. The Getty Museum in Malibu, the exploding Venice neo-bohemian scene, the revitalized Los Angeles County Museum of Art, all proved that culture was alive and well in Southern California.

It didn't hurt that architecture, music, and film—the traditional leading triumvirate of the Los Angeles scene—remained strong or became even stronger throughout the eighties. Hollywood went on an outrageous roll, culminating in the $250-million-plus grossing *Batman*. There was a whisper on everyone's lips that suddenly Los Angeles, not New York, had become the place to be. Even something as banal and basic as eating contributed its share, with California Cuisine becoming famous the world over.

The Walking Center in Beverly Hills: Who says no one walks in L.A.?

There remains a charming, self-deprecating tone to Southern California, captured by Steve Martin's love poem to the area, *L.A. Story.* The movie's moral—Romance does exist, deep in the heart of L.A.—supplies an antidote to the horror stories of smog, racial tension, and over-development.

Martin rollerskates through his role of Harris K. Telemacher, who has the most unenviable job in the world: that of an L.A. weatherman. Black waiters rap out the menu offerings in restaurants which require bank credit interviews just to get into; sculptured roadside hot-dog stands float in midair; freeway signs give out advice to the lonely and lovelorn.

The L.A. of *L.A. Story* is a phantasmagoric world, much of it silly, but all of it human and therefore somehow endearing. The real star of the movie is Los Angeles itself, a place where the worst thing that can happen is to lock your keys in your car, and where, according to Martin's freeway-sign guru, "Sing Doo Wah Diddy" is the meaning of the universe. But perhaps a truer, deeper sentiment is voiced by Martin's love interest in the film (and his wife in real life) Victoria Tennant. It serves as a fitting summation for the whole history of Los Angeles: "A place where they've taken a desert and turned it into their dreams."

L.A. vs. New York City

In the perennial duke-out between Los Angeles and New York City, the battle has already been decided. That's because New Yorkers are voting with their feet. It has been estimated that every day, 85 New Yorkers move to the greater Los Angeles area —that's one every 17 minutes. To the transplanted New Yorker, we offer this verbal map of L.A., always with the acknowledgment that when you're comparing New York with Los Angeles, you're comparing apples and oranges.

THE NEW YORKER'S MAP OF L.A.

East Village	=	Venice	Astoria	= Culver City
West Village	=	West Hollywood	Harlem	= Watts
Midtown	=	Downtown	South Bronx	= Compton
Wall Street	=	Spring Street	East Harlem	= East L.A.
Central Park	=	Griffith Park	Boat Basin	= Marina del Rey
Upper East Side	=	Beverly Hills	Brooklyn	= Santa Monica
Upper West Side	=	Hollywood Hills	Staten Island	= Long Beach
Garment District	=	Garment Center	Orange County,	= Orange County,
Queens	=	San Fernando	NJ	CA
		Valley	Williamsburg	= Fairfax District

EQUIVALENCIES

L.A.	New York
The Music Center	Lincoln Center
The Forum	Madison Square Garden
Anaheim Stadium	Yankee Stadium
Dodger Stadium	Shea Stadium
Exposition Park	Flushing Fairgrounds
Wiltern Theater	Carnegie Hall
Wiltern Theater	Radio City Music Hall
Century City	Rockefeller Center
Venice Boardwalk	St. Mark's Place
Biltmore Hotel	Waldorf Astoria
Cantor's Deli	Carnegie Deli
Pacific Coast Highway (PCH)	FDR Drive
The Ambassador	The Plaza
Harbor Freeway Interchange	Triborough Bridge

STATS AND FACTS

	L.A.	New York
Population	3,458,400	7,322,600
Greater metropolitan area	13,759,700	18,120,200
Population density per square mile	6,830	23,494
Average age of population	33.9	36.3
Days of sun each year	186	107
Crimes per 100,000 population	9,272	9,667
Number of parks	355	1,701
Number of phone calls daily	42 million	58 million
Fortune 500 headquarters	16	52
Number of visitors per year	27.8 million	25 million
Number of pet cemeteries	3	11

QUOTES

In Hollywood, actors learn to act from watching television.
In New York, people learn to act by walking down the street.
—Sidney Lumet

New York is live, not on tape. I'd rather run a Chock Full O' Nuts in
New York than a studio in Hollywood. At least the talk would be better.
—Mel Brooks

When it's 20 below in New York, it's 78 in L.A. When it's 110 in New York,
it's 78 in L.A. Of course, there are 8 million interesting people
in New York, and only 78 in L.A.
—Neil Simon

New York is a wart-hog from hell.
—Marlon Brando

If New York is the Big Apple, L.A. is the Big Nipple.
—Louis Malle

H O L L Y W O O D

BASED ON THE PHYSICAL EVIDENCE AVAILABLE TODAY, it's difficult to understand just why "Hollywood" is a word that barely needs translation into any of the world's 3,000 languages. Sidewalks and souvenir shops still declare the place to be the entertainment capital of the world, but at first blush there's not much substance to back that claim up.

Paramount Studios—the last remaining major studio within the precincts of Hollywood—is a gated fortress, inaccessible to the average tourist. Hollywood Boulevard is loud and garish but short on real appeal, like a carnival barker whose sideshow has packed up and moved on. Of course, after all the grousing about lack of glamor and downright shabbiness is done with, the Hollywood of today has a vast nostalgic attraction. The place was once a movie stars' heaven, and that makes it a mecca for the fan.

■ HOLLYWOOD AND VINE

There are a few musty "must-sees" in downtown Hollywood, and no better place to begin than the corner of **Hollywood and Vine** itself. Right from the get-go, we run into a minor mystery, since there's little agreement about just how and why the corner came to symbolize Hollywood glamor.

Some say it was because of the **Taft Building**, still standing on the southeast corner, which housed many agents' offices and drew many young acting hopefuls to the vicinity. This was the office building that held the notorious "Hays Office," headquarters of William Hays, for years the chief Hollywood censor. Ronald Reagan beamed his radio show from here, and in the movie, *Earthquake*, we see the Taft collapse—or at least, a model of it.

Others point to the **Equitable Building**, located across the street at the northeast corner of Hollywood and Vine. The Equitable was crammed with glamor during the glory days of Hollywood. Such luminaries as Garbo, Gable, and Loretta Young were in and out of the building because their agents all had offices here. Gable's dentist was here also, and this cements the Equitable's claim to fame: it was here that the most famous false teeth in Hollywood were constructed.

"The people are very strange. They seem to have fronts and no backs.
They're just like the sets." —Brandon de Wilde

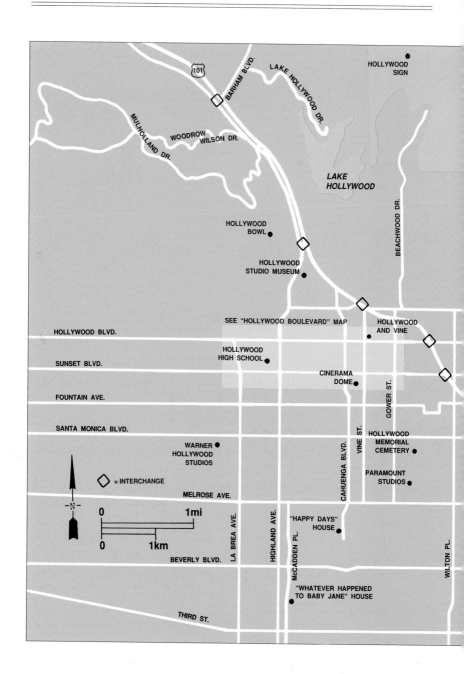

HOLLYWOOD
SIGN

101

BARHAM BLVD.

LAKE HOLLYWOOD DR.

MULHOLLAND DR.

WOODROW WILSON DR.

LAKE HOLLYWOOD

BEACHWOOD DR.

HOLLYWOOD
BOWL

HOLLYWOOD
STUDIO MUSEUM

SEE "HOLLYWOOD BOULEVARD" MAP

HOLLYWOOD
AND VINE

HOLLYWOOD BLVD.

SUNSET BLVD.

HOLLYWOOD
HIGH SCHOOL

CINERAMA
DOME

GOWER ST.

FOUNTAIN AVE.

SANTA MONICA BLVD.

VINE ST.

HOLLYWOOD
MEMORIAL
CEMETERY

WARNER
HOLLYWOOD
STUDIOS

CAHUENGA BLVD.

PARAMOUNT
STUDIOS

◇ = INTERCHANGE

MELROSE AVE.

-N-

0   1mi

0   1km

LA BREA AVE.

HIGHLAND AVE.

"HAPPY DAYS"
HOUSE

McCADDEN PL.

WILTON PL.

BEVERLY BLVD.

"WHATEVER HAPPENED
TO BABY JANE" HOUSE

THIRD ST.

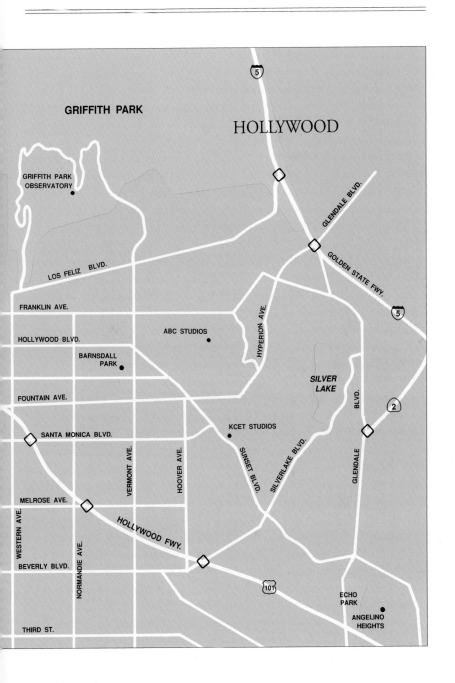

Whatever the provenance of its fame, the intersection today gives up its treasures only haltingly. Among locals, Hollywood and Vine is known for "THE LOOK": the pained bafflement fixed on the faces of tourists who have trekked halfway around the globe to see this spot and once there are unable to understand why. It doesn't help that this section of the **Hollywood Walk of Fame** inexplicably features the names of the Apollo moonshot astronauts.

But there was a day when the Hollywood and Vine area was called "Little Paris," when it was the hub of a radio and movie industry that employed thousands, and the intersection came to symbolize it all. And a symbol it remains, as when director Paul Mazursky staged a cinematic apocalypse in his film, *Alex in Wonderland,* with Donald Sutherland playing a deranged director (Paul Mazursky?) bathing the corner in blood.

East from Hollywood and Vine, the Art Deco riot of the **Pantages Theater** (6233 Hollywood Boulevard) interior is dazzling, but current management has a strict policy of allowing only ticket-holders inside. The Pantages was the site of the Academy Awards ceremonies during the fifties, when Howard Hughes owned it and had his office there. The lobby, lounges, and mezzanines are in superb condition, furnishing a rare look at a surviving thirties movie palace.

North from Hollywood and Vine, there is the **Palace Theater** (1735 N. Vine Street) which as the El Capitan hosted *This Is Your Life* in the fifties, Bing Crosby's *Hollywood Palace* variety show in the late sixties, and *The Merv Griffin Show* in the seventies. Its current incarnation is as a rock'n'roll nightclub. Farther north is the **Capitol Records Building**, built to look like a stack of 45s and sporting a mural of the company's great recording artists on its first story. The Capitol Building has been featured in many films and television shows—it's cinematic shorthand for "we are now in Hollywood." Just down the street, at 1708 N. Vine, is **Collectors Bookstore**, a Hollywood institution and great for books, posters, souvenirs, and photos.

South from Hollywood and Vine, at 1628 N. Vine, is the shuttered hulk of the **Brown Derby**, one of the famous lunch spots back when Hollywood was still Hollywood. This wasn't the one shaped like a hat and visible in *What Price Hollywood?* (that one was and is on Wilshire), but it was the most prominent of the four Brown Derby restaurants run by Herbert Somborn, husband of Gloria Swanson. Cecil B. De Mille was the landlord, and Clark Gable was supposed to have proposed to Carole Lombard here—or was that just P.R.? Closed in 1985 by ownership squabbles, given the coup de grace by fire in 1988, the restaurant tried to revive itself in 1989 on the northwest corner of Hollywood and Vine, where the movie-themed eatery **Premieres** is located. With the initials "B.D." still spelled out on its grillwork doors, the Derby building stands (barely) as mute testimony to a Hollywood that once was.

Across the street, at 1637 N. Vine, is more of the same: the **Plaza**, once a premier Hollywood hotel. It was, for example, the place where neophyte contract player Ronald Reagan stayed when he first arrived in Hollywood from Des Moines. The Plaza was also briefly the site of one of Clara Bow's attempted comebacks, *The It Cafe.* In 1937, however, the "It Girl" no longer had "it," and the club didn't last the year. The Plaza is now an old-age home, an oddly fitting comment on glories past and the fate of many of the area's once-fabled hostelries.

If there is any claim to fame that Hollywood and Vine still has, today it's as a burgeoning Off-Broadway-style theater district. When the Pantages and the **Henry Fonda** (Hollywood and Gower) theaters are lit, they augment the smaller theaters of the area, the **Stella Adler** and the **West Coast Ensemble** (both at Hollywood and Argyle Avenue), the **Ivar** (1605 Ivar Avenue), and the **Theatre Theater** (1715 Cahuenga Boulevard). The **James A. Doolittle** (1615 Vine Street) has the most history to it: as the CBS Playhouse Theater, it hosted Cecil B. De Mille's "Lux Radio Theater" in the thirties and forties.

■ GOWER GULCH

From Hollywood and Vine the tendency is to follow the Walk of Fame west along the Boulevard, but there is a short, worthy side trip down Vine to Sunset and east to Gower Street. Some would argue that this area, bounded by Vine, Selma, and Sunset, is the most historic turf in Hollywood. A misplaced plaque on the northeast corner of Selma and Vine (it should be on the southeast corner) commemorates the fact that it was here that Sam Goldwyn and Jesse Lasky produced the town's first full-length feature, *The Squaw Man.*

The success of that film—plus a merger with Adolph Zukor's Famous Players—allowed Lasky's studio, Feature Play Company, to grow and grow until it ate up the whole block. The company would eventually metamorphose into Paramount, but the studio itself was torn down to make way for a huge broadcasting studio, Radio City, built by NBC. The complex was torn down in 1964 and replaced by a bank and office building and, inevitably, a parking lot.

The bank on the Lasky lot, **Home Savings of America**, gives a spirited corporate nod to the history of the area. On its front facade, diagonally facing the corner of Sunset and Vine, is Millard Sheets's huge mosaic, featuring early Hollywood stars and luminaries. Inside, there is Sheets's mural of *The Squaw Man*, plus a large, movie-themed stained-glass creation by Susan Hertel, called "The Chase." Another corporate spin on Hollywood tradition is given by the **McDonald's** outlet at 1413 N. Vine Street, where the Golden Arches are transformed into Rick's Cafe, from the movie *Casablanca*.

The still-vibrant **Hollywood Palladium**, at 6215 Sunset Boulevard, was the city's premier big-band showcase in the forties, later hosting the bubble-machines of *The Lawrence Welk Show*. Across the street and further down the boulevard is **Aquarius Theater** (at 6230 Sunset), opened in 1938 as a showcase for impresario Earl Carroll's "Most Beautiful Girls in the World." A bronze idealization of beauty still stands in the lobby. Fifties TV fans know it as the Moulin Rouge, the nightclub which hosted the series *Queen for a Day*.

The section of Gower Street extending north and south from Sunset Boulevard used to be known as **Gower Gulch**, due to the large number of small "Poverty Row" studios located there. These churned out B-movie horse operas by the hundreds, and all this action would attract cowboy extras and bit players, who hung about waiting for calls. These few blocks of Gower thus came to resemble a surreal portion of Tombstone, Arizona, lifted up and dropped into Hollywood.

The same block is now occupied by a Gower Gulch shopping center and **Columbia Square**, a CBS facility at 6121 Sunset. It was here that the first "studio" in Hollywood was established, back when Al Christie and David Horsley of the Nestor Film Company rented Blondeau Tavern. Columbia Square was the main CBS studio during the golden age of radio, and two famous duos—Burns and Allen, and Edgar Bergen and Charlie McCarthy—operated from there.

Sunset-Gower Studios (1438 N. Gower Street), kitty-corner from CBS, was through most of its existence the home of Columbia Studios. Here was a Poverty Row studio made good, due to the astute but rapacious business sense of Harry and Jack Cohn. They took over California Studios here in 1927, and soon gobbled up many of the other struggling Poverty Row minors. Almost in spite of themselves, the Cohn brothers made great movies: all of **Frank Capra's** classics came from this studio, although the *Three Stooges* might have been more the demotic Cohns' style. Columbia moved to Burbank in 1972, and has had a peripatetic history since, winding up on a portion of the old MGM lot in Culver City.

Director Tony Scott takes a break.

■ HOLLYWOOD BOULEVARD

In the thirties, a fast, young, hip crowd of people like Cornelius Vanderbilt, Jr. used to call Hollywood Boulevard "**Hollywood Bull**." "The Golden Road, Hardened Artery, Santa Claus Lane, Main Street in Slacks," added gossip columnist Hedda Hopper in 1941. It's fitting that it takes a film as perverse as *Myra Breckenridge* to exploit Hollywood Boulevard to its fullest: man/woman Myron/Myra's waltz down the Walk of Fame opens and closes that jazzy tribute to the glory of the Hollywood dream. The stretch of Hollywood Boulevard between Vine and La Brea is packed thick with movie memories, plus the occasional present-day site you won't need a time warp to appreciate.

Progressing west from Hollywood and Vine, a worthy side trip presents itself immediately. Head up Ivar Avenue, past the faded glory of the **Knickerbocker Hotel** (another retirement home) at 1714 N. Ivar, one of the former grand hotels of Hollywood, erected in 1926. Once temporary home to such luminaries as

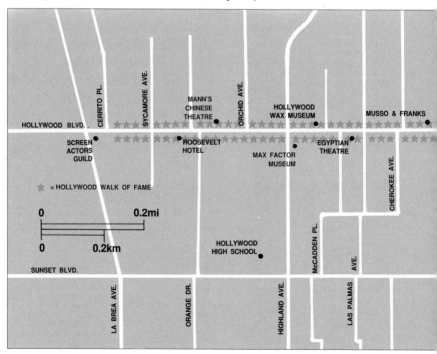

Norma Shearer, Frank Sinatra, Elvis Presley, Bette Davis, and Dick Powell, the Knickerbocker was where **William Faulkner** holed up when he was writing *Absalom, Absalom!* at night and the screenplay for Howard Hawks's *The Road to Glory* during the day.

Farther north, in the curious *quartier perdu* block between Yucca and the Hollywood Freeway, there are two small, oddly named apartment buildings, each with a bit of Hollywood history lingering around them. **Alto Nido**, a blocky white apartment house at 1851 N. Ivar, is where Joe Gillis, the William Holden character in *Sunset Boulevard,* lived before moving into the freakhouse of Norma Desmond. The red brick **Parva Sed-Apta**—the name is Latin for "small but perfect"—at 1817 N. Ivar, is where **Nathanael West** wrote *The Day of the Locust,* one of the finest, certainly the most viciously funny, Hollywood novels ever written. Thus within blocks of each other Faulkner and West committed two of America's literary landmarks to paper, both on innocent Ivar Street.

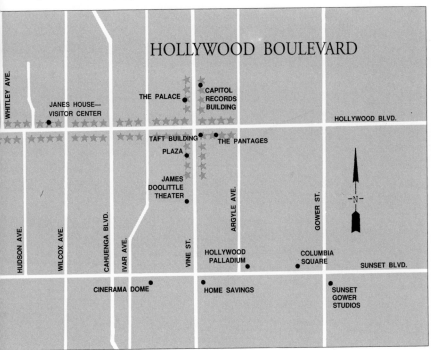

Back on the Boulevard, we pass the **Hollywood Pacific Theatre** (6433 Hollywood Boulevard), unremarkable except for a curious bit of showbiz serendipity. The Hollywood Pacific was originally the Warner Brothers Theater, and a young usherette named Carol Burnett could be said to have gotten her start in show business there. Sure enough, a few decades and a solid Hollywood career later, she would see her star enshrined in the Walk of Fame in front of her old workplace.

On the same side of the street is the charming Victorian **Janes House** (6541 Hollywood Boulevard), utterly out of place in the middle of a mini-mall. Named after three sisters who ran a school on the premises in the early days of Hollywood —children of Cecil B. De Mille, Charlie Chaplin, and Douglas Fairbanks were pupils—the house remained home to the surviving member of the trio as late as the early 1980s. It is now a Visitors Information Center (see "PRACTICAL INFORMATION" for details).

Across the street is **Frederick's of Hollywood** (6608 Hollywood Boulevard), headquarters of a see-through empire. Founded by Frederick Mellinger, the company did a bang-up business selling lingerie to men to give to women—the kind of frilly, outlandish stuff women rarely buy themselves. The garish purple building has a free Lingerie Museum inside, featuring an intimate look at such celebrity unmentionables as Cher's bra, Mae West's peignoir, and Madonna's corset, as well as contributions from Tony Curtis (*Some Like It Hot*) and the king of the TV drag queens, Milton Berle. Down the block at 6644 Hollywood Boulevard is **Larry Edmunds Cinema Bookshop**, the aficionado's first choice not only for film literature but memorabilia as well.

Musso and Frank's (6667 Hollywood Boulevard) is a classic old-style chophouse, the last remaining entertainment industry watering hole in Hollywood. John Musso and Frank Toulet opened their original place in 1919, one door to the west, but it was "enlarged" to its present quarters in 1937. The menu, the decor, even the waiters seem a throwback to an earlier age, backing up the place's claim to be the oldest restaurant in Hollywood. The martinis, at least, seem unchanged from the time in the forties when Musso and Frank's was the rendezvous of literary types like F. Scott Fitzgerald, Ernest Hemingway, and William Faulkner, many of them in town to sell their souls to the studios.

Across the street is the **Egyptian Theatre** (6712 Hollywood Boulevard), which was the predecessor to the Chinese Theatre further down, and one of a string of exotic-themed movie palaces run by impresario Sid Grauman (another was the

The Lingerie Museum at Frederick's of Hollywood is one of many unusual L.A. museums.

AN ARRAY
OF COLOR

1965

1960

1987

Mayan, in downtown Los Angeles). When the Egyptian opened in 1922, showman Sid hired an actor to dress in Roman garb and patrol the theater's ramparts. Somewhat faded today, the Egyptian still boasts unlikely architectural embellishments, such as the huge scarab above the proscenium. After you leave the Egyptian, you might want to bow your head for the passing of the **Montmartre Cafe**, the original in-spot of the twenties movie crowd, formerly located on the second floor of 6763 Hollywood Boulevard.

The best way to gauge if you are ready for the **Hollywood Wax Museum** (6767 Hollywood Boulevard) is to know yourself and your tolerance of kitsch. It's here that Kenneth Anger begins *Hollywood Babylon*, his great catalog of the underbelly of movie culture. Somehow that's fitting, since to visit this somewhat shabby sucker-bin is to make one nostalgic for the days when Hollywood was still a fig ranch. All the usual suspects are rounded up, but some of them are virtually unrecognizable in paraffin: Michael Jackson, Madonna, Marilyn Monroe—in her famous *Seven Year Itch* dress-lifting pose, which finally allows tourists a chance to peek underneath. The museum is also home to a film loop on the Academy Awards, as well as to several non-Hollywood celebrity exhibits, like the Hall of Presidents and the Last Supper.

Highland Avenue and Hollywood Boulevard form one of the busiest intersections on the Boulevard, but its glory is faded today. The northwest corner was once the site of the fabled **Hollywood Hotel**, built at the turn of the century for Easterners wintering in the West, and soon taken over by the film community. Rudolph Valentino performed the tango at the hotel's celebrated Thursday afternoon tea dances, and sparked a scandal when his honeymoon to first wife Jean Acker blew up in a hotel suite in 1919. The Hollywood Hotel was demolished in 1957, and the site is now occupied by a bank.

It was from another bank across the street, **Security Pacific** (6777 Hollywood Boulevard), that television's Superman used to fly off to protect Truth, Justice, and The American Way. Down the street, at 1666 N. Highland, is the **Max Factor Beauty Museum**, a great and kitschy tribute to Hollywood gloss that features make-up memorabilia through the ages, archival celebrity ads, photos, and autographs. "Strip away the phony tinsel in Hollywood and you'll find the real tinsel underneath," Oscar Levant once said, and at Max Factor you'll see the real thing.

The stretch of Hollywood Boulevard from Highland to La Brea finishes off the main Hollywood strip. The blocks yield one landmark—the **Chinese Theatre**, between Orange Drive and Orchid Avenue—and one refreshing blast from the past, the restored **Roosevelt Hotel**, across the street at 7000 Hollywood Boulevard. Along the way, a tip o' the hat to the **El Capitan** (6838 Hollywood Boulevard), built in 1926 as a legitimate theater themed, in the fashion of the day, in East Indian decor and benefiting from a recent facelift sponsored by the Disney Company. The Roosevelt is a real gem, its Spanish colonial interior, refurbished in the mid-eighties, bringing back the plush surroundings of its glory days. In 1929 the Roosevelt was the site of the **first official Academy Awards ceremony**. They were called "Merit Awards" back then, and by all accounts the evening was a flop. The Roosevelt, however, has been a success through most of its existence.

In the lobby mezzanine, an exhibit of movie memorabilia is displayed, showing the breadth of the attachment between the film community and the hotel. Those were the days when Bill "Bojangles" Robinson taught Shirley Temple to tap dance on the lobby staircase, and when Montgomery Clift, in town to star in *From Here to Eternity*, fell in love with the bugle and bugled in the hallways of the Roosevelt at all hours. The Roosevelt's **Cinegrill** is a cabaret with a history, too: it used to be a favorite of Marilyn Monroe—her booth was the darkest one, in the northwest corner. *This Is Your Life* originated from the Cinegrill in the fifties and sixties.

Grauman's Chinese Theatre is now officially known as Mann's Chinese Theatre, after the chain that owns it, but there is a faint air of impresario Sid Grauman's promotional savvy still hanging about the place. Grauman was a wheeler-dealer who got others to build his movie palaces, then give him long-term leases. He had this one built in 1927, and gave it an ornamental chinoiserie decor which lasts—a little faded, a little cracked—to this day. If you're buying a ticket to see the interior, be sure the movie is in the main theater, not the uninteresting twins added in 1980. You can also join a **Starline Tour**, which has the run of the place every forenoon, before the shows open. Finally, you can rent *Fade to Black,* a film which features the Chinese Theatre, a great Marilyn Monroe look-alike named Linda Keridge, and a murderous film buff.

Exactly how and why the theater's courtyard became full of cement footprints is the stuff of myth. Did silent star Norma Talmadge "accidentally" step in cement on her way into the theater? Did Sid step in the muck himself? Press agent folderol. Here's the real story: Grauman came upon stone mason Jean Klossner as he laid the cement in the Chinese Theatre courtyard. The French workman was putting his handprint in the cement, a sign for posterity, he explained, that his French ancestors had made when they built Notre Dame cathedral.

HOLLYWOOD WALK OF FAME

All of us are in the gutter, but some of us are looking up at the stars.

—Oscar Wilde

The **Hollywood Walk of Fame**, a series of star-shaped brass plaques embedded in the sidewalk, is the nearest Hollywood comes to an official Hall of Fame. Extending for a block north, east, and south, and for a dozen blocks west, from the corner of Hollywood and Vine, this celebrated but finally baffling promotional device is sponsored by the Hollywood Chamber of Commerce. Perhaps sponsored is too strong a term: the stars pay for their "stars" at the rate of $3,500, while the Chamber of Commerce oversees the process and runs the screening committee.

There are 2,518 stars in all, of which 1,935 have been engraved with names of the stars, leaving enough blanks to last well into the next century if they are filled at their present rate. The categories are motion pictures, television, recording, radio, and theater, with Gene Autry being the only "five-star" star (6384, 6520, 6644, 6667, and 7000 Hollywood Boulevard).

Rin Tin Tin, the dog whose films saved Warner Brothers from bankruptcy in the twenties, rates a star (1627 N. Vine Street), but not King Kong (rejected by the nominating committee in 1986). Mickey Mouse (6925 Hollywood Boulevard) and Snow White (6910 Hollywood Boulevard) both have stars, but not Donald Duck. The Beatles don't have one, but the Beach Boys do (at Sunset and Vine). Other unstarred worthies include Paul Newman, Richard Burton, Peter Sellers, Howard Hughes, and Chico, Harpo, and Zeppo of the Marx Brothers. A personal favorite: "Maurice Diller," enshrined in front of 1713 N. Vine Street This was supposed to be Mauritz Stiller, the Swedish director who brought Greta Garbo to America. A rueful sort of good news-bad news joke, to be given what passes for immortality in Hollywood but then have them get your name wrong!

The Walk of Fame, together with the cement footprints in front of the Chinese Theatre, represent a metaphorical flip-flop, whereby the stars of heaven are literally under our feet. Since the idea of having the public plod over you every day is unappetizing to say the least—in Malaysia it is considered a deadly insult to draw a name in the dirt and stamp on it—a common sight on the Walk of Fame are fervent souls with buckets of soapy water and cleanser, busily erasing the gum-blots and heelmarks from the names of their gods. They are volunteers who have "adopted" their favorite star, and are committed to polishing it at least once a month, even though the Chamber of Commerce itself cleans the walk every day.

The making of a star . . .

Stars are required to be at their installation (so far, Barbra Streisand, enshrined at 6925 Hollywood Boulevard, has been the only no-show), usually held at noon the third Wednesday of each month. This is probably the one way to get an in-the-flesh star to downtown Hollywood. It's a rare sure-fire method to catch a glimpse of celebrity (contact the Chamber of Commerce at 469-8311 for schedule and names of stars).

STARS AND THEIR ADDRESSES

Louis Armstrong	7000 Hollywood
Marlon Brando	1717 Vine
Johnny Carson	1749 Vine
Charles Chaplin	6751 Hollywood
Tom Cruise	6912 Hollywood
Sammy Davis, Jr.	6254 Hollywood
Marlene Dietrich	6400 Hollywood
Harrison Ford	6667 Hollywood
Clark Gable	1610 Vine
Greta Garbo	6901 Hollywood
Rita Hayworth	1645 Vine
Michael Jackson	6927 Hollywood (not to be confused with Michael Jackson, the British-born broadcaster, at 1541 Vine)
Groucho Marx	1735 Vine
Marilyn Monroe	6776 Hollywood
Elvis Presley	6777 Hollywood
Ronald Reagan	6374 Hollywood
Frank Sinatra	1600 Vine
Sylvester Stallone	6712 Hollywood
Elizabeth Taylor	6336 Hollywood
Rudolph Valentino	6166 Hollywood
John Wayne	1541 Vine

. . . a star is born.

If it is was good enough for Notre Dame, it was good enough for Sid Grauman, and the showman offered a lifelong contract to Klossner on the spot. Then, on May 17, 1927, he summoned Talmadge, Douglas Fairbanks, and Mary Pickford to be the first to commit themselves to posterity. When not enough members of the press showed up, Sid had them do it all over again the next day.

Oddities among these fossilized celebrity imprints include R2D2 and C-3PO, the *Star Wars* robots, as well as Harold Lloyd's glasses, Trigger's horseshoes, Sonja Henie's skate blades, Harpo Marx's harp, etc. There are dark rumors, unsubstantiated here, of rejects in the theater basement, has-beens whose squares of cement were ripped up as their stars faded from the firmament.

Next door to the Chinese Theatre, on the corner of Sycamore and Hollywood Boulevard, is the cinema complex **Hollywood Galaxy**, housing the American Cinematheque, a film program modeled after the famous French series and run by the Directors Guild. The site itself is a sore subject, since it was here that the fabulous **Garden Court Apartments** breathed their last, demolished after a furious preservationist fight.

For aspiring stars only: near the Chinese Theatre are the headquarters of two of Hollywood's powerful entertainment unions, the **Screen Actors Guild** (SAG) (7065 Hollywood Boulevard) and the **American Federation of Television and Radio Artists** (AFTRA) (6922 Hollywood Boulevard). Both are famous for the sight of industry hopefuls with their noses pressed up against the glass. SAG also has a fascinating bulletin board, with ads for apartment shares and airline tickets giving a hint of life at the margins of show business.

The corner of Hollywood and La Brea represents the west end of "The Bull" proper. On the corner stands the impressive HQ of Stephen J. Cannell Productions, the house built by *The Rockford Files, The A-Team,* and many other TV shows.

■ SUNSET BOULEVARD

Parallel to Hollywood Boulevard two blocks to the south, Sunset Boulevard on its run through Hollywood isn't quite as densely packed with history but does hold a few interesting places. To the east, near the Hollywood Freeway at 5800 Sunset Boulevard, is KTLA, once Warner Brothers headquarters in Hollywood. It was here that the sound age was ushered into the movies, with such patented Vita-phone-process epics as *Don Juan* and *The Jazz Singer.* The advent of talkies came too late to save Warner Brothers from an expensive mistake: it once paid the opera star Enrico Caruso a quarter of a million dollars to star in a silent movie! After Warner moved to Burbank in 1929, the handsome, colonnaded building was used by several studios, including Paramount, before finally being transformed into a television station by "Singing Cowboy" Gene Autry.

Just west of Sunset and Vine, the geodesic roof of the **Pacific Cinerama Dome** (6360 Sunset) stands out like an oversized golf ball. Designed for the ill-fated Cin-erama projection system, this wrap-around, wide-screen theater was supposed to be the wave of the future back then; now the place has a techno-pop fifties air to it, and an immensity at odds with the age of the crackerbox multiplex.

Further west, at 6525 Sunset Boulevard, the **Hollywood Athletic Club**, now a pleasant but staid office building, restaurant, and billiards parlor, was once an oasis of clubby male bonding, a place where men were men and women were provided by the bellhops. Charlie Chaplin came from his nearby studios, Rudolph Valenti-no hid from his fans there, and Buster Crabbe—who later did a turn as Tarzan—gave swimming lessons.

At the intersection of Sunset and Highland Avenue is an immediately recogniz-able landmark, **Hollywood High School**. The school boasts many famous gradu-ates, including Jason Robards, Lana Turner, Carol Burnett, the Nelson Brothers, and James Garner. *M*A*S*H*'s Sally Kellerman and Mike Farrel both went to Hollywood High, as did *Dallas*'s Linda Evans and Charlene Tilton.

The myth of Lana Turner being discovered at Schwab's Drugstore originated with gossip columnist Sidney Skolsky, who was a Schwab's fixture at the time. The troll-like Skolsky transferred the legend to his home turf from where it really hap-pened: at **Top Hat Malt Shop**, formerly located diagonally across from Holly-wood High. W.R. "Billy" Wilkerson, publisher of the *Hollywood Reporter,* asked the 16-year-old Turner if she'd like to be in pictures. "I don't know," came Lana's immortal reply, "I'll have to ask my mother."

Bringing us to the end of Hollywood, geographically and figuratively, is the **A&M Recording Studios** just south of Sunset at 1416 N. La Brea Avenue. This was the site of Charlie Chaplin's studios before he moved to the United Artists lot. Chaplin wanted a homey feel to his place of work, so he designed small Tudor-style bungalows for his offices, most of which survive—the Little Tramp's

(following pages) The quest for the perfect body has long been an Angeleno obsession.

footprints can still be seen imbedded in the cement on Soundstage 3. After Chaplin's tenure, a number of television shows were taped here, including *The Perry Mason Show* and *Superman.*

■ AROUND HOLLYWOOD

A veritable necklace of historical sites and other places of note rings downtown Hollywood, but even more than the boulevards it is best pursued on wheels. Just north of La Brea and Hollywood off Franklin Avenue is a bonafide cultural artifact: the **Ozzie and Harriet house** (1822 Camino Palmero Drive). Farther east at 7001 Franklin is the **Magic Castle**, a private club in a pseudo-French chateau which caters to prestidigitators of every stripe. Above it, at 1999 N. Sycamore, is **Yamashiro**, a Japanese restaurant with arguably the best view in Los Angeles. Built around 1910 by two brothers who were import-export moguls, it originally served as a private club for something called the "Hollywood 400," yesterday's version of the A-list. The restaurant has served as an ersatz Oriental movie set many times, most notably in *Sayonara.*

A short detour for James Dean fans: proceed east on Franklin and dip down to Yucca Street just past Highland Avenue, where the KFAC radio building is the **site of the Villa Capri** (6735 Yucca Street). The Capri was a home away from home for Dean, who was such a regular he entered the place through the kitchen. The "Rat Pack"—Humphrey Bogart, Frank Sinatra, Lauren Bacall, Judy Garland, and Sammy Davis Jr., among others—also held court at the Villa Capri, which closed in the early eighties.

William Randolph Hearst.
(Academy of Motion Picture Arts and Sciences)

On the corner of Highland and Franklin there is the immediately recognizable **Hollywood United Methodist Church**, familiar from many movies and TV shows, including *What Price Hollywood?* and *War of the Worlds*. Farther along, there is the **Montecito Apartments** (6650 Franklin), Ronald Reagan's first digs in Hollywood and also the model for Raymond Chandler's Chateau Bercy in *The Little Sister*. The grandest chateau of all is farther east, at Franklin and Bronson. This is the magnificent **Chateau Elysee**, now an outpost of the Church of Scientology, but once a glittering mansion of the widow of Thomas Ince, one of Hollywood's earliest producers.

Legend has it that the Elysee was part of William Randolph Hearst's clandestine pay-off to Mrs. Ince, stemming from a bizarre 1924 incident on Hearst's yacht, the Oneida. The immensely rich and powerful newspaper magnate was immensely jealous of his mistress, Marion Davies, and he suspected Charlie Chaplin of making love to her. Hearst burst into Davies's chambers on the yacht and shot a man he thought was Chaplin, only to find it was Ince.

Ince died, officially of a heart attack (more likely a "Hearst attack"!), and the whole sordid affair was covered up. Louella Parsons, the gossip columnist who was on the Oneida that night, dated her career in the Hearst papers from that night. The Elysee supposedly represented Mrs. Ince's hush money. Lost in all this is the stature of Thomas Ince himself, a true film pioneer who virtually invented the movie Western. He was destined to be a great producer-mogul, only to have his career cut short by "Citizen Hearst" instead.

Head south on Gower Street from Franklin to reach **Paramount Studios** (5451 Marathon), the last major studio left in Hollywood and the one with the longest tradition. Paramount

Marion Davies.
(Academy of Motion Picture Arts and Sciences)

traces its roots back to the company which filmed *The Squaw Man* at Selma and Vine. A Hollywood superstition is that young hopefuls must hug the wrought-iron gate of the Paramount lot at Marathon and Bronson, repeating, à la *Sunset Boulevard,* the magic incantation: "I'm ready for my close-up, Mr. De Mille."

Paramount became a director's studio, allowing the genius of Preston Sturges, Ernst Lubitsch, and Billy Wilder to achieve full flower. It was the studio of Valentino and Dietrich, of Mae West and Cecil B. De Mille, of Lewis and Martin, of Hope and Crosby's "Road" movies. Today Paramount is an entertainment conglomerate wholly owned by another conglomerate, Gulf & Western. It is famous as the *Godfather* studio, and for its television: *Mork and Mindy, Laverne and Shirley,* and *Happy Days* were all shot here.

The Gulf & Western alliance gave Paramount the cash to gobble up the neighboring RKO **Studios** at Melrose Avenue and Gower Street. This studio lot, long a rich-man's plaything (it was owned first by Joseph P. Kennedy and later by Howard Hughes), was bought by Lucille Ball in 1957, forming the base of her Desilu entertainment empire. The old RKO globe, famous from the original company logo, is still visible on top of the studio.

"I'm the girl who works at Paramount all day and Fox all night." —Mae West.
Mae West and Humphrey Bogart take a stroll during a Hollywood lookalike party.

The area to the southwest of Paramount Studios is dense with old sound stages, support industries, and historical sites. **Raleigh Studios**, a quaint-looking rental lot at 650 N. Bronson Avenue, reaches all the way back to 1914 for its first production, Adolph Zukor's *The Girl From Yesterday*, starring Mary Pickford. The place is also known for its production of *Death Valley Days*, with Ronald Reagan as host. One of the most preservation-minded of all Hollywood studios, Raleigh still maintains Mary Pickford's little cottage on its lot.

Farther away, in a quiet enclave at 565 N. Cahuenga Boulevard, is the *Happy Days* house, so immediately recognizable that you expect the Fonz to step up to the door and ask for Richie. One reason why this house was chosen for exteriors is that it was close to Paramount Studios, where *Happy Days* was taped, on the old Desilu-RKO lot. Legend has it the house was once owned by actress Lupe Velez, the "Mexican Spitfire."

Nearby are two more unassuming houses, both of which were used in versions of the camp horror classic, *What Ever Happened to Baby Jane?* Aficionados will recognize **172 S. McCadden Place** from the original 1962 film, starring Joan Crawford and Bette Davis. A few blocks away, at 501 S. Hudson Avenue, is the house used in the 1991 television remake, starring real-life sisters, Lynn and Vanessa Redgrave. Next door to this Spanish-style manse is a Tudor home used for exteriors in Warren Beatty's gangster epic, *Bugsy*, as well as for episodes of *Murder, She Wrote*.

For die-hard fans of Rudolph Valentino, there is a worthy side trip up to **De-Longpre Park** (Cherokee and DeLongpre Avenues). The park itself is named after Paul DeLongpre, whose lush gardens (formerly at 1721 Cahuenga) attracted thousands of visitors annually in the early days of Hollywood. In the middle of this rather seedy downtown park are two sculptures erected in honor of the Sheik: a bust and a more abstract torso called "Aspiration."

More directly west of Paramount is the UCLA **Film Archives** (6311 Romaine Street), closed to the public but famous as the site of the old Technicolor Building. Just off Romaine, at 1040 N. Las Palmas Avenue, is **Hollywood Center Studios**. It was here that Francis Coppola, flush with the success of *The Godfather* founded Zoetrope Studios in 1980, hoping to base an independent, quality-oriented production facility there. A few post-*Apocalypse Now* bombs later, Zoetrope went down in flames, and with it the dream of an alternative to the majors and their death-lock on Hollywood. Before Zoetrope, the lot had a succession of tenants, including Jean Harlow in Howard Hughes's first movie, *Hell's Angels*, and Shirley Temple in her debut. Today it is a rental lot.

Hughes figures into another site, farther west on Romaine Street. The squat, ugly, fortress-like building at 7010 Romaine is the **former headquarters of Howard Hughes** in Hollywood (when he wasn't working out of the bar at the Bel-Air Hotel, that is). Basing himself there beginning with Caddo Pictures in 1927, Hughes slowly transformed the Romaine Street HQ as his personality warped, and ended his Hollywood period as a virtual recluse in the place, directing the operations of the giant Summa Corporation from here. Nearby at 940 N. Mansfield Avenue is a more modern headquar-

"Hollywood always wanted me to be pretty, but I fought for realism." — Bette Davis, shown here with Howard Hughes. (Academy of Motion Picture Arts and Sciences)

ters, the Franklin Israel-designed **offices of Propaganda Films**, makers of music videos and such films as David Lynch's *Wild At Heart*.

■ HOLLYWOOD MEMORIAL AND BETH OLEM CEMETERY

Only a wall separates the life-and-death fortunes of Paramount Studios from the eternal rest of **Hollywood Memorial Cemetery** (6000 Santa Monica Boulevard), and its Jewish counterpart, **Beth Olem Cemetery** next door. These are the quintessential Hollywood burial grounds, not only for the names buried here but for the setting—snuggled tight against Paramount Studios and the vast variety of weird markers, including obelisks, cenotaphs, a rocket ship grave marker(!), temples, and mausoleums.

A map showing who's buried where is available at the entrance, but the main draw is still **the crypt of Valentino**, at number 1205 in the far left-hand corner of the Cathedral Mausoleum. This was the grave that the famous "Lady in Black" visited every year on Valentino's birthday. The Sheik shares his final resting place with such luminaries as Marion Davies, Tyrone Power, Cecil B. De Mille, Jesse Lasky, Douglas Fairbanks, Sr., both Carl "Alfalfa" Switzer and Darla Hood of *Our Gang*, the Talmadge sisters, Peter Lorre, and *Network's* Peter Finch. The visionary Vegas mobster Bugsy Siegel is buried in Beth Olem, near the great director/actor John Huston.

■ SANTA MONICA BOULEVARD

A jog down Santa Monica Boulevard from Hollywood Memorial brings us to what is now called **Warner-Hollywood Studios** (Formosa Avenue and Santa Monica), known for much of its existence as the home of United Artists and Samuel Goldwyn. In 1919, Mary Pickford and Douglas Fairbanks bought the studio when it consisted of only 20 acres and a single stage, naming it Pickford-Fairbanks Studios (she was still getting top billing). Mary and Doug joined Charlie Chaplin and D.W. Griffith, two other disaffected refugees from the town's increasingly restrictive majors, and together the four formed United Artists.

In 1924, after getting elbowed out of an early stake in Paramount and then MGM, Sam Goldwyn came aboard. The facility was officially renamed Goldwyn Studios in 1935, ushering in a golden era of musicals (Eddie Cantor, Danny Kaye, and the Gershwins) and screenwriting (Lillian Hellman and F. Scott Fitzgerald both worked out of the Writer's Building). Classics of the Goldwyn era include *Wuthering Heights, The Best Years of Our Lives,* and *Guys and Dolls.* Marlon Brando, Frank Sinatra, and Jack Lemmon all had bungalows on the lot at one time or another.

From the outside, the studio is easy to miss: a blank and bland tan wall completely surrounds it. The inside, also, is rather undistinguished, and another reminder that Hollywood studios are basically industrial sites—there's nothing to remind you that this was the place Mary and Doug owned, or where Sam Goldwyn retired behind closed doors every day at 2 P.M. for a nap which, unlike Harry Cohn's starlet "naps," didn't have inverted commas around it.

Across the street from the old Goldwyn lot is the **Formosa Cafe** (7156 Santa Monica Boulevard), a longtime industry watering hole with vast Hollywood tradition. The walls of this place tell a story all their own, filled with photos and

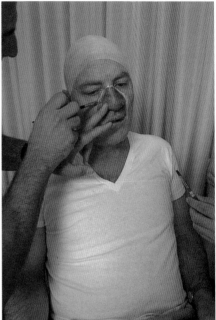
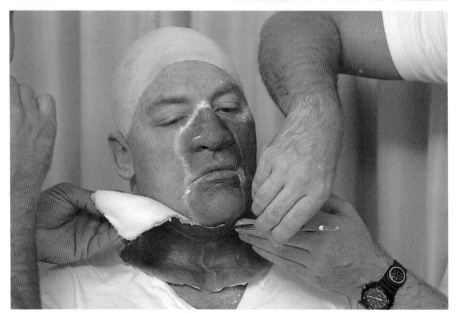

Stacy Keach is transformed for his role in a play in Pasadena.

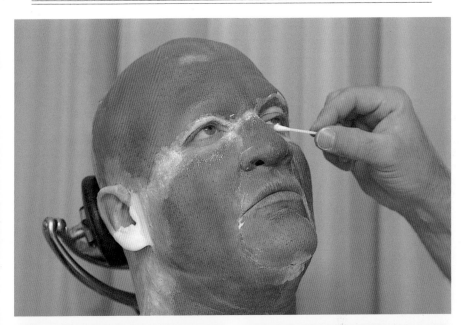

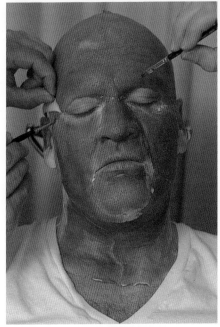

A *VARIETY* OF SLANG

For the entertainment industry, Los Angeles is a two-newspaper town, and that never meant the *L.A. Times* and the now defunct *Herald Examiner*. It meant *Variety* and the *Hollywood Reporter*, two dailies which, taken together with the weekly edition of *Variety*, are known as "the trades." These are the movie industry Bibles, pored over every day by the powers-that-be and the would-bes, sold at corner newsstands and packed with press agent puffery. They are trade magazines, much like *Floor Covering Weekly* or *Spudman, the Magazine of the Potato Grower*. The difference, of course, is that this trade is the entertainment business, and some of the glamor has rubbed off on its unofficial publishing organs.

Variety was there first, gearing up in 1904 in New York City to cover the still-burgeoning vaudeville circuit. W.R. "Billy" Wilkerson started the movie-oriented *Reporter* in 1930, soon augmenting his stake in it with real estate investments, a chain of extremely popular nightclubs, and a horse-breeding enterprise, finally to become one of Hollywood's most recognizable—and wealthiest—men-about-town. The two rags were soon neck-in-neck covering the inside story of the movie industry, and they've been that way ever since.

It was *Variety*, however, which since its inception infused its stories with lively doses of theater slang. Neologisms, nouns used as verbs, street slang—it all went into the rich column broth. Its breeziness burst forth when the trade mag reported on Black Tuesday of October 1929 with the classic headline, "Wall Street Lays an Egg." Then there was "Sticks Nix Hick Pix," which translates as "farm audiences reject rural-based movies."

A *VARIETY* GLOSSARY

author used as a verb
b.o. box-office, ticket sales
bomb to fail
bow to open, debut or premiere
chopsocky a martial arts film
crix critics
ducats tickets
emcee M.C., or master of ceremonies
exex executives
fave favorite
helmer a director

ink used as a verb
jet used as a verb
legit legitimate theater, live on the stage
legs longevity at the box-office
lens used as a verb
nets the television networks, ABC, NBC, CBS
preem to premiere, used as a verb
sez *Variety*-speak for "says"
sked schedule

starrer a film in which a particular actor stars

venue a theater or auditorium

wrap to wrap up, or finish production of, a film

VARIETY COINAGES:

Words used in the trade mag that have since gone on to be part of popular speech.

baloney nonsense, first used in *Variety* in the 1920s.

bimbo originally a synonym for "honey" and other terms of endearment, 1920s

corny sentimental, mid-1930s

freeloader 1940s

gams female legs, 1940s

passion pit a drive-in movie

sex appeal probably the most famous of *Variety's* coinages

sit-com from "situation comedy"

soap opera from when daytime serials used to advertise soaps and detergents, 1930s

whodunit a detective plot

VARIETY GEOGRAPHY

Oz, Down Under Australia

the Hub Boston

Chi Chicago

Beertown Milwaukee

Gotham New York

---

memorabilia that owner Lem Quon has collected over the years. The Formosa represents a bit of non-industry heritage, too, since it was built out of an old Red Car from the city's fabled electric trolley system.

In recent years the Formosa has been in a fight for its life, threatened by the owner of its lease, Warner Brothers. Slated to replace the irreplaceable? A parking lot, of course. But community protest and the formation of a group called Friends of the Formosa have brought the eatery back from the edge of extinction. Plans now call for Warners to preserve the Formosa, eventually moving it to a new site 250 feet away from the old one.

■ SILVER LAKE

East of central Hollywood, the confluence of Sunset and Hollywood Boulevards in Silver Lake furnishes up several landmarks from the early history of film, including the site of one of the largest and most grandiose sets ever built, **D.W. Griffith's** Babylon constructed for his 1916 film, *Intolerance*. The ornate elephant statues, Sumerian columns, and monolithic gates turned out to be too expensive to be torn down when the film failed. The set stood for years on the lot, mute testimony to the outlandish, almost Biblical excess of Hollywood moviemakers; the site, appropriately enough, is now occupied by the **Vista** movie theater, one of Hollywood's best revival houses.

Hollywood Boulevard was originally called Prospect Avenue, and at its eastern end it's still called by its old name. Just north of Sunset, the ABC **Television Center** (Prospect Avenue and Talmadge Street) now hosts game shows and a few sitcom series, but originally was part of Vitagraph Studios, a pioneering company that located here in 1915. Vitagraph was later gobbled up by Warner Brothers, which used this locale to film some scenes of the most famous "talkie" of all time, *The Jazz Singer*.

At 4401 Sunset is KCET, the area's primary public television station. It is situated on the old Monogram studio lot and is one of the few working L.A. studios offering tours—see "Studio Tours" in "MAJOR ATTRACTIONS" for details. Another old Hollywood studio hasn't fared so well: **Walt Disney's** first studio, at 2719 Hyperion Avenue, where he and animator Ub Iwerks labored over the early Mickey

Cecil B. De Mille on the set directing Intolerance. *(Academy of Motion Picture Arts and Sciences)*

Mouse cartoons as well as Snow White and the Seven Dwarfs, is now a supermarket parking lot.

■ ECHO PARK

Echo Park, along Sunset Boulevard just east of Silver Lake, is an exquisitely landscaped oasis in the middle of L.A.'s thriving Mexican community. Early on in its existence the locale was used countless times in the Keystone Kops comedies of **Mack Sennett** (whose studio was close by, Glendale Avenue at Effie Street), and Echo Park is also where Jack Nicholson tails Hollis Mulwray in a rowboat, early on in *Chinatown*. On a hill just east of Echo Park is another of the city's favorite film sets, **Carroll Avenue**. This was an early suburb called Angelino Heights, connected to downtown via the city's first cable car, and present-day residents have banded together to restore the neighborhood and keep it free from modern contaminants like telephone wires and mercury-vapor streetlamps. The most famous use of a Carroll Avenue location was Michael Jackson's

"A moving picture is just an expensive dream. That's all it is, and hardly anybody knows it."
—Jack Warner (Still from Intolerance, *courtesy Academy of Motion Picture Arts and Sciences)*

Thriller video, which featured the house at 1345 Carroll. Also in the Echo Park area, off Sunset at 929 Vendome, are the famed **"Piano Stairs"** of Laurel and Hardy's short, *The Music Box*. In this slapstick farce, which won director Hal Roach an Oscar for best comic short of 1932, the boys set out to deliver a piano but wind up with kindling wood instead.

■ LOS FELIZ

Los Feliz, which climbs up the lower Hollywood Hills above Silver Lake and Echo Park, is another L.A. neighborhood favored by early filmmakers, both as a residence and as a location for studios. **Fox Studios** were first located at Sunset Boulevard and Western Avenue, but the only original building left is now a film lab, with the rest of the site taken up by a mini-mall and a parking lot. Two early Hollywood luminaries lived on a little side street at the end of Normandie Avenue that's now named after one of them: **Cecil B. De Mille's house** was at 2000 De Mille Drive, while **W.C. Fields's house** was across the street, at 2015.

Also in Los Feliz is the **American Film Institute**, on a lovely campus at 2021 N. Western Avenue. The film school holds classes in all phases of filmmaking, and its seminars (open to the public on a limited basis) sound like a Who's Who of Hollywood: Spielberg, Scorcese, Coppola, etc. The Louis B. Mayer Library is a small but significant research facility also open to the public, and the campus as a whole is well worth a visit.

Glendower Avenue, which winds into the hills above Los Feliz at the northern end of Vermont Avenue, holds a one-man private film museum and a Frank Lloyd Wright house that's often used as a film location. At 2495 Glendower is Forrest J. Ackerman's **Science Fiction Collection**, an amazing treasure-trove of stills, posters, props, and memorabilia of the genre's foremost archivist. Ackerman plays genial host most Saturdays, allowing visitors to peruse his 300,000 piece collection. After years of fruitless negotiations with the City of Los Angeles, he has contracted to transfer his priceless "imagi-movie" collection to a specially constructed museum in Berlin, sometime in 1995, so if you want to visit one of the world's finest concentrations of movie memorabilia, act soon.

Ackerman's prop collection is the most visually arresting: he has the full-scale, female robot manikin from *Metropolis*, models from *Star Trek*, *Outer Limits*, *20,000 Leagues Under the Sea* and the original *King Kong*, the star child from *2001: A Space Odyssey*, the "demon" mask of the possessed Linda Blair in *The Exorcist*, the golden head Harrison Ford found at the beginning of *Raiders of the Lost*

Ark, Jane Fonda's latex breasts from *Barbarella,* the *Phantom of the Opera* cape that Claude Rains inherited from Lon Chaney, and—well, any listing of Ackerman's astounding array must necessarily be partial. Call (213) MOON-FAN for more information.

Farther up Glendower is the **Ennis House** (at 2607), a proto-Mayan concrete-block hulk designed by Frank Lloyd Wright and used in *Black Rain* and *The Day of the Locust,* among other movies. If it looks familiar, it may be because the art director of *Blade Runner* copied the exterior molds of the Ennis facade and reproduced them for the interior of Harrison Ford's apartment. For a glimpse of the house's actual interior, try the scene in Lawrence Kasdan's *Grand Canyon,* where Steve Martin and Mary McDonnell have their tête à tête in what is supposed to be a movie producer's palatial home.

Below the Ennis House, standing like a watchtower on a bump of land at the foot of the Hollywood Hills, is another beautiful Wright-designed residence, the **Hollyhock House.** Completed in 1920 as Wright's first commission in Los Angeles, it is the centerpiece of Barnsdall Park, overlooking Hollywood Boulevard at Vermont. The wood-ornamented, Mayan-inspired house is a pleasure to tour

Sci-fi aficionado Forrest J. Ackerman shows off parts of his collection of movie memorabilia, which may be visited by the public at his Los Feliz home.

(Tuesday and Thursday by appointment, call [213] 485-4580) or just enjoy from the surrounding gardens—noting always the hollyhock motif used throughout. Aline Barnsdall, who built the house, was an oil heiress with leftist leanings, and she bequeathed her entire estate to "the people." Today, the house is surrounded by what amounts to a municipal arts colony, including an art gallery and an art-and-crafts center. If you don't get around to seeing it in person, the Hollyhock House has been seen in such disparate motion pictures as *Cannibal Women in the Avocado Jungle of Death* and *Hedda Hopper's Hollywood.*

OLD SPANISH CALIFORNIA

*D*oña Ina had followed my glance and nodded acquiescence to my thought. 'In dressing for *baile,* one would have as soon left off the rose as one's fan. One wore it even when the dress was wreathed with flowers.'

'And did you, then, go wreathed in flowers?'

'Assuredly; from the garden if we had them, or from the field. I remember once I was all blue larkspurs, here and here . . .' she illustrated on her person. 'And long flat festoons of the *yerba buena* holding them together.'

'It would have taken hoopskirts for that?' I opined.

'That also. It was the time that the waltz had been learned from the officers of the American ships, and we were quite wild about it. The good padre had threatened to excommunicate us all if we danced it . . . but we danced . . . we danced . . .' Doña Ina's pretty feet twitched reminiscently.

They danced *La Varzoviana* also, the *caballeros* most attractive in their blue vests with gold tassels and white rolling collars, red sashes, and black velvet, silver-buttoned trousers, slit up the outside seam to show the white underdrawers. There were spurs also, a foot long with six-inch rowels, but no *caballero* who valued his reputation as a gentleman would dance in spurs. They made *coplas* as they danced *La Jota,* impromptu rhyming compliments which were sung to the music of the dance. Doña Ina . . . tried, for my benefit, to recall the dictionary of the fan—there had actually been a book in which the whole alphabet of lovemaking had been spelled out on finger-joints with touches of *el abanico,* but Doña Ina scarcely recalled it. Her mother had been an adept, one of those women of her time who was not deterred from dancing or discreet flirtations by the appearance at regular intervals of a full dozen and a half children.

—Mary Austin, *The Lands of the Sun,* 1927

In Los Angeles, home of the stars, Liberace's swimming pool should come as no surprise. At top is producer Aaron Spelling's Bel-Air spread, seen from a safe distance.

THE HOLLYWOOD HILLS

IN THE MIDDLE OF NO OTHER METROPOLIS CAN ONE enter a vast half-wild expanse of terrain such as the **Hollywood Hills**. Home to coyote, opossum, and raccoon, their skies are graced by the lazy circling of red-tail hawks. Riven by canyons, washes, and the occasional pass, these low hills separate Hollywood proper from the deep-dish expanse of the San Fernando Valley.

On stilts and gravity-defying foundations, the wealthy have colonized these hills with a stunning array of houses. The styles vary so widely—Mission haciendas abutting Japanese tea-houses—that the final effect is often derided as an architectural mishmash. But with stunning, above-the-smog views, the Hollywood Hills offer some of the most prestigious addresses in L.A.

A good entry into the Hollywood Hills is Laurel Canyon, north from the corner of Sunset and Crescent Heights Boulevards. Midway up the canyon, at Lookout Mountain Avenue, is the corner where cowboy star **Tom Mix's log cabin** once stood, one of many vacation cottages that made the canyon a popular weekend getaway for basin-dwellers. Only later, when the likes of Frank Zappa and Timothy Leary moved in, did Laurel Canyon turn into the countercultural mecca it styles itself today, with flower-children refugees hitchiking out of the Canyon Store parking lot. Opposite the Lookout Mountain turn-off is **the site of Harry Houdini's mansion**, with ruins of stone archways and balustrades still visible along the right-hand side of the the road.

■ MULHOLLAND DRIVE

At the top of Laurel Canyon, just before it drops down into the Valley, is **Mulholland Drive**. This beautiful summit road was named after William Mulholland, the chief engineer of the Los Angeles County water district and model for the murdered man in the Roman Polanski film *Chinatown*. The drive, which stretches all the way west to Malibu, boasts spectacular views of the Valley and most of Los Angeles, as well as a few sites of interest to movie lovers.

To the west of Laurel Canyon on Mulholland are some of the richest precincts of Los Angeles, where the drive lines the top of Beverly Hills and Bel-Air. So many stars inhabit Mulholland on this stretch that a portion of it has been nicknamed

"Bad Boy Drive," after the estates of one-time party boys Jack Nicholson (12850 Mulholland), Warren Beatty (13671 Mulholland), and Marlon Brando. If the present-day reputations of this out-to-stud triumvirate is to be believed, this stretch should perhaps now be called Reformed Boy Drive.

Turn right from Laurel Canyon, and the eastern stretch of Mulholland Drive also yields spectacular views and cinematic sites. Above Mulholland, on the right or "city" side, you can easily see the space-age **Chemosphere** house at 3105 Torreyson Place, featured in the film *Body Double* (where it was "dressed," or modeled, very differently). Torreyson Place was also the site of Errol Flynn's **Mulholland House**, torn down in 1988. With two-way mirrors on the ceilings of the guest bedrooms, a swimming pool, and stunning Valley vistas, Mulholland House fit well with Flynn's hedonistic lifestyle.

The sleek, modern abode on stilts at 7436 Mulholland is instantly recognizable as the **Lethal Weapon 2 house**, which Mel Gibson was supposed to have demolished with his pickup. The actual house is still standing, of course, testimony to special effects wizardry. A mock-up of the place was built on a hillside above the Six Flags Magic Mountain amusement park in Valencia, and it was this stand-in which bit the dust, the Mulholland Drive original being used only for interiors and establishing shots.

■ HOLLYWOOD BOWL

A more direct way to climb up into the hills is to follow Highland Avenue from the center of Hollywood, a route which will bring you right past the **Hollywood Bowl** (2301 N. Highland). A Los Angeles institution, the Bowl is sited in a natural amphitheater that was sacred to the Cahuenga Pass Gabrieleños, and later named Daisy Dell by white settlers. The shell-like building that stands here today is a much-modified version of a structure originally designed by Frank Lloyd Wright's son, Lloyd Wright, and built, legend has it, with materials left over from Douglas Fairbanks, Sr.'s *Robin Hood* sets. Complete with a museum on the grounds, the Bowl is familiar to film buffs, who've seen it featured many times in movies, most notably in the 1937 version of *A Star is Born*. In a memorable sequence at the beginning of that film, Frederic March as the bottle-bitten Norman Maine disrupts a concert, his crapulous antics witnessed by the then-unknown Esther Blodgett, soon to be Vicki Lester.

The Hollywood Bowl experience remains a touchstone for tourists and locals alike. Even though there are complaints about the elusive, quickly dissipating quality of the sound, the Bowl is an essential Southern California experience—sitting under the stars on a warm night, eating a gourmet picnic, and listening to great music. The Hollywood Bowl is, along with the Capitol Records Building, a symbolic landmark of Los Angeles.

Across busy Highland Avenue from the Hollywood Bowl is the **Hollywood Studio Museum** (2100 N. Highland Avenue). A restored sign reading "Jesse Lasky's Feature Play Co." stands atop the famous De Mille barn used as a setting, a dressing room, and a stable for *The Squaw Man,* the first feature-length movie shot in Hollywood. The barn now houses a small museum devoted to the early days of the movies.

Within walking distance of the Bowl and museum is a view of the **High Tower**, west of Highland off Camrose Drive, at the end of High Tower Drive. This architecturally eclectic apartment complex, in which an outdoor elevator is disguised as a castle tower, was used by Robert Altman for his version of Raymond Chandler's *The Long Goodbye,* and later was put to good use in the climactic scenes of Kenneth Brannagh's homage to L.A., *Dead Again.*

Also within easy striking distance of the Hollywood Bowl (but perhaps more comfortably visited by car) is **Whitley Heights**, a posh neighborhood for the early Hollywood elite. Modeled on an Italian hilltop village by developer Hobart Whitley, this enclave was once home to Marion Davies, Ethel Barrymore, Jean Harlow, and Gloria Swanson among others. The area still has a cul-de-sac feel to it, cut off as it is by the Hollywood Freeway to the west (access is up Milner Road, south of the Studio Museum). Location scouts love it, and it has been seen in many films, from *Now, Voyager* to *The Day of the Locust.*

■ LAKE HOLLYWOOD AND THE HOLLYWOOD SIGN

Perhaps the most astounding place hidden away in the Hollywood Hills is **Lake Hollywood**, a beautiful, lushly landscaped reservoir that's just off the Hollywood Freeway at Barham Boulevard. A jogging circuit around the perimeter of the lake is a favorite of area residents, and the lake itself is often used as an accessible "wilderness" location by filmmakers, notably in *Out of Bounds* and *Earthquake,* when a dam break threatens to flood the city. In *Chinatown,* Lake Hollywood was

(following pages) L.A. by night, as seen from Mulholland Drive.

the site where water commissioner Hollis Mulwray met his violent death—an intentional reference, no doubt, to the fact that William Mulholland, model for the Mulwray character, designed and built the reservoir dam. Along the base of the dam there are beautiful bear-head sculptures built into the cement face. From the freeway take Barham east to Hollywood Drive, then turn right onto Lake Hollywood Drive.

A detailed street map may be necessary to find the **Double Indemnity House,** above Lake Hollywood at 6301 Quebec Street. Although it's presented as the home of a "Los Feliz" oilman, the Spanish Revival house, perched on a steep grade above the intersection of Franklin and Argyle avenues, is a good mile away from the actual Los Feliz neighborhood. But it looks little different than from when insurance man Walter Neff walks up its front stairs and finds Barbara Stanwyck smoldering inside.

From Franklin Avenue on the east side of Hollywood, Beachwood Drive climbs up the hills toward the universally familiar **Hollywood sign.** Rising from the slopes of Mount Lee, the sign was first erected in 1923 to publicize a housing development of *Los Angeles Times* publisher Harry Chandler and originally spelt out "Hollywoodland," the name of the enterprise. The last syllable was torn off and the remainder deeded to the Hollywood Chamber of Commerce in 1945 as a sort of civic symbol. Thus a real estate come-on was transformed into an emblem for a city, an industry, and a cultural phenomenon. Given the sway real estate has always held over Angelenos, it's somehow fitting.

Over the years, the Hollywood sign has undergone a series of travails and transformations itself. It was originally lit with 5,000 electric bulbs, but that proved too expensive, as well as too obnoxious for residents immediately below. In 1932, an unsuccessful actress proved that suicide could be an excellent career move when she leapt to her death from the letter "H." Peg Entwistle was soon a household name, symbol of all the young girls headed for heartbreak in Hollywood.

Prank modifications of the sign have included the doper's HOLLYWEED and (during the Iran-Contra hearings, which starred Col. Oliver North) OLLYWOOD, as well as the HOLYWOOD suggested by the press whenever evangelist Aimee Semple McPherson was in town. Collegiate boosters have also draped the sign with banners reading CAL TECH and GO NAVY. In a dream sequence in the movie *Grand Canyon,* the sign bids a personal HULLO MACK to a flying Kevin Kline.

A successful renovation was completed in 1978, when restoring the sign became something of a cause célèbre. Donors could sponsor a letter for $27,000, and the opportunity attracted such diverse luminaries as Hugh Hefner, Gene Autry, and rocker Alice Cooper, who donated an "O" in memory of pal Groucho Marx. Physical specifications are impressive: the sign is 50 feet high, 450 feet long and weighs 480,000 pounds (15 m by 137 m/218 kg). Though it's visible from all over L.A., the sign itself is basically inaccessible, unless you're willing to scramble cross-country through the dense undergrowth—there's no trail.

On your way back down Beachwood Canyon, stop at the intersection of Belden Drive and see if you recognize the area. In the original *Invasion of the Body Snatchers,* this area stood in for the small town that was supposedly being taken over by alien pod creatures. In the film, the hero and heroine (Kevin McCarthy and Dana Wynter) flee from the aliens up the steps located at 2744 Westshire Drive. Suddenly, through the space-warp known as film editing, they are in **Bronson Canyon**, a part of Griffith Park a short drive to the east.

■ GRIFFITH PARK

Some 4,000 prime acres of the Hollywood Hills have been set aside as **Griffith Park**, the centerpiece of the Los Angeles park system. No, it wasn't named after D.W. Griffith, although he often used it as a location. A wealthy eccentric with the odd monicker of Col. Griffith J. Griffith bought the land in the late 1880s and donated it to the city. With hiking trails crisscrossing the mountainous terrain, and attractions like the **Gene Autry Museum** (see "Museums" in "MAJOR ATTRACTIONS" for more) occupying the flatter portions, Griffith Park has since become a sort of communal backyard for Hollywood and urban Los Angeles.

Backyard, and backlot, too. For ease of access and the availability of country vistas in the middle of the city, Griffith Park is still in constant use as a location, as it has been since filmmakers began coming to Hollywood. The early rule of thumb, often attributed to Samuel Goldwyn but actually formulated by producer Abe Stern: "A tree is a tree, a rock is a rock—shoot it in Griffith Park!" The directors did, so often that someone once waggishly proposed the addition of permanent tripods pre-set for the park's favorite shooting angles, in order that film crews not waste so much time setting up.

(following pages) A rare clear day at the Griffith Park Observatory.

Dominating the park from a promontory overlooking Los Feliz is its most famous movie location of all: the **Griffith Park Observatory.** Director Nicholas Ray used it as a backdrop for several dramatic scenes in the James Dean epic of teenage angst, *Rebel Without a Cause.* Rarely has a setting played more effectively off the action, with the monumental copper-domed observatory throwing into high relief the painful thrashings of James Dean, Sal Mineo, and Natalie Wood. The observatory also played a starring role in the Arnold Schwarzenegger sci-fi spectacular *The Terminator.*

The southwestern corner of Griffith Park, known originally as Brush Canyon and still wild and undeveloped, has been the setting of films from *The Squaw Man* and *King Kong* on, as well as episodes of *Gunsmoke* and *Bonanza.* The **Bronson Canyon caves** in the old rock quarry here have doubled as the **Batcave** for both the movie and television versions of *Batman,* as well as being used for the underground haunts ("10,000 feet beneath the surface of the Earth!") of the Muranians in the 1935 Mascot serial, *Phantom Empire.* The caves were also used as hideouts from the aliens in the original *Invasion of the Body Snatchers.*

WEST HOLLYWOOD

WEST HOLLYWOOD, AS FITZGERALD SAID about rich people, is different from you and me. It's also very different from Hollywood proper. Until it became an independent city in November 1984, the area was a small, unincorporated pocket administered by the county of Los Angeles, which sounds like a purely jurisdictional distinction, but had very real consequences. County authority meant fewer police officers patrolling the area, and looser laws regarding gambling, alcohol, and prostitution.

Although famous for the nightclub-packed **Sunset Strip**, West Hollywood today incorporates large residential areas, also. It is the home of many retirees, pushing the median age to among the highest of any greater L.A. community, as well as a politically active gay population. With its booming nightlife and progressive government, West Hollywood is more Hollywood than Hollywood itself, and one of the liveliest communities in Los Angeles.

■ SUNSET STRIP

The most famous consequence of West Hollywood's unincorporated legal status was the **Sunset Strip:** a mile-long section of Sunset Boulevard between Crescent Heights Boulevard and Doheny Drive that was once a neon gulch of flashy nightclubs, drop-dead *Pretty Woman*-style streetwalkers, and illicit casinos. Another factor might have contributed to the area's reputation for lax morals: many agents had their residences here, due to a loophole in county revenue laws which taxed their commissions at a low rate.

Sunset Strip has tamed down today. There are nightclubs here, but they tend to be rock and comedy clubs, not speakeasies. The streetwalkers are gone (the film *Pretty Woman* was anachronistic in that respect), chased out by incorporation and stricter police control. But there is still a flamboyance to the area, and the huge billboards along the Strip lend it an awesome graphic sizzle.

West Hollywood is known for its excitement and life, but also for its celebrity deaths. Art Linkletter's daughter Diane leapt to her death in 1969 from a building overlooking the Strip at 8787 Shoreham Drive. Reports say she was reliving a bad LSD experience at the time; her father later became an active anti-drug crusader.

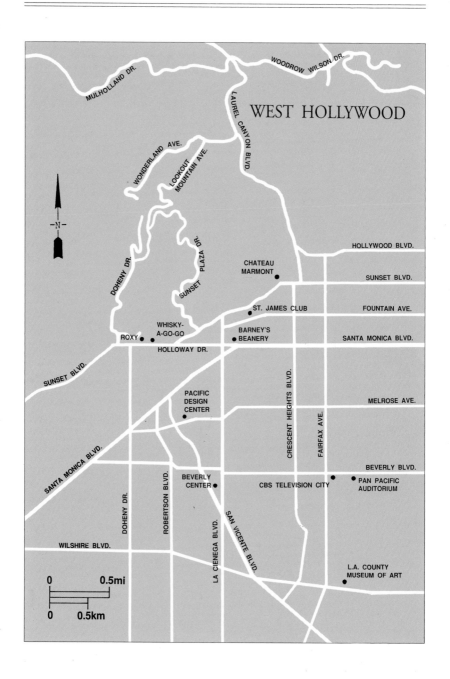

A death that was clearly drug-related was that of comedian **Lenny Bruce**, who still had a needle in his arm when they found him at a hilltop house at the intersection of Sunset Plaza and Hollywood Boulevard. Actor **Sal Mineo** had run-ins with the law over drugs, but his death (at 8563 Holloway Drive) occurred when a mugger stabbed him in the carport of his West Hollywood apartment.

Perhaps the most famous death-site in West Hollywood is the **Chateau Marmont** hotel (8221 Sunset Boulevard), where comedian John Belushi succumbed to a lethal cocktail of heroin and cocaine. It's unfortunate that Belushi's death overshadows the history of the hotel, which has quite a bit of Hollywood tradition behind it—it's one of two hotels in town that have had books written about them (the Beverly Hills Hotel is the other).

The seclusion, casualness and downright funkiness of the Marmont have attracted stars from the time of Jean Harlow and Boris Karloff. Karloff lived there for years, evidently feeling that the somewhat gothic Marmont fitted his image. Director Billy Wilder used his own apartment in the Marmont as the model for Fred MacMurray's modest digs in *Double Indemnity*.

Two famous movie romances ignited here were those of Paul Newman and Joanne Woodward, and Jessica Lange and Sam Shepard. But it was always a place for illicit assignations and wild romance. "If you must get into trouble," Columbia mogul Harry Cohn told bad-boy stars William Holden and Glenn Ford in 1939, "do it at the Marmont."

Marilyn Monroe, Robert De Niro, Dustin Hoffman, and Jim Morrison are all stars who have made the Chateau Marmont home at one time or another. You can see the real thing in Oliver Stone's movie, *The Doors:* it's the place where Val Kilmer as Jim Morrison stumbles drunkenly on the hotel rooftop, high above the Strip.

Across Sunset Boulevard from the Marmont, two mini-malls stand on what was once the second most famous corner (after Hollywood and Vine) in Tinseltown. Throughout the thirties and forties, the **Garden of Allah Hotel**, was *the* place to be and be seen. The social scene was especially lively around the hotel swimming pool, where transient stars and screenwriters would receive their guests and gather for a West Coast version of Dorothy Parker's "Round Table." The hotel itself was a quaint collection of small, Mission-style bungalows, opened by the dramatic Russian actress Nazimova in 1929. Robert Benchley was a famous Garden of Allah resident; so dismayed was he by the traffic on Sunset Boulevard he used to take a taxi to get across the street to the Marmont.

On the southeast corner of Crescent Heights and Sunset stood **Schwab's Drug Store**, a rather nondescript coffee shop that gained brilliance reflected off the nearby Gardens and the Marmont. As partygoers struggled into Schwab's for breakfast, they would be set upon by columnists like Sidney Skolsky, who used the place as an unofficial office. The myth of Lana Turner being discovered here attracted hundreds of would-be ingenues, who'd sit around sipping malts and hoping to be touched by God, or at least a casting agent. *M*A*S*H*'s Sally Kellerman reports she did the whole sipping-sodas-in-Schwab's routine, and all she got for her trouble was "pudgy."

There may have been magic to Schwab's, after all, since Howard Arlen supposedly wrote the melody to "Somewhere Over the Rainbow" there, inspired, wags say, by the drugstore's famous neon sign. The building was demolished in 1987, and though the owners of the replacement structure say they are negotiating with Schwab's old owners to reincarnate it, the feeling just won't be the same. Just down the street from the site is another blast from the past, **Jay Ward Productions** (8218 Sunset), complete with a fiberglass statue of Ward's most famous cartoon creation, Bullwinkle the Moose.

Another famous address in the area was fictional. **Seventy-Seven Sunset Strip** was actually 8433 Sunset Boulevard—or at least this was the parking lot where Ed "Kookie" Barnes parked cars. The restaurant was really Dino's Lodge, owned by Dean Martin. The door to "77" was upstairs and next door, and was actually a fire exit for the Tiffany Theater. Other clubs along the Strip included the Trocadero, Ciro's, and the Mocambo, as well as the Player's Club, owned by Preston Sturges, the Clover Club, the Colony Club (named after Al Capone's notorious Chicago speakeasy), and the Villa Nova.

This last is now the **Rainbow Bar and Grill** at 9015 Sunset. In its earlier incarnation, the restaurant saw one of the most famous blind dates in history: Joe DiMaggio and Marilyn Monroe met there in 1953. In 1945, Vincente Minnelli proposed to Judy Garland there.

Not all the action on the Strip today is historical or fictional. There are distinct sections, or neighborhoods, to this area of Sunset. The shops and restaurants around Sunset Plaza, for example, are home to the sophisticated European and Middle Eastern jet-setters whose L.A. headquarters, the posh English residential hotel **St. James' Club** at 8563 Sunset, was recently restored to its original Art Deco glory. A setting used in *Murder, My Sweet,* among other films, the hotel was once famous for hosting John Wayne—and his pet steer!—in one of its penthouse suites.

Farther west, in the long, looping curve from La Cienega Boulevard to Holloway Drive, movieland's movers and shakers assemble in tony eateries like **Spago** (overlooking Sunset at 1114 Horn Avenue), **Nicky Blair's** (8730 Sunset), and **Le Dome** (8720 Sunset). An elegant *boîte* famous for high-profile romances (Sylvester Stallone/Brigitte Nielsen, Don Johnson/Melanie Griffith), Le Dome was previously the showroom of thirties Hollywood's premier interior decorator, William "Billy" Haines. Hounded out of an MGM contract because of his open homosexuality, Haines had a second career as the decorator of choice for star homes and studio offices—some of the same offices from which he had been banished as an actor.

Just off this section of the Strip is **Bel Age** (1020 N. San Vicente Boulevard), a hotel that's rather unprepossessing on the outside but very luxurious inside. This all-suite hostelry is the choice for the industry folk who stay in the area, as well as some who are perhaps not exactly in any industry at all. In *Prizzi's Honor,* the hilarious send-up of Mafia manners, "I'll meet you at the Bel Age," is given a Brooklynese spin by professional contract hitman Jack Nicholson.

Finally, on the short straightaway just before Sunset drops down into the hushed precincts of Beverly Hills, there is the rock'n'roll paradise filling the block between the **Roxy** (9009 Sunset) and the **Whisky A Go Go** (8901 Sunset). On weekend nights, this stretch of Sunset becomes an outrageous parade of cerulean-haired punks, tattooed bikers, and random voidoids—one of the few verifiable pedestrian scenes in Los Angeles. The out-of-town rockers' hotel-of-choice is the **Sunset Marquis** (1200 Alta Loma Road), with parklike grounds and aviary to go along with compulsory MTV cable service and multi-line phones in every room.

■ SANTA MONICA BOULEVARD

Although Sunset gets all the play, the backbone of West Hollywood is really Santa Monica Boulevard, a four-lane artery (oftentimes clogged) to the south. Here we have such landmarks as **Barney's Beanery** (8447 Santa Monica), one of the longest-running restaurants in the area (Harlow loved to do her slumming there). Located a few blocks away is Steven Seagal's **Aikido Ten Shin Dojo** (8505 Santa

"Hollywood is America's show window." —Charles Laughton.
West Hollywood is packed with trendy nightclubs and designer stores.

Monica), the karate school owned by the martial arts star. He was discovered there by one of his pupils, the super-agent Michael Ovitz of Creative Artists Agency. At 8612 Santa Monica is **The Sports Connection**, the ultimate West Hollywood workout spa, where the imperfect movie *Perfect* was set.

Between Sunset and Santa Monica Boulevards and running parallel to them both is **Fountain Avenue**, justly celebrated for its string of Norman-style chateaus and one of the area's great residential streets. Just off Fountain are several sites of cinematic interest, such as **Villa D'Este** (1355 N. Laurel Avenue), a charming Mediterranean apartment building featured in the film *Under the Yum Yum Tree*. On the other side of Fountain, at 1401 N. Laurel, is the residence of F. Scott

---

SUNSET STRIP NIGHTCLUBS

During the Golden Age of Hollywood, in the thirties and forties, the Sunset Strip was known for its elegant nightclubs, strung like jewels down its length and glittering with excitement. Well, the setting is still there, but somebody has stolen the gems. The trio of greats—Ciro's, Mocambo, and the Trocadero Cafe—is no more, but they, and their cinematic stand-ins, have done double duty on- and off-screen, showing up most recently in Warren Beatty's gangster epic *Bugsy.*

The Mocambo's main rival, **Ciro's**, at 8433 Sunset Boulevard, was one of two clubs started by W.R. Wilkerson, publisher of the *Hollywood Reporter,* who could conveniently provide publicity for enterprises in the pages of his own paper. In its heyday, after a P.R. genius named Herbert Hover took it over, Ciro's was the place to be seen—and even more the place to be photographed—for all the Hollywood celebs. Ciro's is now the Comedy Store, one of chain owned by Mitzi Shore (Mitzi's husband, Sammy, was Elvis's opening act in Las Vegas.)

The "old favorite" (opened in 1934, also owned by Wilkerson) was the **Trocadero Cafe** at 8610 Sunset. For a long time, all that remained of the famous nightclub was a set of steps at the southeast corner of Sunset Plaza Drive. These too were destroyed, when after the incorporation of West Hollywood the owners got wind of a movement to lend the site some sort of landmark status. Fearing their development opportunities would be diminished, they hustled in workmen to tear out the famous Trocadero steps. Thus goes the preservation of the past in Hollywood. Some of the glamor and ambience of the "Troc" has been preserved forever, in the 1937 version of *A Star Is Born,* which features both interiors and exteriors from the club.

Fitzgerald during his sad last years in Hollywood, as seen in the movie *Beloved Infidels*, starring Gregory Peck. A little farther off Fountain, at 1428 N. Genesee Avenue, is the *Nightmare on Elm Street* **house**, used in all the Freddie Kreuger movies.

■ MELROSE AVENUE

Another east-to-west avenue, Melrose, is home to one of L.A.'s trendiest shopping districts, with most of the shops located between La Brea Avenue and San Vicente Boulevard. One indication of the highs and lows Melrose Avenue embraces is the fact that it is home to the power dining of **Morton's** (8800 Melrose) as well as **Pink's** (Melrose at La Brea). Morton's is the place Julia Philips was referring to in her Hollywood tell-all *You'll Never Eat Lunch in This Town Again*, (see the "Power Dining" sidebar for the ins and outs of eating in L.A.) while Pink's is a hot-dog joint where Eddie Murphy pulls up in a limo, and where Sean Penn proposed to Madonna.

Melrose is braced at its west end by the gigantic **Pacific Design Center** (at San Vicente Boulevard), which used to be referred to as "The Blue Whale" until it was expanded by a huge green addition that dwarfed the blue original. Most of the design showrooms are closed to the public, but the **Melrose Bar and Grill**, on the fourth level of the blue building, is open to all.

■ BEVERLY BOULEVARD

Beverly Boulevard echoes the variety of West Hollywood's better known boulevards while being much less congested. Just west of La Brea Avenue, **El Coyote restaurant** (Beverly at Detroit Street) is where Sharon Tate had her last meal before being brutally murdered by the Manson clan. The headquarters of Heinsbergen and Company (7415 Beverly) is on the north side of the street. Now run by A.T. Heinsbergen, son of founder A.B. Heinsbergen, the firm was responsible for the interior designs of many of the great **movie palaces** along Broadway and elsewhere —United Artists Theater, Los Angeles Theater, and the Wiltern Theater are just three. The company offices show off their founder's flair for fantasy, although now the firm is involved in restoration work as much as in original design.

A passing nod as we proceed west on Beverly at Gardner to the forlorn facade of the **Pan Pacific Auditorium**, still standing after a 1989 fire gutted the building. Developers are working with preservationists to incorporate the streamlined Art Moderne facade—which movie fans will remember from the 1980 roller skating musical *Xanadu*—into the site's new building.

The intersection of Fairfax Avenue and Beverly Boulevard is dominated by CBS **Television City**, occupying a huge site adjacent to the famed **Farmers Market**. A side-jaunt up Fairfax is very worthwhile: not only will you pass by the predominantly Jewish Fairfax district's shops and restaurants—**Canter's Delicatessen**, at 419 N. Fairfax, is Hollywood's favorite spot for a pastrami sandwich —but at 611 Fairfax is **Silent Movie**, the only area theater-museum still regularly showing archival silents from the early age of cinema. (See "Movie Theaters" under "Nightlife" in "PRACTICAL INFORMATION" for details.)

At Beverly and La Cienega Boulevard is the huge **Beverly Center**, setting of the Woody Allen-Bette Midler comedy, *Scenes from a Mall*. The Beverly Center was used in only a few establishing scenes, because Allen refused to do the movie if he had to stay in Los Angeles. A mall in Connecticut was used for the majority of the filming.

The Pacific Design Center, a West Hollywood landmark.

The Sunset Tower, a favorite locale of Raymond Chandler's private eye, Philip Marlowe, is now the exclusive St. James' Club.

On the San Vicente Boulevard side of the Beverly Center is the **Hard Rock Cafe**, featured prominently in *L.A. Story* and still with a line outside most weekend nights. If the Hard Rock is too loud or too crowded, head up San Vicente a short ways to the **Tail-o'-the-Pup**, a hot-dog stand that looks like a giant hot-dog; a mock-up of it flew through the air in the opening scenes of *L.A. Story.*

THE WEIRDEST PLACE

Hollywood, 2 June 1930

*T*his is the weirdest place. We have taken Elsie Janis's house. It has a small but very pretty garden, with a big pool. I have arranged with the studio to work at home, so I sometimes don't get out of the garden for three of four days on end. If you asked me, I would say I loved Hollywood. Then I would reflect and have to admit that Hollywood is about the most loathsome place but that, never going near it, I enjoy being out here.

My days follow each other in a regular procession. I get up, swim, breakfast, work till two, swim again, work till seven, swim for a the third time, then dinner and the day is over. When I get a summons from the studio, I motor over there, stay for a couple of hours and come back. Add incessant sunshine and it's all rather jolly. It is only occasionally that one feels one is serving a term on Devil's Island. We go out very little. Just an occasional dinner at the house of some other exile, e.g. some New York theatrical friend. Except for one party at Marion Davies's house, I've not met any movie stars.

The actual work is negligible. I altered all the characters to earls and butlers with such success that they called a conference and changed the entire plot, starring the earl and the butler. So I'm still working on it. So far I've had eight collaborators. The system is A gets the original idea, B comes in to work with him on it, C makes the scenario, D does preliminary dialogue, and they send for me to insert class and what not, then E and F, scenario writers, alter the plot and off we go again. I could have done all my part of it in a morning but they took it for granted that I should need six weeks.

The latest news is that they are going to start shooting quite soon. In fact there are ugly rumours that I'm to be set to work on something else. I resent this as it will cut into my short story writing. It is odd how soon one comes to look upon every minute wasted that is given to earning one's salary. (Now don't go making a comic article out of this and queering me with the bosses.)

—P.G Wodehouse, letter to Denis Mackail, from *Abroad In America*, 1930

B E V E R L Y   H I L L S

WHEN WILLIAM GOLDMAN, SCREENWRITER OF *Harper, Butch Cassidy and the Sundance Kid,* and *Marathon Man* first came to Los Angeles on a writing assignment, he was picked up at the airport by a studio limousine. As he looked out upon this alien city, one neighborhood in particular struck him, and he wondered aloud to the driver about what kind of housing development it was. The driver laughed and told him it was **Beverly Hills.**

The mistake is less surprising than it sounds. For all its vaunted distinction as embracing some of the toniest—and priciest—precincts in L.A., Beverly Hills is the product of illusion. The name bespeaks soaring incomes, extravagant residential architecture, and chauffeur-driven poodle trips to the local pet salon. But the reality is, on first inspection, surprisingly mundane. The trees do not drip money, the streets are not paved in gold. Just houses, chock-a-block with one another, some with (gasp!) older-model cars parked in their driveways.

One reason for this first impression is that the city of Beverly Hills (and it is a city, with a government distinct from that of the behemoth which surrounds it, Los Angeles), is divided into two areas. The residential neighborhood to the south of Sunset Boulevard is the one most visible, most accessible—the Beverly Hills that Goldman and other passers-by can see. It looks pretty much like any other upper-middle-class American neighborhood, Oak Park in Chicago, say, or parts of Westchester County. Very nice, very well-kept, with broad, leafy streets. Because it is Beverly Hills, it qualifies as some of the most expensive real estate on earth. But it is not the Beverly Hills of the imagination.

That Beverly Hills is located in the canyons above Sunset Boulevard, nestled in the foothills of the Santa Monica Mountains. It is here that the rich and super-rich have their lavish estates, and it is, in its way, just as much of a let-down as the Beverly Hills of the flatlands below. Most of the riches, most of the conspicuous consumption, are walled off from prying eyes, hidden behind high-security hedges, invisible at the end of endless driveways. There are a few exceptions, and I'll try to point them out, but anyone heading for Beverly Hills "**to see where the movie stars live**" is bound to come in for a modicum of disappointment.

As with Hollywood, what we are dealing with here is two distinct entities. There is Beverly Hills, the place. Then there is Beverly Hills, the brand name for Hollywood's premium products, the worldwide symbol for movie-money wealth.

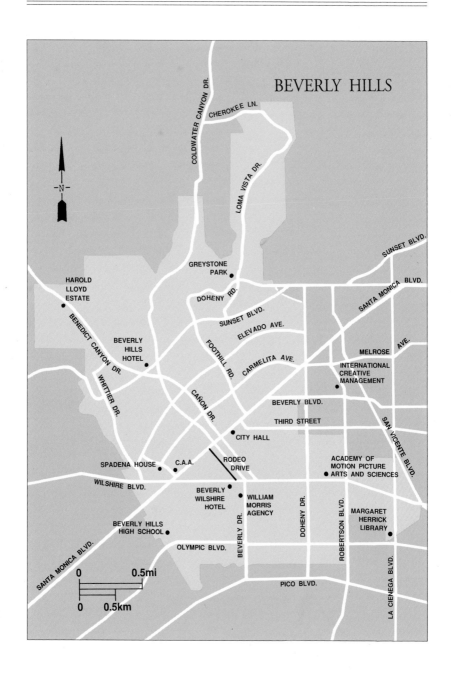

BEVERLY HILLS

Along Sunset, vendors set up shop with nothing more than a lawn chair, a cardboard sign, and a supply of ersatz "Maps to the Stars' Homes," doing a brisk business hawking glimpses of the dream. They are cashing in on the illusion, when all they have to sell is brief stolen glimpses of the reality.

Yet more disappointment is in store for you upon your first glimpse of **Rodeo Drive**, which, if you buy the hype, is a shopping mecca rivaling Fifth Avenue and Via Condotti. What the neophyte finds instead is a few blocks of screamingly banal architecture. Again, the appearance cheats reality. Rodeo Drive—and remember to pronounce it Spanish style, "Row-DAY-oh"—is indeed a world-class concentration of high-ticket shops, but one needs to penetrate those appointment-only boutiques to get a real taste of its glamor. From the outside, it just looks tacky.

All of which is not to say that Beverly Hills is a sham. Ever since Mary Pickford and Douglas Fairbanks, Sr. established Pickfair here, it has been home to the major concentration of movie wealth (which is to say movie power) on the planet. Like so many pilot fishes attending that monstrous wealth, the offices of high-powered producers, actors, and agents are also located here, not to mention the high-style restaurants where the movers and shakers sometimes meet. Also, while

Even some of the storefronts on Rodeo Drive are copyright protected.

the shopping district of Rodeo Drive is best seen on foot, walking the streets of Beverly Hills can attract the attention of the authorities—not for nothing is it known as the "**best-policed six square miles on earth.**"

■ SWIMMING POOLS . . . MOVIE STARS

Crossing the border into Beverly Hills from the Sunset Strip is like entering another dimension—serious money. The flash and cash of Hollywood is left behind as you pass by one sedate manor after another along Sunset Boulevard. The **Beverly Hills Hotel**, probably the best-known hostelry in Los Angeles, looms over Sunset Boulevard in the middle of this parade.

Above the hotel, two lushly vegetated canyons, Coldwater and Benedict, cut up into the Santa Monica Mountains. Up **Coldwater Canyon**, at 1011 N. Beverly Drive, is the former home of Marion Davies, where **William Randolph Hearst** died in 1951. **Rock Hudson** fans might want to proceed up Coldwater to 9402 Beverly Crest Road. It was there, at an imposing home he called "**The Castle**," that the screen idol died of AIDS at age 59. At 1120 Wallace Ridge is the former home of **Warren Beatty**, familiar from its appearance (as Jack Warden's mansion) in *Shampoo.*

Benedict Canyon is hallowed ground for star-tour aficionados, not the least because **Pickfair** is there, located at 1143 Summit Drive, the end of the road. Not much has been preserved of the home where America's sweethearts, Mary Pickford and Douglas Fairbanks, Sr., put down stakes in 1918, expanding and upgrading an old hunting lodge he owned. The wall surrounding the grounds is there, and the impressive sweep of the gated estate is visible.The house itself, remodeled into a faintly Tudor mansion, can barely be seen. After Mary and Doug, it passed to the hands of Jerry Buss, owner of the Los Angeles Lakers, and then to Pia Zadora and her wealthy husband, Meshulam Riklis.

Across the canyon is **Green Acres** (1740 Green Acres Place) the palatial estate of another early Hollywood star, Harold Lloyd. The comedian's house, which after Lloyd's death was turned into a museum for a short time, is a little better preserved than Pickfair, with a lion brooding down at visitors from the gates. The extensive grounds, however, have been chopped up into a multi-million-dollar hillside subdivision.

BEVERLY HILLS HOTEL

One of the best and cheapest shows in Beverly Hills is in one of the most expensive hotels in the world, the **Beverly Hills Hotel** at 9641 Sunset Boulevard. Even if you can't afford the prices (and the possible humiliation) of the hotel's famous *Polo Lounge* bar, try the all-pink coffee shop: you can order the wheat pancakes (delicious, and favored by Jaclyn Smith and Jackie Collins) and a cup of coffee, pay a couple dollars for valet parking, and still get away for under ten dollars. You get a liberal dose of the heady atmosphere, and can stroll around the 12-acre grounds until you feel at home; who knows, you may even run into a movie star or two. Provided, that is, that the hotel is still open—major renovations are planned, which may close it for as long as two years.

continues

"Nobody is allowed to fail within a two-mile radius of the Beverly Hills Hotel."
—Gore Vidal

The stars still come to this fabled hotel, fondly called the Pink Palace, whose garish Mission Revival architecture stands for everything top-drawer in Hollywood. That may be because it was there at the beginning, way back in 1912, when Beverly Hills was known mostly for its lima bean fields. The area had been called Morocco Junction until then, but a developer named Burton Green bought it and renamed it after Beverly Farms, a Massachusetts retreat then-President Taft favored. The hotel was built to attract the one ingredient the new development lacked: people. The "Toonerville Trolley" took guests and visitors from the Morocco Junction Red Car station to the doors of the Pink Palace.

The hotel, and the city of Beverly Hills, both would have failed were it not for Mary Pickford and Douglas Fairbanks who made the area fashionable by moving into Pickfair, the hillside mansion just above the hotel. Where Mary and Doug went, the movie crowd—and eventually the rest of America—followed. Even so, the hotel enjoyed only a brief currency, actually closing for a few years during the Depression. Recent owners of the hotel include Marvin Davis, the Denver oil baron, and the Sultan of Brunei, the world's richest man.

Gable and Lombard made Bungalow Number Four their illicit love nest, before his divorce. Howard Hughes rented Bungalow Three year-round (cost, about $350,000), and was extremely secretive: he used to leave messages for the hotel staff in a tree outside his door. Liz Taylor's father had an art gallery in the hotel, so she knew the place intimately even before she came to stay there as a star.

The Polo Lounge, once the children's dining room, now hears the lunchtime dealings of the grown-up children of Hollywood—this is one place the phone jacks at the tables aren't only for show. The hotel itself has been shown off in *A Star Is Born* (the 1937 version), *Designing Women, American Gigolo, Shampoo, The Way We Were,* and *California Suite,* but you haven't seen it in films recently because the management has instituted a strict no movie policy, ever since the hot lights of a movie crew set off the sprinkler system in the Crystal Room, ruining thousands of dollars worth of furnishings. There is a fairly strict no-photos policy, also.

The upper reaches of Benedict Canyon is tragic turf, with the death sites of Sharon Tate, Rudolph Valentino, and George "Superman" Reeves clustered close together. Whether from superstition or to discourage curiosity seekers, they've changed the address of the **Manson murder site**, from 10050 Cielo Drive to 10048, but the house is just as secluded as it was when followers of Charlie Manson walked up the driveway in the morning hours of August 9, 1969.

Off Cielo is Bella Drive and the aptly named aerie of Rudolph Valentino, **Falcon Lair** (1436 Bella Drive). Less violent but just as sad, in its way, as the Tate house, this fortress-like redoubt was bought by Valentino in 1925 so he might escape from his hellish fans. He lived only another year, dying in 1926, but visible signs of his residence remain, including the "falcon" weather vane and the words "Falcon Lair" over the gate. Down the hill, at 1579 Benedict Canyon, is the house where George Reeves committed suicide, despondent over his career (he had been over-identified with the role of Superman). One mass murder, one premature death, one suicide—one bad-luck neighborhood!

East of the canyons, high up in the hills, **Trousdale Estates** were carved up in the fifties from the estate of oil baron Edward Doheny. Two sites along Hillcrest Drive are prominent on star maps: **Elvis Presley's former mansion** at 1174 was famous for the graffiti his admirers would etch into its massive front gates; the chapel at Danny Thomas's Villa Rosa (1187 Hillcrest), visible from the street, was where his daughter Marlo and talk-show host Phil Donahue were married.

Snaking back down the steep streets brings us to **Greystone Park and Mansion** (905 Loma Vista Drive), the original Doheny estate manor, built for the oil baron's only son. Soon after that son moved in, Beverly Hills was shocked by the murder-suicide of the young Doheny and his secretary, Hugh Plunkett, both of whom were found dead in the master bedroom. The 55-room English Tudor manor house was later the home of the American Film Institute, but is not open to the public, though the 16-acre grounds are now one of the city's most attractive public spaces. Greystone has been much used in movies, most notably in *The Loved One*, the hilarious send-up of life and death in Hollywood, in which the gardens served as the Whispering Glades cemetery.

At the mouth of Benedict Canyon, across Sunset from the Beverly Hills Hotel, is a pretty green triangle, filled with fountains and fish ponds and called **Will Rogers Memorial Park**. It's the oldest park in Beverly Hills, and named for the genial cowboy who was once made honorary mayor of Beverly Hills, but it is not to be confused with his Pacific Palisades ranch, now Will Rogers State Park and a long way west on Sunset (see "WEST L.A." chapter for more).

The well-kept residential area around the park features more of the astronomically expensive real estate for which Beverly Hills is famous. **Bedford Drive** is typical of the area, and rich in star-lore sites. Lana Turner's lover Johnny Stompanato was stabbed to death with a kitchen knife wielded by Turner's daughter, Cheryl Crane, at 730 N. Bedford. Stompanato was a gangster who had been physically abusing Turner, and his killing was ruled "justifiable homicide." Among the revelations that came out at the trial, however, one is that Lana made it a practice to hand out gold boudoir keys to all her lovers. A few doors down, at 802 N. Bedford, is the house used in *Down and Out in Beverly Hills*—for once, a film site represented as being in Beverly Hills actually is. Close by is the former home of **Clara Bow** (512 N. Bedford), where the "It Girl" was supposed to have taken on the whole USC football team in a 1927 Roman-style orgy. The coach is said to have later declared the house—and the star—"off-limits."

One street west of Bedford is **Roxbury Drive**, which features a string of star homes. Jimmy Stewart has the house and gardens at 918 N. Roxbury; Lucille Ball's home until her death was at 1000 N. Roxbury; and next door, at 1002, was

Beverly Hills City Hall.

The gates of the stars' homes are the closest most people can get to seeing their idols. The golden girl (Madonna, above) and bad boy (Michael Jackson, below) reside behind these two entranceways.

Jack Benny's residence, sometimes used in his television show. A few sites farther west: the **Bugsy Siegel death house** (810 Linden Drive), where the gangster portrayed in Warren Beatty's *Bugsy* was killed by gun blasts through the window as he sat on his living room couch. Visually more arresting is the **Spadena House** at 515 Walden Drive, a fairy-tale "witch's house" in mock-Bavarian style, complete with a steeply pitched roof and quaintly paned windows. Originally built in 1921 as a combination film set and production company office in Culver City, the house was later moved here for use as a private residence but may soon ping-pong back, part of the moveable feast that is Hollywood.

■ RODEO DRIVE AND THE REST OF BEVERLY HILLS

Though some of Beverly Hills's most impressive palaces sit on the hills that give the city its name, you may want to resist the compulsion to cruise in on Sunset Boulevard; instead slip in through the back door, on Beverly Boulevard. This will take you past ICM, **International Creative Management** (8899 Beverly), along

"I'm ready for my close-up, Mr. De Mille." —*Gloria Swanson.*
(Still from Sunset Boulevard, *courtesy Academy of Motion Picture Arts and Sciences)*

with William Morris and CAA, one of the big-three talent agencies. When the agents of ICM want to take their clients to lunch, they go down the street to **Chasen's** (9039 Beverly), a Hollywood institution dating from 1936. Chasen's is known for its clubby, red-banquette-and-knotty-pine atmosphere, for its pricey chili, and for such star regulars as Jack Nicholson, Frank Sinatra, and Liz Taylor.

The Beverly Hills Civic Center, just west of where Beverly runs into Santa Monica Boulevard, is focused upon the **Beverly Hills City Hall**. This Spanish baroque masterpiece appeared prominently in both *Beverly Hills Cop* pictures, as well as in the obsessive Nicholas Ray drama *In A Lonely Place,* in which screenwriter Humphrey Bogart found himself in trouble with the law. Across Santa Monica Boulevard, "Our Lady of the Cadillacs" is the profane nickname for the **Church of the Good Shepherd**, at 505 N. Bedford. This was where Liz Taylor married Nicky Hilton, conveniently timing their wedding to coincide with the release of the original version of *The Father of the Bride.* You can also see this church in the funeral scene of *A Star Is Born* (1954 version). Another famous movie church is nearby: **All Saints Episcopal** (Camden Drive and Santa Monica Boulevard), where Dudley Moore first laid eyes on Bo Derek in *10.*

South of the City Hall, on Little Santa Monica Boulevard just west of Rodeo Drive, check out the small building tucked away from the main boulevard. This is the **Artists and Writers Building**, founded by Will Rogers for use by Hollywood writers, composers, and set designers. At the end of Little Santa Monica, which runs parallel to and south of the main boulevard, are the offices of **Creative Artists Agency**, an I.M. Pei-designed building which reflects the power of CAA and its head, **Michael Ovitz**.

Rodeo Drive itself is a looping avenue which heads up toward the hills, but the well-known shopping district is a short strip running between Santa Monica Boulevard and Wilshire Boulevard. More hype than substance, the buildings along Rodeo are surprisingly undistinguished-looking, with no "anchor," no sun-dappled plaza, no noticeable aesthetic sense at all. Glamorous stores like Celine (designer duds from Paris), Giorgio Armani (ditto, from Italy), Cartier (where Zsa Zsa buys her jewels), and Hammacher Sclemmer (gadgets for the super-rich) are all housed behind dumpy, steel-and-glass facades. The one slight exception is the fake European street that winds behind Two Rodeo Drive, designed mainly to enable even more retailers to crowd into the tiny shopping district. Rodeo Drive's celebrity status is based in no small measure on the exposure it has received in films, *Beverly Hills Cop, Down and Out in Beverly Hills,* and *Maid to Order* among them.

At the foot of Rodeo Drive, the **Beverly Wilshire Hotel** (9500 Wilshire Boulevard) was described by long-time guest Warren Beatty as "the only place to stay in Beverly Hills"—a pointed slap at the Beverly Hills Hotel, its competition. A graceful, imposing Italian Renaissance structure with a touch of Beaux Arts extravagance, the Wilshire has recently undergone a total refurbishing, and is well worth a look for its cooly lavish, marble-columned lobby.

Given a big boost by its appearance in the hit film *Pretty Woman,* the hotel even has a weekend "Pretty Woman" package for couples. Manager Alain Longatte tells of a Texas oil millionaire who flew in and wanted to reenact scenes from the film, asking to have the dressmaker who made Julia Roberts's evening dress make a duplicate for his girlfriend. The service offered by this four-star hostelry is such that the Texan's requests were fulfilled.

East of the Beverly Wilshire, the **Academy of Motion Picture Arts and Sciences** administrative building (8949 Wilshire) houses the offices of the "academy" responsible for the Academy Awards. There's not much to see here, though the Samuel Goldwyn auditorium has occasional public screenings. This is also where the Oscar-winners go to pick up their statuettes after they are engraved.

On the corner of Crescent and Wilshire is the mammoth corporate headquarters of **Kirk Kerkorian**, formerly head of MGM/UA. Kerkorian bailed out of the studio in a $1.3 billion buy-out deal in November of 1990, and this building was part of his golden parachute. For a long

"A place where you spend more than you make on things you don't need to impress people you don't like." —Ken Murray

The Playboy Mansion, Hugh Hefner's Bel-Air manor.

time, Kerkorian was the building's only tenant, and the joke around town was that it was his "deadquarters." Knowing Kerkorian's past as a Hollywood player (a quirky one, however—as MGM'S CEO he used to buy a ticket and stand in line like everyone else), it's a good bet the corner of Crescent and Wilshire will see some major action soon.

Two blocks away, at 151 S. El Camino Drive, is the **William Morris Agency**, still one of Hollywood's "Big Three" and with a history that stretches the furthest back of any talent agency, to the turn of the century. Their most famous agent-client match-up was Johnny Hyde and Marilyn Monroe, a romantic and business partnership that had pushed Marilyn into the big-time before Hyde died in 1950. North of Wilshire is the **Bistro** (240 N. Canon Drive), where Julie Christie made her notorious offer (of under-the-table fellatio) to Warren Beatty in *Shampoo.*

Two blocks south of Wilshire, on an island at the intersection of Beverly Drive and Olympic Boulevard, the **Monument to the Stars** was erected in 1959 to honor those movieland celebrities who "saved" Beverly Hills from annexation. In April 1923, the question was whether or not Beverly Hills was to follow other area communities (Hollywood among them) and be annexed to the City of Los

Angeles, which would have brought L.A. city services—most importantly, L.A. city water—but also L.A. city control and L.A. city taxes. The developers were all for it, but a group of movie stars thought Beverly Hills was doing fine on its own, thank you very much. Led by "mayor" Will Rogers and "king and queen"

HOLLYWOOD HUMOR

A producer and a screenwriter were stranded in the desert, their throats parched, dying of thirst. They're about to die, when suddenly they see a large, ice-cold glass of lemonade materialize before them. The screenwriter clutches at it gratefully, but just as he is about to drink, the producer says, "Wait, let's piss in it first."

A screenwriter is driving home, but when he comes to his street, he finds it blocked off with fire engines and police cars. "But officer," he tells the cop in charge, "I live down there." He is let through, only to find his house burned to the ground. "You the owner?" says the lieutenant. "Yes," says the writer, "my God, what happened?" "Well, it seems that your agent came to your house, raped your wife, killed your kids and set fire to the place." "Really?" asks the writer, dumbfounded. "My agent came to my house?"

Q. You're in an elevator, a pistol in your pocket with two bullets in it. Suddenly Saddam Hussein, Adolph Hitler and a Hollywood agent get on the elevator. What do you do?
A. Shoot the Hollywood agent twice.

The devil materializes before a Hollywood producer, promising him a string of hundred-million-dollar-grossing hits, with full profit participation, plus control of a studio. "The only thing you must do," say the devil, "is give me your soul, and the souls of your wife and children." "What's the catch?" asks the producer.

An agent and his mistress are sailing in shark-infested waters when the agent suddenly falls overboard. As he is swimming nonchalantly back to the boat, his mistress calls out, "Why aren't the sharks attacking you?" "Professional courtesy," the agent calls back.

Douglas Fairbanks and Mary Pickford, the celebrities memorialized with this statue canvassed the voters and turned back the annexation attempt.

East on Olympic, the intersection of La Cienega is the site where **Zsa Zsa Gabor was arrested** in June 1989 for slapping a police officer during a routine traffic citation. Gabor spent three days in *durance vile* for that one. But the serious attraction of the area is the **Margaret Herrick Library of the Academy of Motion Picture Arts and Sciences** (333 S. La Cienega), a treasure trove of film resources from scripts to books to press clippings. Located in a beautifully restored water purification plant originally modeled on La Giralda in Seville, the Academy's film vaults have been ingeniously located in the old storage tanks of the building. Note the programmatic touch of the giant film reel above the front door. The library is for research only—no lending of materials—but it is open to the public and a great way to track down information on your favorite actor or director.

Olympic Boulevard exits the western boundaries of Beverly Hills at the 26-acre grounds of **Beverly Hills High School** (255 S. Lasky Drive). The school is known for, among other things, having its own oil wells. These revenue-producers have underwritten lavish facilities, including the famous gymnasium-over-a-swimming-pool seen in Frank Capra's *It's a Wonderful Life*. (Movie trivia note: the guy who pushed the button that pulled the floor out from under Jimmy Stewart and Donna Reed was Carl Switzer, "Alfalfa" in the *Our Gang* series.) Established in 1928, the real Beverly Hills High School is far fancier than the one seen in the TV show *Beverly Hills 90210* (which is actually shot at nondescript Torrance High in the South Bay), and has graduated hundreds of people who've gone on to fame and fortune in Hollywood, including Rob Reiner, Carrie Fisher, Richard Dreyfuss, and Richard Chamberlain.

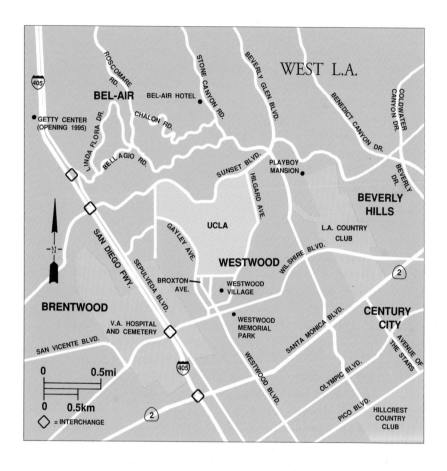

W E S T L . A .

WEST OF BEVERLY HILLS, THE SOUTHERN SLOPES of the Santa Monica Mountains form a fertile crescent into which the rich have dug their badger-holes. Bel-Air, Brentwood, Pacific Palisades—these are the communities, less showy but equally high-priced as Beverly Hills, which make up the heart of **West L.A.** Their restraint is that of the aristocratic snob in the face of nouveau riche extravagance. **Brentwood**, for example, is so inconspicuous that it could be any anonymous upscale town in the Midwest. But don't let the aura confuse you: this is extremely valuable real estate.

There are a few exceptions to West L.A.'s somnolent air, none more startling than Century City, perhaps the single most chilling vision of what L.A. would be like if we started all over and let the developers have their way. Built in the sixties on the old Twentieth Century-Fox backlot, **Century City** is more film business than film industry, since its antiseptic highrises are where entertainment lawyers and agents ply their trade.

In contrast, **Westwood**, a Mission-style retail village near the UCLA campus, is the Los Angeles equivalent of a college town. It also has the most concentrated collection of first-run theaters in the city, perhaps the world, and on weekends the movie lines (and the occasional movie riot) have become a cliché. For pedestrian sightseeing and the odd evening stroll, it is unparalleled in L.A. The shops and boutiques offer first-rate opportunities to lighten your wallet, although Westwood's true charm is that it offers something all too rare in the area: street life.

The San Diego Freeway runs through the heart of West L.A., separating the sleepy residential neighborhoods from the lively beachfront communities of **Venice** and **Santa Monica**, both of which, like Westwood, are exceptions to L.A.'s rule by automobile. Venice in particular has an engagingly bohemian air, residue of its founding as an arts-oriented seaside utopia. From Venice, a broad golden beach, and the Pacific Coast Highway, stretches north along the Santa Monica Bay to **Malibu**, whose ramshackle center belies its status as the home of Hollywood's elite.

RONALD REAGAN IN HOLLYWOOD

Ronald Reagan first came to Los Angeles from Des Moines, Iowa as a sportscaster covering the Chicago Cubs. William Wrigley, the chewing gum mogul who owned the team, also owned Catalina Island, so he ordained that the Cubs should take spring training there. In 1937, young Reagan came, took a screen test and conquered: he was in Hollywood for the next three decades, until he took up residence in Sacramento as governor of California in 1965.

Contract player, perennial second lead, union representative, erstwhile politico, Ronald Reagan has had a long and variegated Hollywood history. During his time there, he left behind a string of addresses, many of them to buildings still standing, which trace the history of the man who went from playing straight man to a chimpanzee to become President of the United States.

Selected Reagan sites:

Catalina Island. The Cubs 1937 spring training camp was held at Catalina Baseball Park at Fremont Street and Avalon Boulevard.

Warner Brothers Studio, 4000 Warner Boulevard, Burbank. Beginning June 1, 1937, Reagan was a $200-a-week contract player there. First film: *Love Is On the Air.*

Barney's Beanery, 8477 Santa Monica Boulevard. Where Reagan hung out in his early days in Hollywood. "Barney is a kindly soul, who recognized our need for a pub to call our own," he wrote in *Where's the Rest of Me?*

Wee Kirk o' the Heather, Forest Lawn, 1712 S. Glendale Avenue. Where the wedding of Jane Wyman and Ronald Reagan took place on Jane 26, 1940. The wedding reception was at the home of gossip columnist Louella Parsons.

Coconut Grove, in the Ambassador Hotel at 3400 Wilshire Boulevard. Where Ronald Reagan and Jane Wyman made their social debut after their honeymoon.

1326 Londonderry View, apartment #5. Reagan first lived with Jane Wyman here. After his divorce from Wyman in 1948, he moved back into same apartment.

Lakeside Country Club, 4500 Lakeside Drive, Burbank. Reagan resigned his membership after learning (because they refused Jack Warner) that the place had an exclusionary policy toward Jews. He joined the Hillcrest County Club, 10000 W. Pico Boulevard, Century City, instead.

"**Fort Roach,**" 8822 Washington Boulevard. Where Reagan made training and propaganda films during World War II.

Chasen's, 9039 Beverly Boulevard. Where a waiter once called Reagan, his post-war career on the wane, "Mr. Wyman."

Ciro's, (now the Comedy Store), 8433 Sunset Boulevard. *Silver Screen* magazine caption, April 1951: "Ronald Reagan and Nancy Davis at Ciro's. Their romance is a big thing." It was "their" place, the nightclub to which they repaired when their first business dinner (he was Screen Actors Guild president, she was an aspiring actress and union member with a billing problem) turned romantic. That first night, they saw Sophie Tucker and "laughed till we cried."

The Little Brown Church in the Valley, 4418 Coldwater Canyon Boulevard. Ronald Reagan married Nancy Davis here on March 4, 1952.

All-Electric House, 1669 San Onofre Drive, Pacific Palisades. General Electric erected this house for the Reagans because Ron was the company spokesperson. The street it's on is named for Southern California's main nuclear power plant.

Home of Nancy and Ronald Reagan today, 668 St. Cloud Road, Bel-Air. A group of supporters pitched in and bought the Reagans this home when he retired from the presidency in 1988.

"I came to Hollywood to act, not to charm society." —James Dean (Still from Bedtime for Bonzo, *courtesy Academy of Motion Picture Arts and Sciences*)

■ BEL-AIR

There is still a gate to the once-private development of Bel-Air, founded by Alphonzo E. Bell in the twenties, but the area is open to the public now, and only the name symbolizes exclusivity. Exclusivity, and the type of mindlessness brought on by too much wealth, as evidenced in such films as *The Prince of Bel-Air*, and the television series *Fresh Prince of Bel-Air*. The large estates are thickly landscaped, effectively shutting them off from the peering eyes of the public.

The *Beverly Hillbillies* mansion (750 Bel-Air Road) was bought and leveled, rows of 50-year-old laurel trees uprooted, and the land combined with two other estates to make a new home for Jerry Perenchio, the producing partner to Norman *"All in the Family"* Lear. That's progress, Bel-Air style. The original mansion seen in the long-running television series was built in 1935 by Lyman Atkinson, an engineer who designed the Hoover Dam before striking it rich in oil. The house featured gold oil derricks for faucets in one bathroom, but the person Atkinson built it for—his wife—hated the place and refused to move in. So the Clampetts did. Jed would have been proud that the **home of Nancy and Ronald Reagan** (668 St. Cloud Road) is just down the hill—the number used to be 666, sign of the Antichrist in Revelations, but numerological Nancy had it changed.

High up on Bel-Air Road (at 938) is the mansion of the self-crowned Queen of Bel-Air, **Zsa Zsa Gabor**. She took an old mansion owned by Howard Hughes ("it looked like a whorehouse," she says) and totally remade it, even putting in an in-house nightclub, the Moulin Rouge. Zsa Zsa is famous for her pronouncements on the superiority of Bel-Air, especially vis-à-vis Beverly Hills: "Bel-Air is not like Beverly Hills at all. It's very chic, elegant. Underplayed people live here. Beverly Hills is all showoff, showoff, showoff."

Chic, elegant, and underplayed is definitely the way to describe the cooly stunning grounds of the **Bel-Air Hotel** (701 Stone Canyon Road), a place that redefines the word "seclusion." The English writer Evelyn Waugh communicated the slightly mysterious, Mediterranean air of the place, circa 1947: "It was more like Egypt, the suburbs of Cairo, or Alexandria than anything in Europe. We arrived at the Bel-Air Hotel—very Egyptian with a hint of Addis Ababa."

Other guests have been reminded of the the South Seas, Thailand, or the south of France, but there is probably not another place like the Bel-Air on earth. Swans glide in a lake beneath a waterfall as the jacarandas bloom; 11 acres of gardens give guests plenty of room to wander. In fact, the whole lay-out is designed to make you feel as if you are the only guest there, if not the only person on earth. The hotel bar, with its lustrous wood wainscoting, was once the hang-out of Howard Hughes during his movie-producing days, but it is the open-air, flower-scented terrace that is most appealing. The lineup of stars that have taken the rest cure here stretches from the 1920s—when the original Bel-Air development company's real estate offices were converted into a hostelry—down to the present time.

Down amongst the plebes of Sunset Boulevard is the former home of **Jayne Mansfield** (10100 Sunset). The mansion was originally built in 1932 by Rudy Vallee, who called it "Three Palms," but Jayne wanted to put her own stamp on the place. She put in a heart-shaped pool (with "I Love You Jaynie" painted on its bottom) and had the house painted bright pink. A little more down to earth, at 10431 Bellagio Road, is the *9 to 5* **house**, where in the film Lily Tomlin, Jane Fonda, and Dolly Parton conspire to commit Dabney Coleman to bondage.

A number of Hollywood figures have made homes in the leafy neighborhoods at the foot of Bel-Air. Aaron Spelling, the money's-no-object television producer (*The Love Boat, Charlie's Angels,* and *Beverly Hills 90210*) razed Bing Crosby's mansion to erect **The Manor** (594 S. Mapleton Drive). Highly visible, the 56,500-sq-ft Manor (roughly the area of a football field) includes the obligatory gym, bowling alley, swimming pool, and tennis court on its six-acre estate, and also has pluses like a skating rink and a lily pond. Spelling's neighbors are the ghosts of Humphrey Bogart and Lauren "Betty" Bacall, the rare Hollywood star couple who actually seemed to be in love with each other: **Bogey and Bacall's house** was at 232 S. Mapleton Drive; they lived there until he died of cancer in 1957.

A bit more sprightly are Hugh and Kimberly Hefner of the **Playboy Mansion** (10236 Charing Cross Road). More subdued than it was in the swinging sixties, the place still has its security intercom built into a boulder at the front gate, and there's still a small zoo on the grounds. The inside of the mansion can be glimpsed in the movie *Star 80,* starring Mariel Hemingway as soon-to-be murdered "playmate" Dorothy Stratten.

■ WESTWOOD AND UCLA

It is amazing that the sybaritic paradise of Bel-Air is just minutes away from the overpopulated precincts of UCLA and its attendant shopping village, **Westwood**. UCLA (south of Sunset between Hilgard and Veteran avenues) is becoming increasingly recognized as a film school, with its screenwriting programs especially strong. The campus itself—which passed for U.C. Berkeley in the *The Graduate*—is the same scramble of architecture found at public universities everywhere, but there's something delightful and ironic about such a collegiate environment—complete with skateboarders, bicyclists, and downwardly mobile dress codes—in the middle of some of the most expensive real estate on earth. UCLA offers a couple of marvelous free opportunities for unenrolled film aficionados. Its Melnitz Hall theater shows movies day and night throughout the school year, and its University Research Library has extensive collections of film-oriented material—both are open to the public.

Westwood Village, built in the twenties with low-rise, Spanish Colonial-style buildings forming a compact shopping precinct, is one of the few L.A. places that

Sidewalk surfing at sunset.

"Hollywood is the only town where everybody at least thinks they're cute."
—John Waters

seems to have pedestrians in mind, even though it too has become clogged with cars (the best way to avoid traffic is by use of the RTD shuttle). Like many good things in L.A., Westwood has suffered from overuse, but on a quiet weekday evening it can still be a pleasant place to stroll; on the weekends, the movie crowds lend the streets a carnival-like—some say zoo-like—atmosphere. The village is famous for its cinemas, including the **Fox Village** and **The Bruin**, both on Broxton Avenue and both dating from the golden age of theater design. Westwood has more screens and seats than anywhere else in L.A., and is one of the few places where you can still experience anything like the opening-night thrill of a Hollywood premiere.

Tucked away across busy Wilshire Boulevard from the hustle and bustle of Westwood Village is **Westwood Memorial Park**. (It's unmarked and hard to locate, approached by driveways beside the Avco movie theater, to the east and south of the intersection of Wilshire and Glendon Avenue.) The cemetery should be nicknamed "Home of the Doomed Ingenue," since it's the final resting place of such tragedy-struck actresses as Marilyn Monroe, Natalie Wood, Dorothy Stratten, and Heather O'Rourke (the little girl from *Poltergeist*), as well as that collector of starlets, Peter Lawford.

Monroe's crypt, located in the northeast corner of the cemetery, is no longer the beneficiary of weekly roses from her ex-husband, Joe DiMaggio, but fans leave tributes there constantly. Stratten, the Playboy Playmate who appeared in *They All Laughed* but was cut down by a jealous ex-husband, has one of the fiercer epitaphs ever committed to bronze:

> *If* people bring so much courage to this world, the world has to kill them to break them. So of course it kills them. It kills the very good and the very gentle and the very brave impartially. If you are none of these you can be sure it will kill you too, but there will be no special hurry.

■ CENTURY CITY

Century City, West L.A.'s sole high-rise district, was first envisioned by New York real estate mogul William Zeckendorf and Beverly Hills hotelier Hernando Courtright, who negotiated for a huge chunk of the Twentieth Century-Fox backlot and proposed a vertical village, a multi-story megalopolis. They were eventually bought out by the Alcoa Aluminum Corporation, and a canned city sprang up on the lot where Tyrone Power, Shirley Temple, and Marilyn Monroe were once put through their paces.

Much of the office space of Century City is taken up by agents, entertainment lawyers, production companies, and other film-related businesses, and its many glass towers and modernist public spaces have been seen on celluloid countless times, from *The Turning Point* (where it was supposed to be New York's Lincoln Center) to *Conquest of the Planet of the Apes* (where it was a city of the future). The most famous use of a Century City office tower, however, was in *Die Hard*, in which Bruce Willis saved the 34-story **Fox Plaza** (2121 Avenue of the Stars) from terrorists.

Immediately adjacent to Century City (the skyscrapers ruin its sight-lines) is the sole remnant of the **Twentieth Century-Fox** movie lot, at 10201 Pico Boulevard, founded by film pioneer William Fox in 1927 on the site of movie cowboy Tom Mix's old ranch. Fox was forced out and his company merged with Twentieth Century, headed by the hard-nosed Joseph Schenck and the brilliant movie-man Darryl Zanuck. Musicals such as *The King and I* and *The Sound of Music;* comedies such as *How to Marry a Millionaire* and *M*A*S*H;* social dramas such as *The Grapes of Wrath* and *Gentlemen's Agreement;* action adventures like *The French Connection* and *Romancing the Stone*—they all came out of this amazing studio.

Visible through the open gate of Fox is the **New York set**, used in *Hello, Dolly!* as well other films, and modeled after the stretch of Lafayette Street between Fourth Street and Astor Place in Manhattan. Since there are no tours offered to the public, this glimpse through the gate is about the closest you can come to the magic that is Twentieth Century-Fox. One great way to take a whirlwind tour of the lot is to watch the final scenes of *Grand Canyon*, in which Kevin Kline and Steve Martin take a golf-cart journey through this prime cinematic turf.

■ SANTA MONICA

The most famous L.A. beach community of them all, Santa Monica, is the home of progressive politics, trendy restaurants—and a few sites from the nascent California film industry. Even though the city has announced its intention to lure more film-related business to its boundaries, as far as the movies are concerned the past is still weightier than the present. For much of its existence, beginning with its origins as a beach resort in the late 1800s, Santa Monica was a snoozy little place. The coming of the freeway in the mid-sixties changed all that, and Santa Monica swiftly became one of L.A.'s most sought-after addresses.

The **Santa Monica Pier**, which juts out into the Pacific at the end of Colorado Avenue, has been the setting for many period films, but its most notable appearance was in *The Sting*, wherein its 70-year-old carousel was supposedly in Chicago, being operated by Paul Newman. The Depression-era dance marathon of *They Shoot Horses, Don't They?* (starring longtime Santa Monica resident Jane Fonda) and *The Glenn Miller Story* both took advantage of the fact that the pier once featured a nationally famous ballroom, which also was where Lawrence Welk got his start. TV shows—*Charlie's Angels, Three's Company*, and *Fresh Prince of Bel-Air*—

Santa Monica Pier is a playground by day and night.

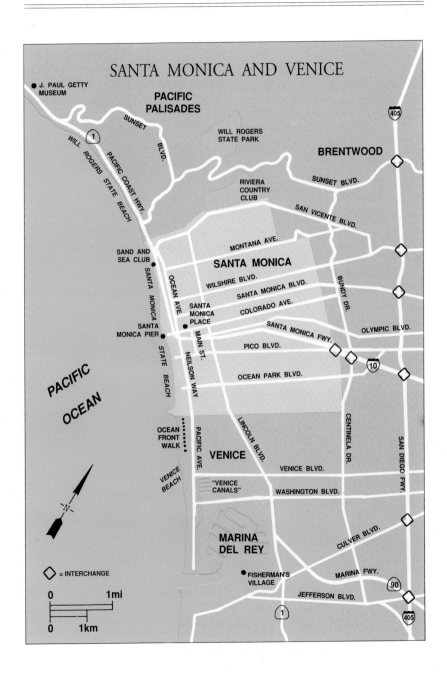

SANTA MONICA AND VENICE

• J. PAUL GETTY
MUSEUM

**PACIFIC
PALISADES**

SUNSET

WILL ROGERS
STATE PARK

BRENTWOOD

405

WILL ROGERS STATE BEACH

PACIFIC COAST HWY.

1

BLVD.

SUNSET BLVD.

RIVIERA
COUNTRY
CLUB

SAN VICENTE BLVD.

MONTANA AVE.

SAND AND
SEA CLUB •

SANTA MONICA

WILSHIRE BLVD.

SANTA MONICA BLVD.

OCEAN AVE.

SANTA
MONICA
PLACE

COLORADO AVE.

BUNDY DR.

OLYMPIC BLVD.

SANTA
MONICA PIER •

SANTA MONICA FWY.

SANTA MONICA BLVD.

MAIN ST.

STATE BEACH

NELSON WAY

PICO BLVD.

OCEAN PARK BLVD.

**PACIFIC
OCEAN**

10

OCEAN
FRONT
WALK

PACIFIC AVE.

LINCOLN BLVD.

VENICE

VENICE
BEACH

"VENICE
CANALS"

VENICE BLVD.

WASHINGTON BLVD.

CENTINELA DR.

SAN DIEGO FWY.

◇N

**MARINA
DEL REY**

CULVER BLVD.

◇ = INTERCHANGE

• FISHERMAN'S
VILLAGE

MARINA FWY.

90

0 ———— 1mi

JEFFERSON BLVD.

1

405

0 ———— 1km

love it as a setting for mindless fun and oceanside antics. From the pier, the beach-front south to Venice was once the heart of Santa Monica's down-market resort area, lined by huge hotels and amusement parks and thinly disguised as "Bay City" by Raymond Chandler, as in this passage from *Farewell, My Lovely:*

> Outside the narrow street fumed, the sidewalks swarmed with fat stomachs. Across the street a bingo parlour was going full blast and beside it a couple of sailors with girls were coming out of a photographer's shop. The voice of the hot dog merchant split the dusk like an axe.
>
> There was a faint smell of ocean. Not very much, but as if they had kept just this much to remind people this had once been a clean open beach where the waves came in and creamed and the wind blew and you could smell something besides the hot fat and the cold sweat.

A different class of leftover from Santa Monica's past stretches along the clean white strand to north of the pier. This was the fabled **Gold Coast**, a string of posh

Marion Davies's Santa Monica beach house was one of early Hollywood's party palaces. (Academy of Motion Picture Arts and Sciences)

homes owned by the wealthiest of the wealthy, many of them in the movie business. A majority of the Gold Coast homes have been demolished, and the few that remain are remodeled or walled in. At 625 Pacific Coast Highway (near the pedestrian crossover) is the former home of Louis B. Mayer, king of MGM; a later tenant was Kennedy in-law Peter Lawford, who provided this luxurious beachfront home as a place for Jack and Bobby to get away from the pressures of politics—and entertain Hollywood starlets like Marilyn Monroe. **The Sand and Sea Club**, at 415 Pacific Coast Highway, was once the servants' quarters for the mansion of another high-living denizen of the Gold Coast, Marion Davies, mistress of William Randolph Hearst.

On the bluffs above the pier and the beach, in the heart of the town of Santa Monica, the "hospital" used on Marcus Welby, M.D. is actually known as the General Telephone Building (Wilshire Boulevard at Ocean Avenue). A block away, one of Santa Monica's oldest buildings was also used briefly as the headquarters of **Vitagraph Films** (1438 Second Street), where the pioneering company had

Pacific Coast Highway in Santa Monica, ca. 1907. (L.A. County Natural History Museum)

its offices from 1911 to 1915. After being one of the country's premier producers of silent shorts, Vitagraph was taken over by Warner Brothers in the wholesale consolidations of the film business in the twenties. Also on Second Street was the original **Gold's Gym**, seen in Arnold Schwarzenegger's debut film, *Pumping Iron*. A block away, the high-style **Santa Monica Place** shopping center played a starring role in Arnie's *Terminator 2*, while the outdoor mall which stretches to the north was the location of the bike shop seen in *Pee Wee's Big Adventure*.

■ BRENTWOOD AND PACIFIC PALISADES

The overlapping communities of Brentwood and Pacific Palisades, which spread over the foothills north of Santa Monica, are yet more affluent West L.A. neighborhoods, more small-town and countrified than Bel-Air but still among the city's most exclusive corners. Along with winding Sunset Boulevard, well-groomed San Vicente Boulevard is the main thoroughfare, a curving green swath popular with joggers and bicyclists.

Most of **Brentwood** is residential, with the exception of fantasy-within-a-fantasy **Mount St. Mary's College** (12001 Chalon Road), a favorite locale of TV shows and also seen in Mel Brooks's *High Anxiety*. The *Mommie Dearest* **house** (426 N. Bristol Avenue) was the site of Joan Crawford's autocratic family rule, as chronicled by daughter Christina in her book. The Faye Dunaway movie did not use this house as a setting, it having passed out of the hands of Crawford and into those of actor Donald O'Connor. A short distance away, at 231 N. Rockingham Road, is a more idyllic childhood home, the **house of Shirley Temple** when she was growing up. Amenities for the child star included her own little cottage, complete with a working soda fountain. Shirley would later move into this cottage with her first husband.

A sadder place is the rather cramped bungalow where **Marilyn Monroe** died, at 12305 Fifth Helena Drive between Sunset and San Vicente. It serves to remind us just how loose and adrift the star was in her last days, that her body lay unclaimed in the morgue after the coroner got through with it. Somehow it's fitting that a short distance away is the house where **Raymond Chandler** (12216 Shetland Lane) lived while he was working on screenplays such as *Double Indemnity* and novels like *High Window* and *The Lady in the Lake*.

MARILYN MONROE'S LOS ANGELES

In the full glamor of her glory years and the tragic spasm of her death, it's easy to forget that Marilyn Monroe was an L. A. girl, born and bred. Or rather, born and thrown to the wolves: Norma Jean Mortensen was in a foster home by the time she was two weeks old, then leapfrogged through a succession of them. When she was nine, she was placed in the Los Angeles Orphan's Home.

After such tumultuous beginnings, it's little wonder that Marilyn's later life was a tangle of broken relationships and missed opportunities. Throughout her adult life, she was looking for something she had lost two weeks out of the womb: a sense of security. She never found it in L.A., and she attempted suicide at least three times before her final, fatal success. Her migrations in the City of Angels can be easily traced, because hers is one of the most well-documented lives in Hollywood.

Los Angeles General Hospital, 1200 S. State Street, downtown. Norma Jean was born here in 1926 to Gladys Baker Mortensen in the charity ward.

continues

"When I remember this desperate, lie-telling, dime-hunting Hollywood I knew only a few years ago, I get a little homesick. It was a more human place than the paradise I dreamed of and found." —Marilyn Monroe

Vine Street School, 955 N. Vine Street, Hollywood. Norma Jean briefly and happily attended school here while living with a foster family.

Los Angeles Orphan's Home, 815 N. El Centro Avenue, Hollywood. Norma Jean arrived sobbing, "But I'm not an orphan!" It was true: her mother was alive, but in an insane asylum.

Adel Precision Products, Olive Avenue at Lake Street, Burbank. The machine shop where Jim Dougherty worked, and where 15-year-old Norma Jean had her first date with him at the company Christmas party in 1941. A year later, they were married.

Florentine Gardens, 5951 Hollywood Boulevard. The downscale nightclub where Norma Jean Dougherty went with her husband to celebrate her wedding.

Ambassador Hotel, 3400 Wilshire Boulevard. In 1944 Norma Jean signed up with the Blue Book Modeling Agency, which had its offices in the Ambassador.

Twentieth Century-Fox, 10202 W. Pico Boulevard, West L.A. The first studio to put her under contract (in 1946), and the one that changed her name to Marilyn Monroe.

Joseph Schenck Mansion, 141 S. Carolwood, Bel-Air. The septuagenarian mogul of Twentieth Century-Fox kept Monroe briefly as a live-in mistress, which no doubt hurt her self-esteem but boosted her career.

William Morris Agency, 151 S. El Camino Drive, Beverly Hills. The agency of Johnny Hyde, Monroe's lover and the man who broke her into the big time.

Shelly Winters' apartment, 8573 Holloway Drive, West Hollywood. Which Monroe shared as a roommate just as her career started to take off, in 1951.

Villa Nova Restaurant, 9015 Sunset Boulevard. Marilyn met Joe DiMaggio here on a blind date. They would marry in January 1954.

Site of Marilyn Monroe's death, 12305 Fifth Helena Drive, Brentwood. Where she was discovered on August 5, 1962.

Westwood Memorial Park Cemetery, 1218 Glendon Avenue. Marilyn's final resting place is a crypt in the mausoleum, where Joe DiMaggio had fresh roses placed three times a week for over two decades.

Norma Jean Mortensen, aka Marilyn Monroe. (Academy of Motion Picture Arts and Sciences)

Much of **Pacific Palisades** stands on slowly deconstructing bluffs above the Pacific Coast Highway. One of the neighborhood's most enticing spots is a mile or so inland, above Sunset Boulevard in the foothills of the Santa Monica Mountains. The home and ranch of Depression-era cowboy-comedian Will Rogers, one of the few Hollywood homes open to the public, is now owned by the state, and protected as the 187-acre **Will Rogers State Historic Park** (14235 Sunset Boulevard). A serene combination of public space and Hollywood history, Rogers's rambling home is well maintained and packed with memorabilia from his show-biz career. A short film in the Visitors Center, housed in the converted carriage house, highlights the good-natured humorist's amazing facility with the lariat, while on the polo field games are still played on the weekends in honor of the man who brought the sport to Hollywood. The surrounding parkland is open to the public for picnics and hiking, with many trails leading up into the neighboring wilderness of Topanga Canyon State Park, giving the common man the chance to enjoy some of the toniest real estate on earth.

Beyond here, Sunset Boulevard continues west to the Pacific, which it meets at Will Rogers State Beach—another of Rogers's legacies. Further along, on the way to Malibu, the J. Paul Getty Museum stands above the shore (see "Museums" in "Major Attractions" for details).

Hollywood aristocrats show up for the polo matches at Will Rogers State Park.

The Getty Museum houses one of the world's finest collections of classical art.
(J. Paul Getty Museum, photo by Jack Ross)

▪ MALIBU

Northwest of Santa Monica along the Pacific are the expensive shorefront estates of **Malibu**, the Gold Coast of this age, a movie-money-encrusted enclave of the "idol rich." Originally a Spanish *rancho*, Malibu was one the last great hold-outs against L.A.'s ever-expanding urban sprawl. A wealthy landowner, Frederic H. Rindge, bought the *rancho* and resisted all efforts of the neighboring metropolis to breach it. Rindge even built his own private railroad to prevent a public one from winning a right-of-way through his land. But the barbarians beat down the gate in 1929 with the building of the Pacific Coast Highway, and since then Malibu has become known for palatial homes, road-tested Lamborghinis, and furious film-colony in-breeding. Movies such as *Mildred Pierce, Kiss Me Deadly,* and *Less Than Zero* have used the beach community here to symbolize success and excess.

In April 1991, Malibu incorporated itself as a separate city, motivated more by the desire to prevent out-of-control development than by any need to be recognized as a civic entity. It's not hard to see what overbuilding has done to this beautiful stretch of the Pacific shore: choked rows of beach houses, pushed chock-a-block upon each other, form a gauntlet along the Pacific Coast Highway. Unless you're here after the annual winter storms, which regularly wipe out at least a couple of these beachfront boxes, one of the few places you can actually see the sea is just north of aging Malibu Pier. The pier itself is emblematic of TV's *The Rockford Files,* and the beach there, officially called **Malibu Surfrider State Beach**, is renowned in Beach Boy circles for its reef-point break.

Beyond the pier, the ultra-exclusive **Malibu Colony** (off Malibu Road east of Webb Way) is one of Malibu's oldest beach communities. "The Colony" is a private, gated and highly secured community, but an agreement with the state to repair breakwaters forced it to make its beach public, so the ocean side of the community is accessible. Paterfamilias of the Colony is Larry Hagman, who lives on Malibu Colony Drive, while its resident psychic is Shirley MacLaine, on Malibu Road.

West of the Colony, past Pepperdine University ("Surfer U."), is **Dan Blocker State Beach**, named for the *Bonanza* star and longtime Malibu resident. Another, newer but equally prestigious beachfront community is the **Malibu Riviera**, up the coast at Point Dume. The most famous Malibu Riviera residences are probably those of the Sheen family on Dume Drive, and Johnny Carson, at the end of Wildlife Road near White Sand Place. Nearby is Carroll O'Connor, on Broad

Beach Road. Again, most of the land is private, but the beaches at least are open to the public.

Art directors of surfing movies love the Malibu beaches, naturally. **Zuma Beach**, on the west side of Point Dume, has been the setting for *Deadman's Curve,* the biopic of the surfin' group **Jan and Dean**, as well as *Beach Blanket Bingo* and its soggy sequel, *Back to the Beach.*

The **canyons above Malibu**, cutting up into the Santa Monica Mountains from Pacific Coast Highway, have in recent years become even more fashionable than the beach. This is because there is much more room to spread out than on the crowded shoreline, and also because a number of top-drawer celebs have put down stakes there. The first and most famous was **Barbra Streisand**, who colonized Ramirez Canyon Road with a huge compound consisting of mansion, guest houses, and sports facilities. Working westward, we find Nick Nolte on Rainsford Place and the late Michael Landon's house on Bonsall Drive, both in the lower reaches of Zuma Canyon, plus the Decker Canyon ranch of **Jack Nicholson**. Many of the roads, such as Malibu Canyon and Kanan-Dume Road, climb over the ridge to the western San Fernando Valley, passing by yet more Hollywood history in the many movie ranches that cover the crest. (See "THE VALLEYS" for more.)

The Malibu Colony, one of L.A.'s most exclusive communities.

BEAUTY ON THE BEACH

"*D*id you always want to be in movies?"

"No. When I was young I wanted to be a chief clerk—the one who knew where everything was."

She smiled.

"That's odd. And now you're much more than that."

"No, I'm still a chief clerk," Stahr said. " That's my gift, if I have one. Only when I got to be it, I found out that no one knew where anything was. And I found out that you had to know why it was where it was and whether it should be left there. They began throwing it all at me, and it was a very complex office. Pretty soon I had all the keys. And they wouldn't have remembered what locks they fitted if I'd given them back."

They stopped for a red light, and a newsboy bleated at him: "Mickey Mouse Murdered! Randolph Hearst declares war on China!"

"We'll have to buy his paper," she said.

As they drove on, she straightened her hat and preened herself. Seeing him looking at her, she smiled.

She was alert and calm—qualities that were currently at a premium. There was lassitude in plenty—California was filling up with weary desperadoes. And there were tense young men and women who lived back East in spirit while they carried on a losing battle against the climate. But it was everyone's secret that sustained effort was difficult here—a secret that Stahr scarcely admitted to himself. But he knew that people from other places spurted a pure rill of new energy for a while.

They were very friendly now. She had not made a move or a gesture that was out of keeping with her beauty, that pressed it out of its contour one way or another. It was all proper to itself. He judged her as he would a shot in a picture. She was not trash, she was not confused but clear—in his special meaning of the word, which implied balance, delicacy and proportion, she was "nice."

They reached Santa Monica, where there were the stately houses of a dozen picture stars, penned in the middle of a crawling Coney Island. They turned downhill into the wide blue sky and sea and went on along the sea till the beach slid out again from under the bathers in a widening and narrowing yellow strand.

—F. Scott Fitzgerald, *The Last Tycoon*, 1940

■ VENICE

Venice, Santa Monica's rowdier, lower-rent neighbor to the south, has been a fairly constant favorite of filmmakers. Not surprising, since this city was a planned beach resort fashioned after its Italian namesake, complete with canals and classical colonnades. Right around the turn of the century, an heir to a cigarette fortune named Abbot Kinney developed the place. It featured a Grand Lagoon and a network of waterways, upon which, on opening day July 4, 1905, there were gondoliers.

Kinney wanted the place to be the forefront of an American Renaissance in the arts, but bad drainage, the exhaustion of his considerable fortune, and the discovery of vast oil reserves caused the dream to abort. The City of Los Angeles took over, paved the **canals** (a few survive just south of Venice Boulevard), and the town settled into a long decline. This was the period when Orson Welles used the seediness to great effect in his *Touch of Evil* in which Venice stood in for a Mexican border town, and Welles himself ended up floating face down in the murky canals. For Venice as itself, try Roger Corman's B-movie classic, *Bucket of Blood,* a perfect (and hilarious) rendering of Venice as the sixties hipster's paradise. Turned into hell, of course, by Corman's gory tendencies.

What Kinney's grand design failed at first to do, low rents eventually accomplished, and during the seventies Venice emerged as an arts community without parallel in L.A. Most of the pseudo-Renaissance trappings of the downtown buildings were brought back to life, and a number of bookstores, cafes, and restaurants sprung up in the increasingly gentrified neighborhood. Film star Dennis Hopper is one of the many Hollywood outlaws who've boosted Venice property values, and it's one of the more interesting corners of L.A. in which to spend time.

Some of the clearest signs of this arts-based revival are the **murals of Venice**, remarkable for their breadth, color, and scope, with two of them—seen in the 1983 remake of *Breathless*—prominently displayed near Windward Avenue and Speedway. Area filmmaker Agnes Varda evoked these splashy samples of public art in a documentary, *Murs Murs.*

Despite its increasingly high-brow image, Venice is still very much a beach city, and the weekend parade of flesh, fetishes, and eccentrics on **Ocean Front Walk** has become a local rite of summer. Muscleboys, roller-derby mamas, sixties time-warp victims, and street performers turn out to be ogled by the tourists. And if you feel

"It is a tremendous playground, . . .

. . . and a lot of people want to get in and play." —Brian DePalma

your inhibitions melting away in the hot California sun, there are plenty of rental places where you can get yourself a pair of Rollerblades and transform yourself from ogler to oglee. This passing parade was showcased in two recent movies, *The Doors* and *L.A. Story*, both of which showed remarkably similar scenes set in what were supposed to be two disparate decades. Sadly, real-life Venice has some distinctly unsafe corners, with much of the Boardwalk and beachfront prone to gang- and drug-related violence, especially after dark.

■ MARINA DEL REY

Immediately south of Venice is Marina del Rey, a marshland transformed in the sixties into a harbor with the world's largest concentration of small boats and pleasure craft. Despite its generally anodyne appearance, parts of the marina have been well-exposed to the cameras, called into play whenever the script calls for a "charming seaside locale." *Mission Impossible* and *Murder, She Wrote*, among other series, used and perhaps overused **Fisherman's Village**, at the end of Fiji Way. And if you're flying out of town, you may want to forget that the *Airplane* movies, take-offs of the disastrous *Airport* and *Airport 1975* movies, were set at **Los Angeles International Airport**, located on the bluffs just south of the marina.

SOUTH BAY
CULVER CITY, LONG BEACH, AND SOUTH-CENTRAL L.A.

SOUTH OF VENICE AND SANTA MONICA, from the airport to the Palos Verdes peninsula, is a string of booming, upmarket communities—Manhattan Beach, Hermosa Beach, and Redondo Beach—collectively known as the **South Bay**, with the kind of fast-and-loose lifestyle portrayed in the movies *Tequila Sunrise* and *Point Break*—the surfer-thriller starring Patrick Swayze—as well as *Big Wednesday* —the seminal surfer movie directed by John Milius. (These and all the other L.A. beaches are described more fully in the "Beaches" section of "PRACTICAL INFORMATION.") Palos Verdes itself, visible from all over L.A., rises above its surrounding communities in two categories: feet-above-sea-level and median income. It is a somewhat insular, deliberately clannish area that retains some of its country ways —it is not uncommon to see people on horseback cantering along its streets. The peninsula also has the most stunning coastline in Los Angeles, terraces and cliffs rising above a rocky, wave-tossed shore.

However, the bulk of the South Bay area is made up not of charming beach towns but of anonymous, semi-industrial sprawl, overlooked and ignored in most discussions of what there is in L.A. One of the most interesting places here, especially from the point of view of the movies, is **Culver City**, home of many early Hollywood studios including MGM, where such classics as *The Wizard of Oz* and *Gone With The Wind* were made. By way of contrast, the bustling port areas to the south of Palos Verdes, around San Pedro and especially **Long Beach**, are about as far as you can get from the high-flying deal-making of Hollywood.

Another, equally unglamorous but, recently at least, much more publicized part of town is the huge spread of **South-Central L.A.**, which fills the 15-mile gap between Long Beach and downtown. South-Central L.A.—made up of distinct, predominantly black communities like Watts and Compton as well as industrial monsters like the City of Industry and its neighbor, the City of Commerce—is most notorious as the crack-addled heartland of the city's warring gangs, portrayed in such gritty films as *Colors* and *Boyz N the Hood*. Despite its recent woes, the area also has a strong if somewhat obscured heritage as a center of L.A.'s music scene: in the thirties and forties, Central Avenue, the main drag, was packed with wall-to-wall nightclubs, home turf to all the great names of jazz and blues.

■ CULVER CITY

Culver City, east of Venice and the airport, and south of the Santa Monica Freeway from Century City, is an incorporated entity that once provided a haven for studios fleeing the high rents of Hollywood. At one time, three studios were located there, busily turning out product: MGM, the giant, plus the lots of David O. Selznick and Hal Roach. "**The Motion Picture Capital of the World**" reads the plaque on the garish **Film Monument** at the intersection of Culver Boulevard and Overland Avenue, which isn't that much of an overstatement: though Culver City has lost much of its luster, back in the forties and fifties this small town was producing half the films released in the United States.

The old **Hal Roach Studios** (Washington and National), torn down in the sixties, churned out countless comedies, including the films of Harold Lloyd, Laurel and Hardy, and *Our Gang*, all of which used Culver City as an anonymous, all-American location. During World War II, the studios became known as "Fort Roach," the official studio of the U.S. military and source of many training and propaganda films featuring Lt. Ronald Reagan among others. The site is now a small park (note the bronze plaque remembering the "Laugh Factory to the World") and a large car dealership.

The jewel of all Hollywood studios, **Metro-Goldwyn-Mayer**, once had five lots and "more stars than there are in heaven," but it is now reduced to a single embattled office building known as MGM-**Pathe** (1000 W. Washington). At one time, however, MGM's backlot, now part of **Columbia Pictures** (10202 W. Washington) produced the finest motion pictures in Hollywood, watched over with loving grace by Irving Thalberg, the boy-wonder head of production, and Louis B. Mayer, a curious combination of autocrat and softie. This was the studio of Gish, Garbo, and Gable, Tracy and Hepburn, of Joan Crawford, Liz Taylor, Judy Garland, and Gene Kelly.

The producer Thomas Ince first sited a studio here, and his 1916 Triangle Building still stands. The huge 1939 Thalberg Building followed a change in taste from the ornamental to the monumental, and illustrated how the fortunes of the studio had skyrocketed. Both buildings are visible from the street.

Many Hollywood studios long ago moved to Culver City and the San Fernando Valley to take advantage of the cheaper real estate.

CHAIN OF COMMAND

*D*espite the apparent casualness of the troops—the shagginess and the sneakers—the film world was as rigidly hierarchical as the military. Richard Sylbert had been right when he'd said that movie-making was like war. The perfect war, in fact. There were uniforms and regiments and communications on walkie-talkies in code, middle-of-the-night maneuvers under grim conditions, and an overwhelming sense of mission. But all that got shot was film.

Approaching the field, it was useful to understand the chain of command. At the very top was the director, commander-in-chief but also the pinnacle of the first unit. He was in charge of the main event, drawing together all the elements—script, cast, cinematography, production design, costumes. The first unit was not to be confused with the first team, the actors with speaking parts. The second team, the stand-ins who did the tedious job of filling in for the actors while the lights and camera were set up, wasn't to be confused with the second unit. The second unit operated entirely independent of everybody else—but, of course, reported to the director.

There was an assistant director, whose job was to orchestrate crowd scenes, help schedule shooting, rehearse the performers, and generally keep order on the set. The second assistant director made sure everyone got to where the first assistant director wanted them to be, and the second to the second did what the second assistant did when the second assistant couldn't.

Every lieutenant had an assistant, and every assistant had assistants. A complex assortment of union rules guaranteed that film sets would be schizophrenic. There would be squadrons of people who never stopped moving from the first call to the final wrap every day. And there would be squadrons of people who never moved at all. The latter group had one job only: simply to be there. For example, because Vilmos Zsigmond belonged to the Los Angeles cinematographers' union, a New York cameraman showed up every day because New York union rules demanded it. The New York "director of photography" was paid $3,850 a week to sit and watch Zsigmond work. . . .

The social stratification was the only certainty on a film set. The players were always different, but status was constant. And almost everyone was angling for better status. The camera operator wanted to be a cinematographer; the cinematographer wanted to direct. The secretaries wanted to be associate producers; the P.A.'s, the production assistants, wanted to be anything that wasn't the lowest rung on the ladder. The stand-ins wanted to act. Everyone was working on a script.

The class distinctions started at the top and ended at the bottom, sometimes they were obvious and sometimes they were subtle, and everyone knew and joked about them. "What's the difference between an electrician and a grip?" the location scouts would ask. The answer: "The electricians take the dishes out of the sink before they pee in it."

—Julie Salamon,
The Devil's Candy—"The Bonfire of the Vanities" Goes to Hollywood, 1991

WHO DOES WHAT ON A FILM SET

ADR Editors. Automatic Dialog Replacement, a process known as "looping," by which muddy, distorted, or otherwise unusable dialog recorded on the set is replaced by that recorded by these editors in a sound studio.

Assistant Director. Popularly (or unpopularly, since they are the ones to call crew and actors to work), they are known as "A.D.'s," and are responsible for keeping track of who must be on the set for each shot, and for how long, and for what needs to be physically present in the shot, etc.—the thousand niggling details of filmwork.

Associate Producer. Comedian Fred Allen gave the following definition: "An associate producer is the only guy in Hollywood who will associate with a producer."

Best Boy. First assistant, usually to the gaffer, but sometimes to the key grip (when the function is called Best Boy Grip).

Camera Operator. When the camera's rolling, he's the one looking through the viewfinder. His assistants are the "focus puller," who adjusts the lens, and the "loader," who tops up the supply of film.

Cinematographer. Responsible for the "look" of the film: will it be soft and gauzy, or hard-edged and realistic? Union rules dictate that the cinematographer may look through, but not operate, the camera.

Director. They've toppled dictators elsewhere in the world, but on the film set the director reigns supreme. On his or her shoulders fall all major decisions and many minor ones about how a film looks, sounds, gets made, edited, etc.

continues

Editor. Takes the footage furnished by the director and cuts and splices it together into a complete film. One of the most underrated functions in all of filmdom.

Foley Artist. "Foley" is the process by which sound effects are recorded and added to the film's soundtrack. These can be quite creative. For example, an old sock filled with sand and beaten against a wooden log becomes, on the soundtrack, the heavy blows of a fistfight.

Gaffer. An Old-English alteration of "godfather," gaffer came to mean foreman or headman. The gaffer is more or less the foreman of the lighting crew.

Key Grip. The head of the grip crew, working underneath the director of photography to physically set up each shot.

Lead Man. As opposed to "leading man." The lead man is one step below set decorator, and directs the "swing gang"—the set dressing crew—to construct or strike sets.

Producer. Producers come in a lot of different flavors, but they all spell "boss." An executive producer is usually the person responsible for bringing the property (story, script, or play) or the money to the project. A line producer does the hiring and firing for the project, takes care of the details, and makes sure the checks get signed.

Production Assistant. "P.A.," or, more accurately, "go-fer." The coffee fetchers, errand runners, whipping kids of the film set. Strictly an entry level position.

Production Designer. What kind of lamp will be on the table in a certain scene? How will the room itself look? The production designer is at the top of a chain of command that creates the physical look of the film.

Screenwriter. The paradox of Hollywood: no good film can be made without a good script, but screenwriters, who are responsible for the scripts, are notoriously low on the cinematic totem pole. This is in part because everyone—from actors, agents, producers to entertainment lawyers—secretly believes they are writers.

Second Unit. A camera crew and director operating independently from the main unit, to film those scenes which do not involve speaking parts or major stars.

Wrangler. Head 'em up, move 'em out. The wranglers are in charge of the animals on a shoot. Sometimes the fauna is exotic: the "spider wranglers" on *Arachnophobia*, for example, or the "worm wranglers" on *Naked Lunch*.

Candice Bergen discusses a scene with fellow actors on the set of Murphy Brown.

Post-Thalberg, MGM's momentum carried it forward for decades, but with the increasing irascibility of Louis Mayer, and the breakdown of the star-contract system, its "heaven" faded. The MGM giant was dealt off piecemeal: it sold its backlot in 1969, its props and costumes a year later, and the studio itself to Lorimar Television in 1987. By that time, it was called MGM-UA, a harbinger of the ineffectual mergers in its future.

The recent history of the lot is much happier. Since the Sony Corporation purchased Columbia Pictures in 1990, it has been pumping massive amounts of money to refurbish and modernize the old MGM Studios. Unfortunately, some of this means that great old buildings, like the massive cyclorama shop (where the backdrops from *The Wizard of Oz* are stored), may soon be replaced.

In 1991, Sony-Columbia also purchased the **Culver City Studios** (9336 W. Washington Boulevard), which will eventually be used for Columbia's television

"'You will have the tallest, darkest leading man in Hollywood.' Those were the first words I heard about King Kong.*"* —Fay Wray. *(Still of* King Kong *onstage at the Shrine Auditorium, Academy of Motion Picture Arts and Sciences.)*

productions. These studios, too, are rich in history: they were once the stomping ground of such giants as King Kong and **Orson Welles**, who ran roughshod over the lot while filming *Citizen Kane* here in 1939.

Once again, it was pioneer Thomas Ince who in 1919 first built on the site, erecting the stately replica of George Washington's home, Mt. Vernon, that went on to become the logo of **David O. Selznick**. Shown at the beginning of all his films, including *Gone With The Wind*, it's often confused with Tara, Scarlett's plantation home. Director Cecil B. De Mille also swept through briefly—it was the leftover sets for De Mille's *King of Kings* that Selznick torched for the unforgettable "Burning of Atlanta" scene.

None of the area's surviving studios is open to the public, but to the south, Culver City's other attractions—its cemeteries—are free and accessible. **Holy Cross Cemetery** (5835 W. Slauson Avenue) is a huge tract set into the neighboring Baldwin Hills. To the immediate left of the entrance are grouped the graves of Charles Boyer, Bing Crosby, Bela "Dracula" Lugosi (said to have been buried in his cape), and Sharon Tate. The great director John Ford is buried at Holy Cross, too, higher up on the hill.

Farther south is the Jewish version of Holy Cross, **Hillside Memorial Park**, at 6001 Centinela Avenue. An imposing mausoleum, with a huge monument to Al Jolson in front of it, dominates the site. Legend has it that Jolson was about to sign up for a burial site elsewhere, when the developers of Hillside offered to pay for his memorial. Jolson jumped ship, and the result is an L.A. landmark—a kneeling, singing-his-heart-out Jolson, visible from the nearby San Diego Freeway. Hillside also contains the remains of Jack Benny, Eddie Cantor, George Jessel, and David Janssen. A recent tragic addition is the actor Vic Morrow, killed while filming the *Twilight Zone* in 1982.

■ LONG BEACH

"A cemetery with lights" is the catty jab at the staid and by-and-large conservative communities clustered on the southeast side of the Palos Verdes peninsula. The port towns of Wilmington and San Pedro offer a blue-collar balance to the more precious settings elsewhere in L.A., while the old U.S. Navy port of **Long Beach** has begun to show a little life with the continued presence of the Queen Mary and Spruce Goose as tourist attractions.

The **Queen Mary**, an overpowering sight in her permanent berth in the Port of Long Beach, has been featured in many films since she docked here in 1964. The 50,000-ton liner, the largest ever floated, stood in for the S.S. Poseidon on the fateful voyage chronicled by *The Poseidon Adventure*—interiors only, of course, since her hull is filled with concrete. In any event it is the interiors that are most impressive: lush Art Deco admixtures of brushed metal and polished wood, with pink marble flooring to set it all off. The liner was also featured in *Under the Rainbow* and *Someone to Watch Over Me*, and is now the site of the Queen Mary Hotel, as well as several shops and restaurants on her refurbished upper decks.

Next door to the ship is a domed structure which houses Howard Hughes's **Spruce Goose**—a name which Hughes himself hated. Built out of Sitka Spruce because of the wartime shortage of metals, it is the world's largest wooden airplane, and when you are up next to it, on platforms built to make the interior visible, it seems the largest airplane ever built, period, with a wingspan of 320 feet and a 219-foot length (97 m by 67 m). The Spruce Goose was designed to take-off and land on water, but was flown only once, skimming the bay for a few seconds in 1947—proof that Hughes did other things during his Hollywood years besides make films and chase starlets. Movie shorts about the Goose and Hughes are shown in the visitors center.

Howard Hughes's Spruce Goose flew only once.

(opposite) The Cunard Line's Queen Mary rests in peace in Long Beach harbor.

■ SOUTH-CENTRAL L.A.

Occupying the heart of the Los Angeles basin, inland from the South Bay beaches and stretching from downtown south to Long Beach, the predominantly black neighborhoods of Watts, Carson, Inglewood, and Compton have, both geographically and symbolically, long been overlooked by the film moguls tucked away in their Hollywood Hills hideaways. This whole section of the city, lumped together under the rubric of **South-Central Los Angeles**, has only in the past few years begun to show up on film.

While *Colors,* the Dennis Hopper/Sean Penn buddy movie, showed contemporary South-Central L.A. from a cop's-eye-view, director John Singleton's *Boyz N the Hood* gave us a cry from the native heart. The "hood" of the title means neighborhood, and Singleton (23 years old when the film was made) grew up here. At one point in his youth, his bedroom window faced a 70-foot drive-in movie screen, and he credits his obsession with film to that—and to repeated, early viewings of *Star Wars.* The specific 'hood of *Boyz N the Hood* is left vague, but Singleton grew up around West 60th Street, hung out in his father's old nabe of 101st Street and Vermont Avenue, and later lived most of his teen years in Inglewood.

The cruising scene featured in *Boyz* still goes on, primarily on Crenshaw Boulevard. The **Crenshaw Mall** is a locus of the black community, as is the **Museum in Black**. The latter, located near Leimert Park at 4327 Degnan Boulevard, is a small but jam-packed collection of African rugs, fabrics, and religious figurines as well as slavery-era documents and artifacts. The **Academy Theater** (Manchester and Crenshaw), a majestic Charles Lee-designed movie palace built in 1939, has been born-again as a church. More up-to-date, the **Baldwin Hills Theater** (La Brea at Rodeo), is the Grauman's Chinese of the African-American community, even to the point of featuring cement handprints of such stars as Louis Gosset, Marvin Gaye, and Billy Dee Williams.

■ WATTS

Because of the 1965 riots which devastated it, the neighborhood of Watts (Central Avenue around Century Boulevard) has a greater notoriety than it deserves, but it remains today a center of artistic and political activism. **Watts Towers** (1765 E. 107th Street) have been adopted as a symbol of the black community, even though they were constructed by an itinerant and enigmatic Italian tile-setter and plasterer variously known as Sabatino Rodella, Simon Rodia (his "official" name), or simply "Sam," who vanished without a trace soon after completing them.'

Featured as a convenient placemark in many films and TV shows, the soaring, 100-foot-tall (30-m) towers (which according to jazz composer Charles Mingus, who grew up nearby when they were still being built, look like upside-down ice cream cones) are one of the folk-art wonders of world. To build them, Rodia worked after-hours and on weekends from 1921 to 1954, building and sculpting, using found objects like seashells, mirrors, and pieces of smashed china to ornament the skin of his delicate towers, which would seem more at home in Gaudi's Barcelona than along the railroad tracks in Southern California. When a move was made to tear the structure down, the towers revealed their true strength, resisting the pull of a bulldozer; they were recently restored, and are now part of a community arts center.

Close by the Watts Towers is the **Will Rogers City Park**, yet another legacy of the film comedian and one which yields the unlikely sight of cricket players alongside the more likely hoop-stuffers of the basketball courts.

The Dunbar Hotel (4225 Central Avenue) is another monument to ethnic Los Angeles—this time black L.A. Built in 1928 by Dr. John Alexander Somerville as the plushest hotel in town catering to blacks, it endures as a symbol of L.A.'s segregated past and the fight for equality. The cultural display lodged in the hotel lobby features an illustrious history of black performers, many of whom (like Bill "Bojangles" Robinson and Steppin' Fetchit) came to Los Angeles to perform in the movies. The building is now a retirement home, a fate shared by many of the great hotels of the Hollywood era.

■ USC AND EXPOSITION PARK

In the no-man's land between South-Central and downtown L.A., southwest of the confluence of the Harbor and Santa Monica freeways, is the campus of the **University of Southern California**. USC's conservative politics, and emphasis on athletic rather than academic excellence, belies the fact that it is also (along with UCLA) one of the premier film schools in the U.S.—where George Lucas and John Singleton, among countless others, learned to make movies.

Across from USC is **Exposition Park**, a world-class concentration of museums

and public spaces. The **Memorial Coliseum**, where both the 1932 and the 1984 Olympics were held, and the Sports Arena are located here, as are the **Afro-American Museum**, the **Aerospace Museum**, the **Museum of Science and Industry**, and the **Los Angeles County Museum of Natural History** (see "Museums" in "MAJOR ATTRACTIONS" for more).

L.A. Lakers star Earvin "Magic" Johnson.

This last, bounded to the east by the marvelously fragrant seven-acre **Exposition Park Rose Garden** (19,000 plants strong), has a majestic interior instantly recognizable from the gala party scene in *Bonfire of the Vanities*. The diorama of the gazelle slaughter featured in the movie was created especially for *Bonfire* and is not seen here, but other, more sedate tableaus of animal life are available for inspection. The stately rotunda, topped by a stained-glass dome, was where a panicked Sherman McCoy (Tom Hanks) wandered through the glittery post-opera party in the film. The museum also features a small display on the motion picture industry, including such exhibits as a bronze of cowboy star William S. Hart and costumes of Charlie Chaplin, Mary Pickford, and Tom Mix.

North and east of USC and Exposition Park is the **Shrine Civic Auditorium** (665 W. Jefferson Boulevard), site of several Academy Awards telecasts but also the place where a captive King Kong was displayed in the original film. In the 1954 *A Star Is Born,* Judy Garland gave the film's climactic line—"This is *Mrs.* Norman Maine"—from the Shrine stage. It was here, also, that in 1984 Michael Jackson accidentally set his hair on fire during the filming of a Pepsi commercial—the commercial later being premiered during a Grammy ceremony telecast from the Shrine Auditorium.

A block west of Figueroa Street, just above Adams Boulevard on the campus of Mount St. Mary's College, is **Chester Place**, one of the many mansions of the early L.A. oil baron Edward Doheny, and often used as film location (*Godfather II,* among other movies). Close by, at 649 W. Adams Boulevard, is the **Theda Bara** house, built by one of the screen's first sex symbols (they called them "vamps" back then) and later owned by silent-film star Norma Talmadge.

Watts Towers rise up from the heart of South-Central Los Angeles.

BETTER THAN SEX

*B*arbara was delirious. She punched the air. She jigged up and down. She hugged her shoulders and made whooping noises like a police siren. She laughed and kissed me, saying: "Let's do something. Let's take crystal Methedrine. Let's call Moss. Let's go to Raging Waters."

I said, "What is Raging Waters?"

"I could party for days."

"What happened?"

"Everything happened. I did a great audition, that's what happened. I did the Jane Fonda thing like you said, you were right about that, then they had me read with this guy, some scene from *Body Heat*, and then they gave me a camera test. Joel said I was the best they'd seen so far. Easily. They'll let me know in a few days. But Joel says I'm home free."

I said, "Who's Joel?"

"He's the director guy I told you about. Isn't it just the greatest? Are you gonna call Moss or shall I?"

I said I'd do it. Moss came round ten minutes later. Barbara told him the news and made more police siren noises. I'd never seen her so excited. Moss offered his congratulations, Barbara grabbed a six-pack from the fridge, and we went outside to the car.

The Cadillac had been serviced: no more infested beer cans on the seats, no more *clunketa-clunketa* rumblings. The bodywork was polished and there were shining new hubcaps. Moss looked guilty, as though he'd betrayed a principle. He said, "The machine was just gonna up and die if I didn't do something. It's not as if I went out and bought a BMW." We cruised south on the Harbor Freeway. The top was down and the sky was dazzling, quivering in the heat. I thought the sky was about to melt. That could have been the effect of the crystal Methedrine, which Barbara had given out as soon as we hit Venice Boulevard and which made me feel weak, light-headed. I was in the back, in a drugged stupor. Barbara was in the front, in high spirits. She imitated the way the Cadillac used to sound, laughing and gesturing with a fantastic energy and enthusiasm. She talked about her happiness and ambition, telling Moss that now at last she'd fixed on something she wanted to do and there would be no stopping her. She tried to describe how she felt in front of the cameras. She said it was better than sex.

—Richard Rayner, *Los Angeles Without a Map*, 1988

D O W N T O W N

"LOS ANGELES IS SEVENTY-TWO SUBURBS in search of a city," Dorothy Parker once said, a formulation that has less truth to it than easy wit. The city has been there all along, symbolized by a vibrant, evolving and historic **downtown**. It's just that downtown L.A. tends to get lost in the low-density sprawl around it, making it seem somehow less important than other metropolitan centers. To some extent, this was according to plan, as city planners had made a conscious decision to de-emphasize downtown in favor of several commercial areas seeded throughout the L.A. area. Also, because of the danger of earthquakes, there was a thirteen-story limit on all buildings until the late fifties, City Hall being the lone exception. In recent decades the spotlight has been turned back on downtown, the boom in Pacific Rim trade reflected in the many glass towers rising up like heavily fortified islands.

Downtown L.A ill-deserves its reputation for being bereft of life: there is a rich, multi-cultural street scene, compelling historical sites, and a burgeoning arts community. Its historic centerpiece is Olvera Street and **El Pueblo de Los Angeles Historic Park**, honoring the original settlement of the area in 1781. Restored in 1929, Olvera Street (across from Union Station) plays a central role in giving L.A. a sense of itself. The ever-expanding Music Center and the attendant auditoriums, museums, and theaters on **Bunker Hill** give downtown L.A. a cultural center the match of any in the world. Spring Street used to be known as "the Wall Street of the West," though Flower Street has taken over as the city's main financial artery.

On downtown's eastern fringes is a loft and warehouse area that is beginning to take on the tone of an artists' neighborhood, as painters and sculptors move into the wide open spaces, bringing with them espresso houses and restaurants as well as small, explosive nightclubs. **Broadway** has historic movie palaces plus some of the highest volume stores in the nation, a largely Hispanic clientele lending the area a distinctive feel. The one finger of downtown wealth stretches west to the Miracle Mile shopping district, following **Wilshire Boulevard** past some of the city's finest Art Deco monuments.

■ BIRTH OF THE MOVIES

The first movies filmed in Los Angeles were shot not in Hollywood but downtown, using, among other makeshift "studios," a rooftop and a Chinese laundry. A
director named Francis Boggs, working for the *Selig Polyscope Company,* is credited
with being on the scene as early as 1907. Unfortunately, film lovers have to turn
part archaeologist and part imaginative-visualizer here, since the **first motion picture location in Los Angeles** is now an empty lot at the northwest corner of Olive
and Eighth streets.

It was here that Boggs completed *In the Sultan's Power,* after having first shot

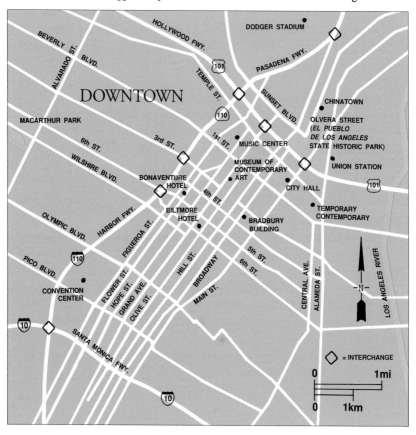

exteriors near San Diego. In a nearby Chinese laundry, Boggs also established what is considered the **first film studio in Los Angeles**, where he filmed *The Heart of a Racing Tout* in 1908. (He also used the roof of Dearden's Department store at 700 S. Main Street.)

A few blocks north, at 501 Spring Street, is downtown's first luxury hotel, the **Alexandria Hotel**, built in 1906 and still featuring the legendary Palm Court, where Charlie Chaplin and Louis B. Mayer were said to have had a fist fight (Chaplin lost). The Alexandria was the favored stop-over for early filmmakers, who had not yet moved on to Hollywood and the Roosevelt, or to the more opulent Biltmore, which opened in the mid-twenties. A recent restoration has brought back some of the hotel's early glamor: suites are named after stars who once stayed in them, and memorabilia of early film celebrities is displayed around the lobby.

Overlooking Pershing Square two blocks west is the beautifully restored **Biltmore Hotel** (506 S. Grand Avenue), another hostelry favored by the early film crowd, and the largest and most opulent hotel west of Chicago when it opened in 1923. This three-towered Beaux Arts landmark is important in movie lore both as a location and because the Academy of Motion Picture Arts and Sciences first convened there on May 11, 1927. No awards were given then—that came two years later, at the Hollywood Roosevelt Hotel—but the dinner at the Biltmore's Crystal Ballroom marked the beginning of the Academy as an industry entity. The Academy Awards were held here half a dozen times in the thirties. Films which used the Biltmore as a location include *Chinatown, The Last Tycoon, A Star Is Born* (1976 version), *Beverly Hills Cop,* and *New York, New York.*

Not a cinematic site per se, but featuring many stars who moved from vaudeville to film is the **Variety Arts Center**, located at 940 S. Figueroa Street. The luxurious wood-paneled bar in this semi-private club is aptly named after W.C. Fields, and the richly detailed, recently restored building was used for locations in the 1985 tribute called *Copacabana,* Barry Manilow's lavish (and slavish) memorial to thirties musicals.

Further south are a couple sites of passing cinematic interest, beginning with **Myron's Ballroom**, at 1024 S. Grand Avenue, where some location work for *Farewell, My Lovely; New York, New York;* and *They Shoot Horses, Don't They?* was done. Also on Grand, at Olympic Boulevard, the **Olympic Auditorium**, built for the 1932 Olympics, is where the climactic fights in the first three *Rocky* pictures were filmed.

■ BROADWAY

During the heyday of downtown in the first half of this century, Broadway was the heart of Los Angeles, lined by posh shops as well as some of the finest movie theaters ever built. From this period hails the **Bradbury Building** (304 S. Broadway), fairly undistinguished from the outside but with an interior that's among the most beautiful in Los Angeles. A skylit Victorian wonderland of intricate ironwork, dark wood and marble, with open-cage elevators adding a further retro touch, the

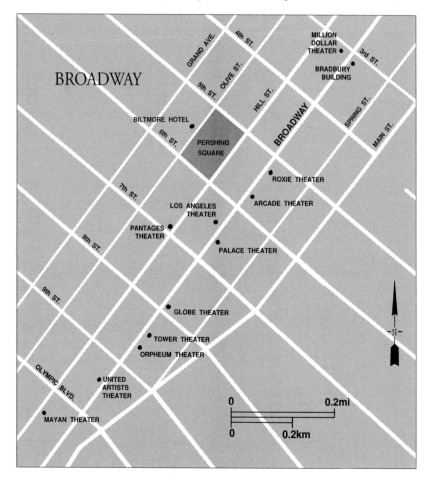

Bradbury has long been a Hollywood set-piece: the first version of *D.O.A.*, as well as all the old Boston Blackie detective films, were shot here. *Blade Runner* represents the most effective recent use of the Bradbury: in the movie, Harrison Ford pursues and is pursued by his android prey through the spookily anachronistic interior, the metal cages of the elevators and the sound of dripping water conveying an effect of decaying grandeur. When *Blade Runner* was shot here, the Bradbury was in state of disrepair, but it has since been restored.

Across the street from the Bradbury, filling the block between Broadway and Hill Street, is another dynamic indoor space, the **Grand Central Public Market** (317 S. Broadway), a bustling bazaar offering an incredible variety of foods, produce, and beverages.

■ HISTORIC BROADWAY THEATERS

The **Broadway Theater District** (Broadway between Third and Ninth streets) is hallowed ground for cinema glamor—although you wouldn't know it at first glance today. Usually, glamor in Hollywood means off-camera tales of life with the stars, but here on Broadway there are examples of another type of cinematic glamor, in different stages of preservation behind a dozen faded, dirty facades.

It was on this stretch of Broadway that the odd hybrid of nickelodeon and opera house known as the "**movie palace**" came to glorious fruition, and a short walking tour will reveal peeks into a past almost totally obliterated in other parts of the country. "Palaces" indeed they were. In the era of the multiplex and of "theaters" the size of living rooms, Broadway's vast movie palaces seem like the temples of another planet.

Broadway theaters were almost all "marqueed" in the fifties, a process which greatly interferes with the impact of the exteriors. By and large, they are now owned by a company called *Cartelera Cinemagraphica*, and show Spanish or subtitled films. Since the Broadway Theater District is in the National Register of Historic Places, one can only hope that these grand movie palaces will be restored, or at least decay no further. The Los Angeles Conservancy publishes a booklet about the theaters, and offers twice-monthly walking tours. Call (213) 623-2489.

Most of the Broadway theaters opened in the late twenties and had their heyday in the dark days of the Depression. Showmen-impresarios like Sid Grauman, Alexander Pantages, or Oliver Morosco backed them, or stars like Mary Pickford herself, and the finest theater architects like S. Charles Lee and C. Howard Crane

(following pages) The annual "Blessing of the Animals" at Olvera Street draws pet-owners from all over L.A.

furnished the designs. The conscious model was the opera house—gaudy, baroque, and lavish—and the intent seemed to be to make the common, everyday, man-off-the-street ticket-buyer feel like a million bucks. Movies as the grand opera of the masses.

Sid Grauman actually called his first palace the **Million Dollar Theater** (Broadway and Third Street), and it's a convenient starting point for a stroll down memory lane. Grauman was a decade away from his masterstroke, the Chinese Theatre on Hollywood Boulevard, when in 1917 he opened the Million Dollar with a Western, William S. Hart's *The Silent Man*. Today, the baroque opulence of the design can be most clearly seen in the delirious portico above the entrance, now partially obscured by the marquee. The lobby has been remodeled, but the theater proper remains in all its splendor.

Continue south on Broadway past the Art Deco **Roxie** (518 S. Broadway) to the **Arcade** (534 S. Broadway), a Beaux Arts gem built in 1911 by impresario Alexander Pantages (his name is still visible behind the marquee). Pantages was one of the top names booking vaudeville, and after the Arcade he went on to build another landmark theater, the still-standing Pantages Theater at Hollywood and Vine.

South of the Arcade, at 615 S. Broadway, is the **Los Angeles Theater**, opened in 1931 and perhaps the most impressive of the movie palaces still showing films. Designed by S. Charles Lee, regarded as the finest theater architect of his time, it is a Baroque masterpiece in the overwrought style of French Second Empire: the exterior features Corinthian columns and an ornate pinnacle arch, and inside, amid the bang and flash of video games and the blasting soundtrack of martial arts films, vestiges of splendor can still be seen.

As usual for Broadway movie palaces, the best touches are in the balcony—most of them well preserved, since they are closed off for lack of business—and the downstairs lounges. The Los Angeles Theater balcony features a hilariously ornate crystal-bead decorative "fountain," while downstairs is paneled in dark wood. Each stall in the ladies room features a different color marble. "Different colored marble," testified my female research scout, "but no toilet paper in any of them"—an indication of the somewhat decayed ambience of the theater. Across the street, at 615 S. Broadway, is the **Palace**, another Baroque phantasm, with a Second Empire facade and sculpture by Domingo Mora inside. It was designed in 1911 by G. Albert Landsburgh, before S. Charles Lee became the premier theater designer of the West Coast (all theater-designers seem required to use first initial only). Sharp-eyed MTV fans will recognize the architectural details of the Palace from Michael Jackson's "Thriller" video, which was partly shot there. Next door to the theater is the outrageous **Clifton's Cafeteria**, styled in what can only be called woodchopper's chic, and a passable place for a bite while on a movie palace tour. It's probably the only cafeteria in the world with its own newsletter.

The **Globe Theater** (744 S. Broadway) has a marquee which advertises "SWAP MEET" nowadays—not an adult film about swingers but a flea market. The gutted and bazaar-like interior still reveals some Beaux Arts touches, and again, the balcony is relatively unchanged and visible from below. The **Tower Theater** (802 S. Broadway), across Eighth Street, is a Spanish-Moorish-Romanesque delight by S. Charles Lee, his first L.A. design, built five years before the Los Angeles Theater. Part of the movie *Mambo Kings* (1992) was shot here. Down the block, the **Orpheum**, another in the chain designed by Landsburgh, is in marvelous condition—again, the balcony and lounges are highlights.

Unreconstructed, with part of its beautifully intricate facade "remodeled" is the **Mayan Theater**, off the beaten Broadway track at 1038 S. Hill. Built during the rage for theme-theaters (the Egyptian and the Chinese theatres in Hollywood are other examples), the Mayan is someone's fantasy—perhaps facade sculptor Francisco Comeja—of pre-Colombian architecture. Now a nightclub, for years it was an X-rated theater, the one that Jack Lemmon visited in the Garment District film, *Save the Tiger*. Next door to the Mayan, and built by the same team of architects, is the **Belasco Theater**.

A fitting end to the Theater District walking tour is the magnificent—and magnificently restored—**United Artists Theater** (933 Broadway). Mary Pickford, U.A.'s leading light, chose the style and the architect (C. Howard Crane) for the company's flagship cinema. Pickford's design sense was inspired by her recently completed tour of Europe, and the result here is an ornamental riot of Spanish Gothic excess. The domed ceiling was set with hundreds of circular, gold-backed mirrors, and everything, from the still-extant lighting system to the organ, was state-of-the-art.

The medieval theme was extended to the Heinsbergen frescoes on both auditorium walls. These heraldic parodies feature the forces of light on the "good" right-side mural, including Mary Pickford, and, on celestial white horses, the faces (if not the bodies) of the United Artists board of directors. On the "sinister" left-side mural, some analysts pick out the faces of U.A. rivals, including Paramount's Adolph Zukor.

The whole theater is a hallucinatory evocation of the cathedrals of Europe (with the plaster finials copied from Segovia), today made all the more enjoyable by a careful restoration job sponsored by the building's new owner, Dr. Gene Scott's University Church. The auditorium is filled every Sunday with parishioners fired by Scott's evangelical fervor, and the baroque details show up nicely broadcast nationwide on his television show. Downstairs, the smoking lounge and Pickford's private screening room (complete with secret passageways and elevators to the street) are now filled with a world-class collection of Bibles. It would be ironic, if it weren't so much like Hollywood, that a movie theater, part of an industry once condemned from the pulpit as sinful, has been reincarnated as a church.

■ BUNKER HILL

On the west side of downtown L.A., a forest of glass towers stands atop **Bunker Hill**, the city's original upmarket residential quarter. Angel's Flight, a funicular cable car, once toiled up and down the hill, but as Los Angeles sprawled Bunker Hill was left behind. The old mansions were divided up into rooming houses, and later provided the backdrops for many of the low-budget B-movie detective stories of the forties. In the fifties, as part of what was then called "urban renewal," everything was torn down. In the sixties, the Music Center complex was constructed, marking Bunker Hill as the center of L.A.'s cultural renaissance. The Dorothy Chandler Pavilion here is the winter home of the L.A. Philharmonic, and is also where the Academy Awards are held every other April. With the construction of the new Disney Auditorium, alongside the Mark Taper Forum and the Ahmanson Theater, the Music Center is set to continue its reign over high-brow L.A.

Another recent addition to Bunker Hill was the **Museum of Contemporary Art** (250 S. Grand Avenue), where Steve Martin did his stand-up send-up of abstract painting in *L.A. Story*. Martin had the run of the museum for the film because he is on the board of directors—he's a serious collector of modern art. The hourglass curve of the museum above its courtyard is supposedly architect Arata Isozaki's "quote" from the figure of Marilyn Monroe. (See "Museums" in "MAJOR ATTRACTIONS" for details of the MOCA collection.)

The Museum of Contemporary Art is the city's most dynamic new museum. (Reproduction of Friend and Foe? ? *by Neil Jenny, courtesy M.O.C.A.)*

Nearer to the Harbor Freeway, at 404 S. Figueroa, is the sleekly futuristic **Bonaventure Hotel.** Sleek futurism is just what filmmakers have used it for, too: *Blade Runner* incorporates it into the film's mock-up of downtown Los Angeles of the future, and *Buck Rogers in the 25th Century* puts the Bonaventure over four centuries hence. It's also used as a generic emblem of modern Los Angeles, in such movies as the remake of *Breathless* and *This Is Spinal Tap.* The area around the Bonaventure is a good place to view the **444 Building** (at 444 Flower Street), familiar as the home of the firm McKenzie Brackman on *L.A. Law.*

Farther south on Flower is the **Seventh and Flower Street Metro Rail Station,** graced with a frieze of movie monsters by artist Joyce Kozloff. Made up of 220 12-inch-square ceramic tiles, mostly in black and white, the mural has the final effect of some comically nightmarish film strip. They are all here, not only the classic archfiends like Dracula and Frankenstein, but also the Creature from the Black Lagoon, the Thing, the Blob, the pod creatures from *Invasion of the Body Snatchers,* and the dinosaurs from *King Kong.* Science fiction is also represented, from Ming the Merciless to the more benign fantasy of R2D2, or Woody Allen in *Sleeper.*

■ City Hall, Chinatown, and Olvera Street

The north side of downtown has a number of film- and TV-related sites, as well as some of the city's most clearly defined ethnic enclaves. A *Dragnet* fan in search of "just the facts" will recognize both **Los Angeles City Hall,** in the Civic Center park at 200 N. Spring Street, and the more modern **Parker Center,** nearby at

150 N. Los Angeles Street, as the turf of Sergeant Joe Friday and Officer Bill Gannon. City Hall was also used as the *Daily Planet* Building in the *Superman* television series, and was seen in the classic Joan Crawford movie, *Mildred Pierce,* and the original *D.O.A.*

A short distance away from the Civic Center park is the entrance to the **Second Street Tunnel** (Hill Street to Figueroa Street), another movie "natural" that sees heavy use. This was the tunnel in which Arnold Schwarzenegger met up with a semi in *The Terminator,* and it has been seen in hundreds of television movies and series episodes.

On the other side of the Hollywood Freeway, at 800 N. Alameda Street, is the stunning **Union Station**, a barrel-vaulted Spanish Revival building still in use as L.A.'s main train station and recognizable from many films. Even though the movie *Union Station* was set in Chicago, it cadged shots from the L.A. station's interior. *The Way We Were* also used the interior extensively, and to a lesser degree so did *Blade Runner, Gable and Lombard,* and *Bugsy.* When a classic public space is required, Union Station can be "dressed" to fit almost any period.

Union Station, which is about to be resuscitated as the terminal of the planned Metrorail system, has a fair chunk of L.A. history buried beneath. The city's original Chinatown was torn down to make way for the station, but before that restaurants and clubs like the Dragon's Den on Los Angeles Street regularly attracted film luminaries like Sidney Greenstreet, Peter Lorre, and Walt Disney. A fake Chinatown, built on Ord Street and surrounded by a "Great Wall," was used in Cecil B. De Mille's version of *The Good Earth.* Today's Chinatown, a vibrant, one-mile-square neighborhood just west of Alameda two blocks north of Union Station, is home to some 12,000 people, and acts as symbolic capital for L.A.'s quarter million Chinese.

Between Union Station and Chinatown is Olvera Street, the symbolic center of historic Los Angeles, a sort of museum mall and traditional bazaar all rolled into one. Closed to vehicular traffic since 1930, Olvera Street asserts itself as a locus of Hispanic culture in Los Angeles, with weekend crowds giving it the air of a fiesta all year long. (It is said there are two centers of mariachi music in the world— Mexico City and Olvera Street.) The Avila Adobe is here, L.A.'s oldest house (built in 1818 by wealthy cattle rancher Don Francisco Avila), as is the impressive 1887 Sepulveda House. Both have been restored and are open to public. Overlooking the Old Plaza at the south end of Olvera Street is La Iglesia, the oldest major public building in L.A., which has become the equivalent of a national church for Mexican Americans.

Just east of downtown is one of the "expected surprises" of L.A.: the bed of the **Los Angeles River**, long ago channeled into a concrete spillway and usually dry as a bone. It was here, below the viaducts between First and Seventh Streets, that the high schoolers in *Grease* raced their rods. It was out of one of these bridge-tunnels, the **Sixth Street viaduct**, that the giant ants of the movie *Them!* came boiling into L.A. from their radioactive birth in the Mojave Desert.

■ EAST LOS ANGELES

East Los Angeles is the heart of the L.A. *barrio,* a concentration of largely Hispanic neighborhoods that stretches from Lincoln Heights to Whittier and beyond. It is the Latino capital of America, home of many of L.A.'s Mexican-Americans, who now comprise well over a quarter of the city's population. While there are

The concrete-lined channel of the L.A. river has starred in many movies including the giant-ant-terror flick Them!

other areas often identified as Hispanic communities—Echo Park and Silver Lake, for example, or the Central American neighborhoods of Pico-Union—the East L.A. *barrio,* celebrated in hundreds of home-town murals, remains the symbol of *raza* L.A.

It has often appeared as such in films, for example in *Born in East L.A.,* Cheech Marin's black farce about a U.S. citizen deported as an illegal immigrant. In *Stand and Deliver,* based on the true exploits of calculus teacher Jaime Escalante (and produced by the local public television station, KCET), East L.A.'s vibrantly diverse Hispanic community shines forth. Escalante (played by James Edward Olmos in the film), taught at Garfield High School, near Sixth and Atlantic, and his tenure there is a continuing source of neighborhood pride. More recently, James Edward Olmos has directed and starred in *American Me,* also featuring the neighborhood.

East L.A.'s Hispanic population celebrates Cinco de Mayo (Mexican Independence Day).

Master muralist Richard Wyatt has brightened many an L.A. building with portraits like this one of jazz great Charlie Parker. (Richard Wyatt)

■ WILSHIRE AND THE MIRACLE MILE

In the twenties, when L.A. began its incessant spread west, most of the building activity was focused along **Wilshire Boulevard**, self-named after the boom-and-bust entrepreneur and land speculator H. Gaylord Wilshire. Another early-day retail hustler, A.W. Ross, began in the late twenties to develop his Miracle Mile, a stretch of Wilshire along which he controlled all construction. Glamorous hotels and opulent department stores graced what just a decade before had been open fields, and a support system of restaurants and nightclubs catered to the Hollywood stars who migrated here from downtown.

The first stop on Wilshire Boulevard's journey west from downtown is **MacArthur Park** (yes, the same MacArthur Park of the Jimmy Webb song, where "someone left the cake out in the rain"). The park itself has seen better days, as indicated by the fact that a police substation has taken over the boathouse, but the **Park Plaza Hotel** (607 S. Parkview), overlooking the park from the west, is used as

The intersection of Wilshire Boulevard and Fairfax Avenue in 1920. This is now the Miracle Mile district. (L.A. County Natural History Museum)

a location exactly because of its down-at-the-heels appeal. Its cavernous lobby has been seen in *New York, New York; Young Doctors in Love;* and *Dr. Detroit;* as well as episodes of *Murder, She Wrote; Lou Grant;* and *Kojak.*

Further west, just past the **Vagabond Cinema**, a revival house at 2509 Wilshire, stands the **Bryson** (2701 Wilshire), a brooding residential hotel used most recently in *The Grifters.* A favorite location for filmmakers seeking L.A. seediness, the Bryson actually looks more decayed than it is, thanks to the gaping rictus of its gutted upper story. Portions of *Barfly* were also filmed there, with Mickey Rourke and Faye Dunaway trying to recreate the world of downmarket hipster Charles Bukowski.

Past **Lafayette Park**, at Wilshire's final curve before it begins its long beeline west, stands the Art Deco tower of **Bullocks Wilshire** (3050 Wilshire), a favorite exterior whenever a film's art director calls for vast bulk or streamlined design. The movie *Topper,* for example, used the rear of the store to double for a New England inn.

The Ambassador Hotel, on Wilshire at Alexandria, was once Wilshire Boulevard's crown jewel, justly celebrated for its gardens, grounds, and grand style—as well as its history. The movie crowd adopted it with a vengeance when it opened in 1921, especially **the Coconut Grove** nightclub, for years the jumpingest joint in town, if you could call a place decorated with palm trees and stuffed monkeys a "joint." Later on, the Ambassador carried a historical onus of another kind, as the place where Robert Kennedy was gunned down during the 1968 presidential campaign. Today the Ambassador has fallen into the hands of Donald Trump, and its future is uncertain.

One of the oddest architectural incongruities in a city of incongruities is the old **Brown Derby** restaurant, now perched atop a mini-mall across Wilshire from the Ambassador. When the hat-shaped restaurant was threatened with demolition, preservationists and the developers compromised, with this unlikely result.

One of Wilshire's strongest connections with Hollywood and the movies, the *Sunset Boulevard* mansion, stood up through the fifties on the northwest corner of Irving and Wilshire. It's now been replaced by a bank, but in 1950 director Billy Wilder used the grand manor, which at the time belonged to the second Mrs. J. Paul Getty, for the home of Norma Desmond. Since Wilder needed a pool for the opening "corpse in the water" scene, in true Hollywood tradition he put in a false one, without any plumbing. That same swimming pool—but not the Getty mansion exteriors—was later used in *Rebel Without a Cause* as the empty pool where James Dean, Sal Mineo, and Natalie Wood—a doomed trio in real life, all of them—frolic near the end of the film.

Not far from the vanished *Sunset Boulevard* mansion is the site of one of the few victories in the battle to preserve a slice of movie history. The **Wiltern Theatre** (3780 Wilshire) was inches from the wrecking ball when Wayne Ratkovich, a developer who has also restored other period masterpieces around town, stepped in and saved it. The Wiltern had a rocky history from the start, when Warner Brothers underwrote its construction in 1931. It closed almost immediately, a victim of the Depression, and sat vacant for many years before being restored by A.T. "Tony" Heinsbergen, son of the original theater muralist and designer. West of Western Avenue, Hancock Park, an upper-class enclave and still a place of graceful residences, saw the growth of the **Miracle Mile** shopping district, the city's first car-orientated shopping district and setting for both the beginning and the end of the satiric end-of-L.A. movie, *Miracle Mile.*

The stage of the resplendent Wiltern Theatre. (Wiltern Theatre Inc., photo by Randall Michaelson)

At La Brea Avenue, the eastern end of the Miracle Mile, Wilshire passes by the **La Brea Tar Pits.** "La Brea" is Spanish for "tar," so the "La Brea tar pits" is actually a redundancy, but there the pits are anyway, with the superb **George C. Page Museum** (Wilshire at Curson) built to commemorate their archaeological finds. Sharing the same chunk of Hancock Park with the Page Museum is the **Los Angeles County Museum of Art** (5905 Wilshire), where Steve Martin did his roller-skating "performance art" in *L.A. Story* (For more on both of these, see "Museums" in "MAJOR ATTRACTIONS").

Scenes from two Hollywood classics, Rebel Without a Cause *(above) and* Sunset Boulevard *(below), were filmed in the same Hancock Park swimming pool. (Academy of Motion Picture Arts and Sciences)*

FILMING WATERLOO

*H*e left the road and climbed across the spine of the hill to look down on the other side. From there he could see a ten-acre field of cockleburs spotted with clumps of sunflowers and wild gum. In the center of the field was a gigantic pile of sets, flats and props. While he watched, a ten-ton truck added another load to it. This was the final dumping ground. He thought of Janvier's "Sargasso Sea." Just as that imaginary body of water has a history of civilization in the form of a marine junkyard, the studio lot was one in the form of a dream dump. A Sargasso of the imagination! And the dump grew continually, for there wasn't a dream afloat somewhere which wouldn't sooner or later turn up on it, having first been made photogenic by plaster, lath and paint. Many boats sink and never reach the Sargasso, but no dream ever entirely disappears. Somewhere it troubles some unfortunate person and some day, when that person has been sufficiently troubled, it will be reproduced on the lot.

When he saw a red glare in the sky and heard the rumble of cannon, he knew it must be Waterloo. From around a bend in the road trotted several cavalry regiments. They wore casques and chest armor of black cardboard and carried long horse pistols in their saddle holsters. They were Victor Hugo's soldiers. He had worked on some of the drawings himself, following carefully the descriptions in *Les Miserables.*

He went in the direction they took. Before long he was passed by the men of Lefebvre-Desnouettes, followed by a regiment of gendarmes d'élite, several companies of chausseurs of the guard and a flying detachment of Rimbaud's lancers.

They must be moving up for the disastrous attack on La Haite Santée. He hadn't read the scenario and wondered if it had rained yesterday. Would Grouchy or Blucher arrive? Grotenstein, the producer, might have changed it.

The sound of the cannon was becoming louder all the time and the red fan in the sky more intense. He could smell the sweet, pungent odor of blank powder. It might be over before he could there. He started to run. When he topped a rise after a sharp bend in the road, he found a great plain below him covered with early nineteenth-century troops, wearing all the gay and elaborate uniforms that used to please him so much when he was a child and spent long hours looking at the soldiers in an old dictionary. At the far end of the field, he could see an enormous hump around which the English and their allies were gathered. It was Mont St. Jean and they were getting ready to defend it gallantly. It wasn't quite finished, however, and swarmed with grips,property men, set dressers, carpenters, and painters.

Tod stood near a eucalyptus tree to watch, concealing himself behind a sign that read, "'Waterloo'—A Charles H. Grotenstein Production." Nearby a youth in a carefully torn horse guard's uniform was being rehearsed in his lines by one of the assistant directors.

"Vive l'Empereur!" the young man shouted, then clutched his breast and fell forward dead. The assistant director was a hard man to please and made him do it over and over again.

—Nathanael West, *The Day of the Locust,* 1933

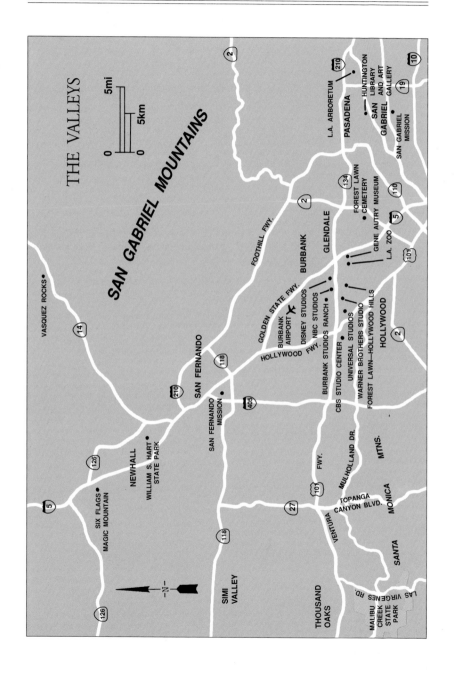

THE VALLEYS

"I LIVE IN THE VALLEY," SAYS A CHARACTER in Steve Martin's *L.A. Story*—and everyone snickers. Though it's a bit of a joke nowadays, serving the same function vis à vis Hollywood and West L.A. as the Outer Boroughs do to Manhattan, there was a time when the San Fernando Valley was fashionable. For folks like John Wayne and Gable and Lombard, it had a reputation for being a sane, countrified alternative for the constricted living south of the Hollywood Hills.

And when the booming studios of early Hollywood looked for places to spread out, more often than not they pulled up stakes and merely moved over the hill to the Valley. Walt Disney, Mack Sennett, the Warner Brothers—all relocated from one side of the Santa Monicas to the other. One area of North Hollywood became so clotted with movie businesses that it renamed itself Studio City; another, around the Universal Studios complex, calls itself Universal City.

Although the San Fernando takes the definitive article (as in "The Valley"), there is more than one valley in Los Angeles. When the Santa Monica Mountains stutter to a stop at Griffith Park, there is a gap which is partially the end of the San Fernando Valley and partly the beginning of the San Gabriel Valley. Glendale and Burbank, the two main cities here, are among L.A.'s oldest constituent communities—both historically and in terms of their current residents. Just east, at the foot of the San Gabriel Mountains, sits Pasadena, the wealthiest pre-Hollywood community in L.A. and symbolic of old society and old money. Today, solidly respectable Pasadena is beset by some of L.A.'s worst smog but still retains its staid, well-established nature, highlighted by the New Year's Day Rose Parade and hymned about by the Beach Boys in "Little Old Lady from Pasadena."

The cities and neighborhoods of the valleys—from Pasadena and Burbank to Van Nuys, Encino, and Newhall—are primarily middle-class, overwhelmingly residential, and by and large suburban. They retain little of the country flavor which just fifty years ago attracted city-weary Angelenos to the area. But they created a new culture, based on the auto and anchored by the shopping mall, for which they have become famous.

■ GLENDALE

At the east end of the San Fernando Valley, just north of downtown, Glendale offers a concentration of active studio sites and historical landmarks. At the end of Cerritos Avenue, is the Glendale AMTRAK Station, used by Billy Wilder in *Double Indemnity* to substitute for the nearby (but unavailable) Pasadena station. When Fred MacMurray boards the "10:15 from Glendale," he was really still in Glendale. Across the dry-as-bone Los Angeles River and the never-empty Golden State Freeway (I-5) from the station is the **Los Angeles Zoo** (5333 Zoo Drive), featured in the motion picture *Body and Soul*, but probably better known for providing the backdrop to the title sequence of the long-running sitcom, *Three's Company.* Next door to the zoo is the brand-spanking new, very well-heeled **Gene Autry Western Heritage Museum**, at 4700 Zoo Drive, (See "Museums" in "Major Attractions.")

Casablanca in The Valley: the unforgettable climax of the 1942 classic was actually shot at the Glendale airport. (Academy of Motion Picture Arts and Sciences)

■ FOREST LAWN MEMORIAL PARK

Perhaps the best place to begin a tour is at the end, at **Forest Lawn Memorial Park** (1712 S. Glendale Avenue). In 1917 founder Hubert Eaton descended upon an undistinguished traditional boneyard called the Tropico and transformed it into Forest Lawn. He said he wanted the "greenest, most enchanting park that you ever saw in your life . . . devoid of misshapen monuments and other customary signs of earthly death . . . vistas of sparkling lawns, with shaded arborways, and garden retreats." Perhaps more succinct is the wag's one-liner about the place: "a country club for the dead."

Whomsoever's point-of-view you accept, Forest Lawn is an amazing place, and not only for the celebrity dead that are there interred. Forest Lawn may be Eaton's dream but it's kitsch central for funereal art, architecture, and statuary. There are full-scale replicas of three churches on the grounds: **The Church of the Recessional**, modeled after a tenth-century English sanctuary; an exact replica of the church described in Thomas Gray's "Elegy in a County Churchyard," and finally **Wee Church o' the Heather**, modelled on a fourteenth-century Scottish church. This last was where Ronald Reagan and Jane Wyman were wed, which goes to show how much Forest Lawn is a place for the living as well as the dead. It's certainly one of those places that has to be believed to be really seen.

There are stained-glass impressions of Michelangelo's *David*, a re-creation of Leonardo da Vinci's *The Last Supper*, and huge murals of the resurrection and crucifixion of Jesus which are re-revealed dramatically, complete with canned crescendo, from behind curtains every half hour. The Court of Freedom contains a mural of the signing of the Declaration of Independence, signalling the element of patriotism that is mixed into the thematic broth, all of it to the tune of Muzak-like inspirational music.

The staff of Forest Lawn has strict instructions not to direct the curious to the various **graves of celebrities**, so here's a brief run-down to help you find your way: In the Great Mausoleum, to the right of the main entrance, Gable and Lombard are in side-by-side crypts in the Sanctuary of Trust. Jean Harlow is here, too, in a huge tomb in the Sanctuary of Benediction. In the Freedom Mausoleum, tucked in the far corner of the cemetery, are the crypts of Clara Bow, Nat "King" Cole, and Gracie Allen of "Burns and Allen," all clustered in the Sanctuary of Heritage. Outside, in the most controversial grave of all—is he really in there, or is his body cryogenically frozen?—Walt Disney's ashes are supposedly interred in the Court of

Freedom. Nearby is the grave of Errol Flynn, rumored to have been buried—in a shockingly un-Forest Lawn manner—with six bottles of whiskey.

The living, driving west on the Ventura Freeway from Glendale, may find themselves experiencing a creeping sense of déjà vu as they near 6300 Forest Lawn Drive, since here is located its less glamorous younger sibling. **Forest Lawn Hollywood Hills Memorial Park** has its share of celebs, including Liberace, Charles Laughton, George Raft, and Freddie Prinze (all in the Court of Remembrance), as well as early comics Buster Keaton and Stan Laurel (both near the George Washington statue). The hills here are also where D.W. Griffith shot many of the exterior-location scenes for his epic, *The Birth of a Nation.*

■ PASADENA

Known to the world through the staid pageantry of the Tournament of Roses Parade—if not the boppin' sounds of "Little Old Lady from Pasadena"—Pasadena, just east of Glendale on the Ventura Freeway, was a symbol of gracious California living almost from its inception. Solidly upper-middle-class, eschewing the flash and bounce of the movie trade, Pasadena first boomed as a winter resort for wealthy Easterners. It has never lost that high-tone patina, although today some of the worst smog in the area has served to tarnish the glow. It's not surprising that Hollywood location scouts have primarily turned to Pasadena for its huge estates and stately homes.

These have included the **Feynes Mansion** (470 W. Walnut Street), presently headquarters of the Pasadena Historical Society but used as early as 1912 for the setting of *The Queen's Necklace.* It appeared in *Being There*, starring Peter Sellers, and has seen constant use in television and commercials as a stand-in for an East Coast mansion. Similarly, the **Arden Villa** (1145 Arden Road) near the campus of the California Institute of Technology (usually known as CalTech) has been used as the Carrington Mansion on *Dynasty*, and appeared on other shows as well. There is also the Gothic-style house at 160 San Rafael Avenue, used as the **Bruce Wayne mansion** on the *Batman* television series, as well as in the movies *Topper* and *True Confessions.*

South of Pasadena, in the town of San Marino, the mansion and grounds of the **Huntington Estate** (1151 Oxford Road) have often attracted filmmakers. Built in

"Another thing that's changed in Hollywood is on accounta the smog. In the days of Garbo and Harlow, you could always tell a star by dark glasses. Now on accounta all the smog, everybody wears sunglasses and nobody sees nuttin'." —Jimmy Durante

RESTRICTED
AREA
KEEP OUT
Hard Hat
AREA

DANGER
HARD HAT
AREA
RESTRICTED
AREA
KEEP OUT

1910 for tycoon Henry E. Huntington, whose father founded the Southern Pacific Railroad, the estate features a world-class museum where, among other treasures, Gainsborough's "Blue Boy" is hung (see "Museums" in "MAJOR ATTRACTIONS" for more). The estate's library has the letters and manuscripts of Hollywood screenwriters, and scripts from the likes of *Gunsmoke*, alongside copies of the Dead Sea Scrolls.

But it is the 207-acre grounds that have sparked the imaginations of location scouts, especially the Oriental garden. Both *Midway* and *The Bad News Bears Go to Japan* have used the Huntington's Japanese garden, with its wonderful Zen courtyard, teahouse, and goldfish pond. More recently, director Peter Bogdonovich used the Huntington for his exuberant flop, *At Long Last Love*.

To the immediate east of the Huntington Estate is Arcadia, site of both the **Los Angeles Arboretum** and Santa Anita Race Track, facing each other across Baldwin Avenue. The two occupy part of the old Rancho Santa Anita, and each has been used many times in film and television. The Arboretum passed as Africa for the Tarzan films of Johnny Weissmuller, including *Tarzan Escapes, Tarzan and the Amazons,* and *Tarzan and the Leopard Woman,* and in 1940 Crosby and Hope softshoed through their first "Road" film here, *The Road to Singapore*.

On the grounds of the Arboretum is the **Queen Anne Cottage**, a guest house of an early owner of the land, E.J. "Lucky" Baldwin. A silver miner who struck it rich in Nevada's Comstock Lode, Baldwin made his ranch famous for experimental horticulture and outrageous architecture, a shred of which survives in the cottage. A favorite of TV shows from *The Love Boat* to *Dallas,* its most famous use came in the series *Fantasy Island*.

The **Santa Anita Racetrack** has been Hollywood's hometown track since it was built in 1934. With the stunning and often snow-capped San Gabriel Mountains in the background, Santa Anita hosts thoroughbred racing in the winter and a mini-season in the fall. Race-horse hobbyists like Louis B. Mayer and the Warner brothers often showed here, and movies made on location include the Marx Brothers' *A Day at the Races* and *A Star is Born* (both the 1937 and 1954 versions).

Before you leave the area, you might want to drive north on Baldwin to its intersection with Sierra Madre Boulevard, in the foothill town of **Sierra Madre**. This was the town square in *The Invasion of the Body Snatchers* (1956 version). In footage shot here, the quick-sighted can glimpse Sam Peckinpah, who would go on to become one of Hollywood's greatest directors, as a bit-part meter reader.

(previous pages) Architect Frank Gehry designed this much-magnified pair of binoculars for admen Chiat-Day's L.A. shop.

■ BURBANK

"Beautiful downtown Burbank," used by NBC-employed comics from Rowan & Martin to Johnny Carson, was a dig at the low-density sprawl of the town, but there are actually quite a few movie-related sites clustered together west of Glendale along either side of the Ventura Freeway.

Across the freeway from Forest Lawn Hollywood Hills, in the section of Burbank known as Toluca Lake, are the **Disney Studios** (500 S. Buena Vista Street). Disney moved here from Silver Lake just before World War II. Although he had *Snow White and the Seven Dwarfs* under his belt by then, he felt insecure enough about his success to insist upon a curious design for his new studio: Walt had all the hallways built especially wide, so that in case things didn't work out, he could sell the place as a hospital (which would need wide halls to turn the gurneys). Other design elements reveal more confidence: Most offices feature northern light, favored by illustrators, and there were underground passages built between all the buildings, so that illustrations and animation cels never had to be exposed to the elements. Unfortunately, the 51-acre site is not open to the public, and lack of television production makes it one of the hardest studios to visit.

Next door to Disney, at 3000 Alameda Avenue, is NBC, home of *The Tonight Show*. When Johnny Carson hosted it, this was the hottest ticket in television. There was also an NBC studio tour, which allowed the public an intimate look at the production side of a busy network studio. Both the tour and Carson's reign are history, but Jay Leno still attracts the faithful to the afternoon tapings of the most popular, longest-running evening talk show in TV history. NBC moved to these studios from its old "Radio City" headquarters at Selma and Vine—yet another example of the Hollywood exodus. Among the more popular programs taped here was Rowan and Martin's *Laugh-In*, the show which originated the "Beautiful Downtown Burbank" tweak. Across the Ventura Freeway from Disney and NBC is **Warner Brothers Studios**, formerly called TBS, for "The Burbank Studios." (See "MAJOR ATTRACTIONS.")

Just north of this concentration of production facilities is the **Burbank Studios Ranch** (Pass and Verdugo avenues), a throwback to the days when Valley land was cheap and rural. Originally, the ranch was developed by Columbia, when its studios were still located at Sunset and Gower in Hollywood, and it required a site for outdoor location work. Now the ranch is in the middle of a residential district, and the lot is used by production crews from nearby studios when they need exterior shots. The lot is fenced, but glimpses of old props can be seen, especially from the Verdugo Avenue side.

Another throwback to the Golden Age of Hollywood, at 11041 Vanowen Street (near the Burbank Airport), is **Western Costume**. For much of its existence it was a virtual adjunct of Paramount Studios, and was located next door to it on Melrose Avenue in Hollywood. In 1990, however, Western moved to cheaper quarters nearer to Burbank, where more movies are made nowadays than in old Hollywood.

The place is still a phantasmagoria of crowns, sabers, royal robes, Second Empire brigadier plumes, ball gowns, livery, and just plain old chaps and Stetsons. What Western Costume can't find in its voluminous, million-piece warehouse, its workshops can fashion. Although the day of the period epic is largely gone, Western is a throwback to the time when audiences thrilled to lavish historical presentations, and when the cut of a man's jacket could signal his station in life.

Western Costume is one of the film industry's principal wardrobe suppliers.

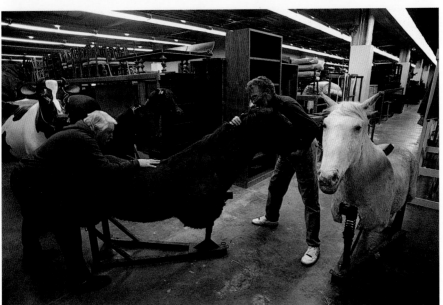

Props are the stuff of Hollywood.

■ UNIVERSAL CITY AND STUDIO CITY

West of Burbank on the edge of **Universal City** (whose mammoth Universal Studios is covered under "MAJOR ATTRACTIONS"), the **headquarters of Hanna Barbera** (3000 W. Cahuenga) is identified by the "Fred Flintstone" sign out front. Further west is the only working studio left in Studio City, **CBS Studio Center** at Ventura and Radford. Built originally by Mack "Keystone Kops" Sennett in 1928, this site was the home of Republic Studios, the greatest source of B-movie Westerns ever. John Wayne, Gene Autry, and Roy Rogers all got their start here, in the great Republic churn-'em-out "B's" of the thirties and forties. Later the studio was purchased by CBS and used by production companies for sitcoms and other TV shows, including *Gunsmoke* and *Hill Street Blues*. *The Mary Tyler Moore Show* was shot here, too, and the lot was long the headquarters of MTM Enterprises, which produced the hit show.

Mary Tyler Moore herself is honored with a bust in the Hall of Fame Plaza of the **Academy of Television Arts and Sciences** (Lankershim and Magnolia) in North Hollywood. Completed in the summer of 1991, the lavish $20 million headquarters features a theater and library (both open to the public on a limited basis) as well as the ATAS administrative offices—the first time in its 44-year history that the organization has had a home.

A huge **Emmy Award** statue in the courtyard is augmented by busts of Milton Berle, Norman Lear, Rod Serling, Sid Caesar, and Paddy Chayefsky—who ironically enough wrote the scathing anti-TV movie, *Network*. Life-sized statues of Johnny Carson, Lucille Ball, and Jack Benny, bas-reliefs of George Burns and Gracie Allen, Walter Cronkite, and Steve Allen—the ATAS is nothing if not tribute-conscious.

■ ENCINO, TARZANA, AND NORTHRIDGE

Farther west along the foothills is **Encino**, home to the **Michael Jackson** compound (4641 Hayvenhurst), complete with its own private menagerie. Jackson rarely shows his rebuilt face, but that doesn't discourage autograph-seekers from besieging the place. Nearby is the **House of Two Gables**, the quaint cottage where Gable and Lombard spent their short happy time together, at 4543 Tara Drive (the street sign is spray-painted over, probably to discourage tourists).

X-RATED L.A.

There is a flip-side to Hollywood that exists in shadowy counterpoint to mainstream moviemaking but is every bit as concentrated in Los Angeles as other sectors of the entertainment business. It is the booming world of adult video, and by some accounts it amounts to a $3 billion-a-year market. Of the some 1,400 X-rated tapes released in the U.S. every year, the huge majority— perhaps 95 percent—are produced in Los Angeles. The San Fernando Valley is the home turf for these tapes, which are sometimes churned out at the rate of two a day.

"For some reason, the Valley is to porn tapes what Washington is to bureaucrats," says Al Goldstein, reviewer of X-rated tapes for *Penthouse* magazine. "They have all the talent out there, most of it drawn to mainstream Hollywood but not making it. Porn rates in the top 100 of California industries."

Like a cracked mirror-image to the studios of Burbank and Hollywood, these small production companies rent houses in North Hollywood, Northridge, or Van Nuys to lens their flesh epics. The California blonde has become a staple of the adult world, and the recent introduction of amateur videos has seen a concomitant boom in private product coming from boudoirs all over Southern California.

In the neighboring town of **Tarzana**, probably the only city in the state named after a fictional character, is the site of the **Edgar Rice Burroughs estate**, now taken over by a nursery farm at 18320 Tarzan Drive. Burroughs, creator of the Tarzan books, founded the city of Tarzana in 1923.

On the other side of the Valley from these sites, the staid community of **Northridge** is where comedian Richard Pryor was living when the ether he was using to freebase cocaine exploded, setting him afire. The stretch of Parthenia Street, immediately to the west of Hayvenhurst, is where the terrified comic ran, trying to out-distance his mortality. Pryor's struggles during this time are brilliantly sketched out in his film, *Jo Jo Dancer, Your Life Is Calling*.

■ MOVIE RANCHES

The western fringes of the San Fernando Valley are interspersed with movie ranches, many of them still in use as extended backlots of the major Hollywood studios. Others were not so lucky: **Warner Brothers Ranch**, for example, is now a housing development around the Calabasas Golf Course—the holes of the course are named after famous Warner Brothers movies, *High Noon, Calamity Jane,* etc.

A better side of Hollywood is expressed by the **Motion Picture Country Lodge, House, and Hospital** at the Mulholland Drive exit of the Ventura Freeway just where it crosses the border from the city to the county of Los Angeles. Sponsored by the industry-supported Motion Picture and Television Fund, this retirement home was founded by Jean Hersholt—of the special Academy Award fame—in 1940. Forty acres of Valley land would cost an astronomical amount today, but the Lodge is the beneficiary of many bequests, like those that underwrote the Louis B. Mayer Theater, where first-run films provided by the studios are shown. George Burns provided the funding for the intensive care unit, and many of the other facilities have famous names attached to them—like the Douglas Fairbanks

Most Hollywood Westerns have been shot in the San Fernando Valley.

Gregory Peck poses in front of the court house used in the filming of To Kill a Mockingbird.

Lounge, for instance. By all accounts, the Lodge is top-of-the-line old-age care, so much so that there's a five year wait to get in. The prerequisite? Twenty years in the movie business. Continuing along the Ventura Freeway, the Las Virgenes Road exit heads up into the Santa Monica Mountains to **Malibu Creek State Park**, formerly Century Ranch of Twentieth Century-Fox. Even today, this area is in almost constant use by movie companies, who prize it for its adaptable wilderness—Century Ranch has stood in for Korea in both the movie and television versions of *M*A*S*H*, for the *Planet of the Apes*, for Mexico in *Viva Zapata!*, and for Connecticut in *Mr. Blandings Builds His Dream House*. In fact, this "dream house" is still there, and it, along with a visitors center well-stocked with memorabilia, makes Century Ranch well worth the visit. You might even catch a location unit in action. Since the wars have moved on, the place is now known as "Little Vietnam," with many wartime episodes of *China Beach* and *War Stories* being shot there.

Further west on the Ventura Freeway, the Kanan Dume Road exit leads to Cornell Road and the **Paramount Ranch**, one of the most accessible of the old movie ranches, primarily because it is now maintained as part of the Santa Monica Mountains National Recreation Area. Movies and television shows are still being filmed at this ranch, and on Sunday evenings during the summer, silent movies are shown outdoors, under the stars.

On the north side of the valley, the area of the Santa Susana Knolls west of Chatsworth yields up a now-silent pair of mountain movie ranches. The first of these is the desolate **Spahn Movie Ranch** (12000 Santa Susana Pass Road), already long-abandoned by the time Charlie Manson and his followers squatted here while planning what they called the "Helter-Skelter" Tate and LaBianca murders. Nearby, at Iverson Lane and Santa Susana Pass Road, the **Iverson Movie Ranch** was the location for such classic films as *The Charge of the Light Brigade*, *Stagecoach*, and *The Grapes of Wrath*, as well as countless episodes of television Westerns like *The Big Valley* and *Gunsmoke*.

■ NEWHALL

Located some 30 miles (48 km) north of Hollywood, **Newhall** was a prime movie location during the golden age of the Hollywood Western. **Melody Ranch** (Oak Creek Avenue at Placerita Canyon Road) was recently sold for development, but the new owners promise that the ranch structures themselves will be kept and restored to the way they looked during the time Gene Autry was America's most popular cowboy. Autry developed the Melody as his own movie ranch, and set many of his films there.

Already in a fine state of restoration is the old ranch of silent movie cowboy William S. Hart, (San Fernando Road at Newhall Avenue). Hart was one of the most popular stars of the silent age, and his home is now a museum on the grounds of the **William S. Hart State Park**. The ranch house, named La Loma de los Vientos, or Hill of the Winds, is a brisk five-minute walk up a small knoll in the middle of the park. Western regalia and mementoes from Hart's career are on display. Down below, there's a petting zoo and, next to it, a cemetery for Hart's dogs.

Finally, farther out on the Antelope Freeway (Highway 14) is **Vasquez Rocks State Park**, a favorite extraterrestrial locale for filmmakers. If these reddish sandstone crags look eerily familiar, that's because the television series *Star Trek* has used them repeatedly to stand in for the surface of alien planets. North of Vasquez Rocks, and even more alien-looking, is the vast expanse of the Mojave Desert, a barren and forbidding emptiness which forms a fitting edge to L.A.'s suburban sprawl.

(following pages) Star date 12-5-91: Captain Kirk and the crew of the Starship Enterprise *search for intelligent life on Hollywood Boulevard.*

LOS ANGELES HISTORICAL SITES THAT ARE NOW PARKING LOTS

Don the Beachcomber	1727 McCadden
D.W. Griffith Studios	4500 Sunset Blvd.
First motion picture location in L.A.	751 S. Olive
Fox Studios	Western & Sunset
Fox Studios	1428 Western
Garden of Allah	8150 Sunset Blvd.
Hal Roach Studios, Culver City	8822 Washington Blvd.
Hollywood Canteen	1451 Cahuenga
Hollywood Hotel	6811 Hollywood Blvd.
Home of Hollywood founder Daeida Wilcox, later the gardens of Paul DeLongpre (Hollywood's first tourist attraction)	1721 Cahuenga
Lasky Feature Play Studios	Vine & Selma
Metro	6300 Romaine
The Mocambo Club	8588 Sunset Blvd.
NBC Studios	Vine & Selma
Nestor Studios	Gower off Sunset
Original site of Hollywood Studio Club	6129 Gower
Walt Disney's Original Studio	2719 Hyperion

MAJOR ATTRACTIONS
THEME PARKS, MUSEUMS, STUDIO TOURS, AND MORE

TO MANY PEOPLE, THE APOTHEOSIS of Southern California culture is **Disneyland**. Built with movie money, and inspired by the same love of illusion, distraction, and excitement that powers Hollywood, Disneyland is at the lead of a host of theme parks and attractions that give Los Angeles a clear shot at the title of fun capital of the world. Close on the heels of Disneyland, and of much greater interest to movie lovers, is the ultimate Hollywood theme park, **Universal Studios**, an old studio backlot turned into a major tourist attraction.

But the popular icons of Disneyland and Universal are only one side of Los Angeles. The city also boasts a world-class collection of **museums**—from the high-profile Getty Museum in Malibu, to the cutting-edge hipness of the downtown Museum of Contemporary Art. For movie tourists, perhaps the greatest attraction of L.A. is the chance to take a **studio tour** or, with a bit more effort, to catch a movie being made **on location**, taking a look at yet another side of this multi-faceted and enigmatic metropolis.

■ UNIVERSAL STUDIOS

Universal Studios is the 500-pound gorilla of movie tourism in Hollywood, huge, obvious, and very hard to avoid. Some snipe at its over-commercialization, saying it delivers only prepackaged thrills for its rather hefty price tag, but the happy smiles on the faces of visitors seem genuine enough. Perhaps the only 500-pound gorilla is a literal one, in Universal's "King Kong" attraction (which actually weighs a mammoth 13,000 pounds!). After all, Universal—which is still a working movie and TV studio—is the world's third most popular theme park, after Disney World and Disneyland, (it gained third place when Jim and Tammy Bakker's Heritage U.S.A. went under). Can 60 million people—over 4 million visitors a year—possibly be wrong?

Shark Attack! at Universal Studios.

The selective approach is perhaps best employed when touring Universal, if you can afford to be selective at these prices—$25 a ticket at time of writing. There are two main areas: the **Entertainment Center**, on the ridge near the main entrance; and the **Studio Center** in the valley below, connected by the world's busiest escalator system, the **Starway**. The real star of Universal, the **Tram Ride** through the backlot and sundry special effects, starts from the Studio Center.

Just inside the main entrance, the Entertainment Center features carefully scripted shows inspired by recent Universal pictures. Recent "spectaculars" here have been based on *E.T.*, *Miami Vice*, *Conan the Barbarian*, *Star Trek*, and *An American Tail*, but equally many are perennials, such as the animal act showcase and the gun-slinging shootouts of the "Riot Act" stunt show. There are also the usual theme-park fixtures, here given a Hollywood spin: restaurants like **Mel's Diner**, modeled after the one in *American Graffiti*, and souvenir shops based on *Star Trek* and Saturday morning cartoons.

The lower part of Universal, the Studio Center, is really three attractions in one: there are more entertainment-type extravaganzas, including the most spectacular of all, the $40 million "E.T.'s Adventure;" a tribute to Lucille Ball; and "The World of Cinemagic," an audience-participation showcase of movie special effects.

On the set of yet another Roger Corman classic.

Finally, there is the famous Tram Ride, the most enjoyable part of the tour, if only because you are sitting down.

The Tram Ride trundles past made-up attractions as well as working movie sets. Universal Studios has been located here ever since 1915, when "Uncle" Carl Laemmle bought out a chicken ranch, and there are large dollops of history throughout the Tram Ride. The **house from** *Psycho* is as chilling as when you first saw it, even at four-fifths life-size. The European Street Set is immediately familiar from Universal's famous monster films, including *Frankenstein* and *Dracula*.

There's been much disagreement as to which side of the tram is best—I suspect it's whatever side you don't happen to be on. For what it's worth, King Kong is on your right; the nearest view of the *Psycho* house is on your left; the *Jaws* shark is on your right; and the flash flood is on your left. Better seats are in the forward cars, but not too close to the terminally jokey, "Universilly" tour guides.

Though technically impressive, the Tram Ride's special effects—"The Big One" earthquake, the aforementioned King Kong, the parting of the Red Sea—are somehow less satisfying than the fleeting glimpses of welders, stage carpenters, and set decorators, working their union 9-to-5s. Universal is known in the industry as being a pain-in-the-ass lot on which to work, since there are dress codes and rules of behavior enforced—all because of the goggle-eyed tourists in the Trams. Another unhyped but engaging attribute of Universal is a plethora of cast-off props, giving the backlot an appealingly dilapidated air: rusted planes, steam engines, space ships, seemingly parked at random in every square inch of unused space.

But for my money (and I was given free promotional passes), the best part of the Universal Tour is that which actually gives you glimpses into hands-on film production. Underneath the glitz, you'll find more glitz, but underneath that, you just might see some TV show or movie being made. Check the large "Shooting Schedule" board to the right of the main entrance as soon as you enter—this lists the actual television shows being produced on the lower lot that day; there's also a booth where you can pick up audience tickets.

You can spend all day or just an afternoon, but you really can't do justice to Universal Studios in under three hours. Besides the main attractions inside the park, there's also a top-notch multiplex movie theater, the *Cineplex Odeon,* as well as the Universal Amphitheater, one of L.A.'s top concert venues. **Tickets** for Universal Studios cost $25 for adults, $19 for children under 12, and the park is open daily 10 A.M. to 8 P.M.; 8 A.M. to 10:30 P.M. in summer. Universal Studios is located just off the Hollywood Freeway (US-101) at 100 Universal City Plaza in the San Fernando Valley. Call (818) 508-9600 for further information.

■ DISNEYLAND

Disneyland, the one, the original, still keeps chugging along, having drawn over a quarter of a billion people since it opened in 1955. Its founder, Walt Disney, knew what people wanted was a seamless, otherworldly experience, so he tucked away all the utilitarian things like food delivery and garbage removal into huge underground streets which run beneath the theme park he called "The Happiest Place on Earth." Visitors get to see only the frothy fantasy, not the hard work that goes into creating it.

If anything is to be said about Walt's approach, it's that it has been too successful, and visitors to Disneyland must battle hordes of other people, equally intent on consuming the fantasy. When it was built in 1955, Disneyland was surrounded by orange groves and farmlands, but the approach now is lined by motel after motel, all thriving on the trade Walt's dream brings in. Dwarfed by its bigger but younger brother in Orlando, (Disneyland is roughly equivalent to a single one of Disney World's burgeoning number of theme parks), Disneyland has announced plans for a $3-billion expansion, but for the moment Disney's "Magic Kingdom" is crammed into its 107-acre spread.

Disneyland is laid out like a triangular pie. The slice where you enter the park is called Main Street, USA, and one of its charms (especially for the movie lover) is the old-time nickelodeon at the Main Street Cinema. Also required for cinemaphiles is "The Walt Disney Story," which has tons of Disney memorabilia on display.

Main Street is just the anteroom to the park as a whole. The biggest slice, and the one people usually head for first, is *Tomorrowland,* to the right (or counterclockwise direction) of Main Street. Continuing around brings us to *Fantasyland, Frontierland, Adventureland,* and then back to Main Street. In the center of it all is the magnificent fairy tale concoction of Sleeping Beauty's Castle. The sixties-modern Monorail, or the chugging Disneyland Railroad, both do a circuit of the park, giving a good introductory overview.

The most popular attractions at Disneyland are easy to determine: they have the longest lines. For good reason, too, since they are by and large some of the best theme-park entertainment available. The following is a short list of favorites:

- **Space Mountain.** Disneyland's fastest and scariest roller-coaster, racing through space, time, and black holes, all in utter darkness. Tomorrowland.

- **Submarine Voyage.** Rather than thrills and spills, this ride takes you on a cruise under the North Pole, dodging giant clams, squids, and sunken treasure-ships. Tomorrowland.

- **The Matterhorn.** A bobsled race around a roller-coaster of a Swiss Alp, terrorized by an abominable snowman. Fantasyland.

- **It's a Small World.** Disney at its most mindlessly cloying. This sing-along tour of the globe is to be avoided by anyone who hates getting tunes stuck in their heads. Fantasyland.

- **Big Thunder Mountain Railroad.** Ride a runaway mining train through tunnels and over trestles, narrowly escaping rock-slides and a waterfall. Frontierland.

- **Haunted Mansion.** Disney being Disney, the ghosts here smile and sing and dance rather than try to scare the daylights out of you. Still, some of the effects—a disembodied head in a crystal ball, for one—are quite unsettling. Adventureland.

- **Pirates of the Caribbean.** The best ride in Disneyland, mixing a few thrills with singing pirates on a drunken rape-and-pillage spree. Adventureland.

- **Jungle Cruise.** People visiting tropical rainforests sometimes feel that the real thing doesn't quite match the Disney version, on which tigers and crocodiles menace a mock-up of the African Queen. Adventureland.

Lines and crowd conditions vary widely through the year in Disneyland, but there are a few ways to avoid excessive delays:

- **Go early.** This will allow you to pace your day, and avoid trying to pack everything into peak hours.

- **Stay late.** The all-time best hours at Disneyland are late summer evenings when most families have gone home.

- **Buy the multi-day passport.** This allows you to spend up to three non-concurrent days sampling Disneyland, so you can bracket your time at Disneyland with visits to the rest of Los Angeles.

- **Plan ahead.** Many rides have a minimum height requirement ("Big Thunder Mountain Railroad," "Autopia," "Space Mountain," and "Splash Mountain"), so don't waste time waiting with a child who's not tall enough.

- **Choose a slow time.** Between Thanksgiving and Christmas (the holiday periods themselves, of course, are quite crowded) is one of the least-crowded times, as is springtime between Easter and Memorial Day.

A good rule of thumb is that a visit to Disneyland, with lunch and dinner in the park, will set you back around $50 per person per day, plus whatever souvenirs you find irresistible. **Admission** fees are always changing, but at time of writing a one-day pass, given unlimited use of all rides and attractions (except arcade games) costs $27.50. A two-day pass goes for $50, and three days cost $72.50; children under 12, and seniors over 60, are given a 20 per cent discount. **Food** within the park is fairly expensive, and you're not allowed to bring any in with you. Disneyland's **opening hours** are variable, ranging from 10 A.M. to 6 P.M. in winter to 8 A.M. to 1 A.M. so it's worthwhile to call before you come. To find out about special events, live entertainment, and which rides may be closed for maintenance or repair, call Disneyland's information number, (714) 999-4565. Disneyland is just off the Santa Ana Freeway (I-5) at 1313 Harbor Boulevard, 25 miles (40 km) south of downtown L.A.

■ OTHER THEME PARKS

Six Flags Magic Mountain. Unlike Disneyland, which has a lot of conceptual attractions, Magic Mountain is famous for one thing: rides, rides, and more rides. Built on the side of a mountain on the northern flank of the San Fernando Valley, Magic Mountain boasts five, count 'em, five roller coasters, including The Colossus, which lays claim to being the largest wooden-framed roller coaster ever built. To the screamers add the soakers, the park's four water rides, and for those who like to get above it all, there's a funicular railway to the top of "Magic Mountain," and a space needle towering over the whole park. There is a small amount of Disneyland-style stuff—"Bugs Bunny World" features creatures from Warner Brothers' cartoons—but Six Flags remains a shrine to velocity and g-forces. In the summer, every night is the 4th of July as the fireworks explode over Mystic Lake.

Six Flags Magic Mountain is located an hour north of downtown L.A. in Valencia, just off I-5 at 26101 Magic Mountain Parkway. The park opens every day at 10 A.M. from Memorial Day to Labor Day, closing at midnight on Friday and Saturday and at 10 P.M. other days. The rest of the year Magic Mountain is open weekends and holidays only. Admission to the park, which gives unlimited access to all rides, costs $24 for adults, $14 for under-12s. Call (805) 255-4111 for more information.

Knott's Berry Farm. This amusement park has perhaps the oddest genesis of any in the nation. It began as a farm stand, selling Mrs. Cordelia Knott's homemade jams, jellies, and preserves. The condiments are still delicious and still for sale, as are the delicious fried-chicken dinners like those Mrs. Knott used to make. (These are now sold in a restaurant outside the park, so you don't have to pay admission just to eat.)

Knott's is above all a family-style place, emphasizing its image of a kinder, gentler, pre-urban America. It is corny and a little makeshift, lacking the smooth, impersonal charm of Disneyland, but some people love it all the more because of that. Knott's has water rides and a 20-story "Sky Jump" parachute ride, but its strength is attractions like Ghost Town and Fiesta Village, *in situ* exhibits that play on nostalgia for the past. The Knott family no longer has an interest in the park; it is now owned by the family of Robert Welch, founder of the John Birch Society, which puts quite a different spin on the obsession with "family values."

Knott's Berry Farm is located at 8039 Beach Boulevard, Buena Park, off the Beach Boulevard exit of the Santa Ana (I-5) and Riverside (Highway 91) freeways. Admission is $22.95 for adults, $9.95 for under-12s, and the park opens at 10 A.M. year round, closing at various times (6 P.M. to 1 A.M.) throughout the year. For further information call (714) 220-5144.

Movieland Wax Museum. A short way from Knott's Berry Farm is the **Movieland Wax Museum**, a much more entertaining paraffin palace than most, and not without its own sleazy charm. Scenes are recreated wholesale here from major movies, including the white-banked steppes of *Dr. Zhivago*, an upside-down *Poseidon*

Adventure cabin, and the bridge of the Starship Enterprise. A "Chamber of Horrors" devoted to Hollywood fright films is very good, as is the "Black Box" tour of flicks like *Alien* and *Altered States.*

Movieland Wax Museum is located at 7711 Beach Boulevard, between La Palma and Orangethorpe, in Buena Park. Admission is $12.95, $6.95 for kids, and it's open daily 9 A.M. to 9 P.M. For further information, call (714) 522-1155.

Raging Waters. A 44-acre water park located deep in the San Gabriel Valley, Raging Waters has slides, swimming pools, and sand "beaches." On hot summer days, it takes on the surreal quality of a beach in the mountains, solving that age-old quandary of which to choose for a vacation. There are picnic spots here, also, and a wide array of fast-food stands. A special evening treat are "dive-in" movies, featuring obvious choices like *Creature from the Black Lagoon.*

Raging Waters is located at 111 Via Verde, off the Via Verde exit from Foothill Freeway (I-210), and is open May–October, 9 A.M. to 10 P.M. weekends, 10 A.M. to 10 P.M. weekdays. General admission costs $16.95, children under four feet tall pay $8.95. Call (714) 592-6453 for further information.

■ MUSEUMS

Gene Autry Western Heritage Museum. "Singing Cowboy" Gene Autry invested his movie money wisely—buying TV stations—and the public reaps the benefits here. This massive museum houses a 16,000-piece archival collection of six-shooters, paintings, Stetson hats, singing cowboy sheet music, Hopalong Cassidy bedspreads—anything and everything to do with the Hollywood Western and with the reality on which it was (loosely) based.

With exhibits designed and produced by Walt Disney Imagineering—the same folks responsible for the Disney theme parks—the six theme exhibit galleries are divided into broad areas, but the whole museum can easily be seen in a half day. "The Spirit of Imagination" is the apt name for the specific gallery dealing with the history of the radio, television, and movie Western. Video loops show clips from dozens of films, from wonderful archival footage of Buffalo Bill to *The Great Train Robbery* to the horse operas of Autry's day to the "spaghetti Westerns" of the sixties. The Museum Theater shows regularly scheduled Hollywood Westerns as well as the occasional documentary and live presentations.

The Gene Autry Western Heritage Museum, located in Glendale at 4700 Western Heritage Drive, (213) 667-2000, is open Tuesday through Sunday, 10 A.M. to 5 P.M. Admission.

General Phineas Banning Residence Museum. A Greek Revival masterpiece commemorating the man who was responsible for constructing Los Angeles Harbor, this is a monument to genteel Victorian lifestyles. Located at 401 E. M Street, Wilmington, (213) 548-777, and open Tuesday–Thursday, Saturday and Sunday, with tours given hourly from 12:30 to 3:30 P.M. Admission.

Exposition Park. What began a century ago as an open-air farmer's market is now an attractively landscaped green space, just south of downtown and home to the city's main collection of museums. The **Natural History Museum** is the gem, a vast space with 26 separate galleries. This has the most visitors of any museum in California, and resplendent displays of dinosaurs, California history, zoology, marine biology, and archaeology, to name but a few. Put these together with the museum's usually superb temporary exhibits, and you have the best place to spend a rainy afternoon in Southern California—and a fine place to spend a sunny one, too.

Chumash Indian diorama at the Natural History Museum.
(L.A. County Natural History Museum)

(opposite) Young patron checks out Marilyn Monroe at the Hollywood Wax Museum.

Across State Drive, the **California Museum of Science and Industry** is itself a complex of museums: the Mark Taper Hall of Economics, the Kinsey Hall of Health (which, without a trace of irony, is right next to the on-site *McDonald's*), and the science and industry section itself. All of these are great fun and packed with push-button exhibits, but perhaps the best part is housed in a new, Frank Gehry-designed structure, the Aerospace Building. Devoted to the technological wonders of flight, from a 1920 Wright Brothers glider to an F-104 Starfighter, the museum also has sections devoted to satellites and the exploration of the universe, as well as holding the wide-screen IMAX Theater.

Next to Science and Industry is the **California Museum of Afro-American History and Culture**, which has art, artifacts, a 13,000 square-foot sculpture garden and a constantly changing menu of exhibits highlighting black culture and achievements. The permanent collection includes works by the Haitian painter F. Turenne de Pres and pencil drawings by Edward Mitchell Bannister, and the small theater hosts a wide variety of educational programs and multi-media events.

All the Exposition Park museums are in separate buildings within a short walk of one another. The Natural History Museum is located at 900 Exposition Boulevard, (213) 744-3466; the Museum of Science and Industry is at 700 State Drive, (213) 744-7400; the Museum of Afro-American History and Culture is at 600 State Drive, (213) 744-7432. All are open daily 10 A.M. to 5 P.M. and are free, except for the Natural History Museum, which is closed Mondays and charges admission.

J. Paul Getty Art Museum. A full-blown reproduction of a Pompeiian villa set into a Pacific hillside just east of Malibu. Crammed with Greek and Roman antiquities, illuminated manuscripts, and a world-class photography collection, the Getty transformed the world art scene with its huge endowment and free-spending ways. Stay tuned for the opening of the Getty Center, on a hillside above Brentwood, where the modern collections will soon be housed.

The Getty Museum is located northwest of Santa Monica at 17985 Pacific Coast Highway, (310) 458-2003, and is open Tuesday through Sunday, 10 A.M. to 5 P.M. Admission is free, but there's very limited on-site parking, so reservations are a must—or you can ride the bus: RTD #434 stops a half-mile (1 km) away.

Armand Hammer Museum of Art. Features the late Occidental Petroleum czar Armand Hammer's world-class art collection, controversial because it was originally promised to the Los Angeles County Museum of Art). In Westwood at 10889 Wilshire Boulevard, (310) 443-7020, and open 11 A.M. to 7 P.M. Admission.

Heritage Square Museum. Sprawling historical development that features eight vintage Victorian houses, as well as cars from the original Angel's Flight and other "living museum" style exhibits. Within walking distance of the Southwest Museum. Located alongside the Pasadena Freeway at 3800 Homer Street, (818) 449-0193, and open Friday through Sunday 11 A.M. to 4 P.M. Admission.

Huntington Beach International Surfing Museum. People who would write surfing off as a frivolous pastime don't realize the rich tradition that lies behind the simple acts of "hangin' ten" and "gettin' tubed, dude." This small museum sets the record straight, tracing the sport's history (it was imported to Huntington Beach from Hawaii by real estate promoters, for example) and emphasizing its competition side. The Surfing Museum is at 411 Olive Avenue in Huntington Beach, (714) 960-3483, and is open Wednesday through Sunday, noon to 5 P.M. Admission.

Huntington Library and Art Gallery. This is everyone's favorite spot in the San Gabriel Valley, a lush 207-acre oasis of blooming horticulture and rampant botanical displays. The library-cum-museum itself is no slouch either, proudly displaying English portraits like Gainsborough's *Blue Boy* and an extensive assembly of historic books, including a Gutenberg Bible, an original folio of Audubon's *Birds of America,* and a controversial copy of the Dead Sea Scrolls. The Huntington is at 1151 Oxford Road in San Marino, (818) 405-2141, and is open Tuesday through Sunday 1 to 4:30 P.M. Reservations are required on Sundays. Admission.

Long Beach Museum of Art. This may be the museum of the future with its emphasis on video art, and its beach-side setting gives a panoramic backdrop to the art. Located at 2300 E. Ocean Boulevard in Long Beach, (310) 439-2119. Open Wednesday through Sunday, noon to 5 P.M., Thursdays till 8 P.M. Admission.

Los Angeles Contemporary Exhibitions (LACE). Downtown art space that features performance, film, and video as well as examples from more traditional graphic and plastic art forms. It also has an excellent bookstore. Located at 1804 Industrial Street, (213) 624-5650, LACE is open Wednesday through Friday, 11 A.M. to 5 P.M., weekends noon to 5 P.M. Free.

Los Angeles County Museum of Art (LACMA). More of a collection of collections, this impressive linked jumble of architecture proves that culture has come to Southern California to stay. Grouped around a central courtyard are five wings, buildings and galleries, including an extravagant Japanese Pavilion that houses the best collection of Japanese art in the U.S. The permanent collection is especially strong in German Expressionism, Oriental art, and costume art. LACMA is located at 5905 Wilshire Boulevard, (213) 857-6111, and is open Tuesday through Thursday 10 A.M. to 5 P.M., Friday 10 A.M. to 9 P.M., and weekends 11 A.M. to 6 P.M. Admission.

Lummis House. Well-preserved residence of the "first citizen" of early Los Angeles, Charles Fletcher Lummis. Writer, publisher, booster extraordinaire, Lummis's centrality in L.A.'s history is the focus of exhibits here. Located at 200 E. Avenue 43 in Highland Park, (213) 222-0546, the Lummis House (also known as "El Alisal") is open weekends 1 to 4 P.M., with extended hours in summer. Free.

Museum of Contemporary Art (MOCA) and the **Temporary Contemporary** (TC). These two sister museums, the latter of which originated as a makeshift space put into service when the original was not ready to open for the 1984 Olympics, show off the best in international contemporary art. The coolly stylish

Treasures from the Getty: (right) Cameo Glass, First Century A.D. (opposite) Bathing Venus by Jean Boulogne, ca. 1559. (J. Paul Getty Museum)

MOCA gallery, designed by Arata Isozaki, uses crisp geometry to highlight the museum's collection of abstract, Pop, Minimalist, and neo-figurative works by the likes of Rauschenberg, Rothko, Oldenberg, Kiefer, and many more. The Frank Gehry-designed "temporary" quarters, converted from an old L.A. police department garage, have proved so popular they were retained, giving MOCA two exhibition spaces.

MOCA is on Bunker Hill at 250 S. Grand Avenue, and the Temporary Contemporary is east of City Hall at 152 N. Central Avenue. Both galleries are open Tuesday through Sunday 11 A.M. to 6 P.M., Thursdays till 8 P.M. The phone for both is (213) 626-6222. Admission.

Museum of Neon Art. Located near LACE, and featuring an explosive display of the signs that make Las Vegas—and vast sections of L.A.—great. The museum is at 704 Traction Avenue, downtown, (213) 617-1580, and open Tuesday through Saturday, 11 A.M. to 6 P.M. Admission.

Merle Norman Museum. Calling all car fans, this collection has dozens of fabulous automobiles from the golden age of luxury, alongside an eclectic display of mechanical music-making machines, from phonographs to huge Wurlitzer organs. The museum is located at 15180 Bledsoe Street in the northern San Fernando Valley. Reservations are necessary, phone (818) 367-2251. Admission.

George C. Page Museum of the La Brea Discoveries. Arguably the world's most innovative paleontology museum, featuring the remains of Ice Age flora and fauna (and one human) recovered from the adjacent La Brea tar pits. The Page Museum is next to LACMA at 5801 Wilshire Boulevard, (213) 936-2230, and is open Tuesday through Sunday, 10 A.M. to 5 P.M. Admission.

Norton Simon Museum. Rated as one of the finest museums in the U.S., but surprisingly low-profile in L.A., the Simon collection contains hundreds of major works ranging from classics by Rembrandt, Rubens, and Raphael to more modern masterpieces by Renoir, Manet, Cézanne, van Gogh, Picasso, Klee, and many more. The gallery also has a world-class assembly of sculpture from Southeast Asia, many of them collected by Simon's wife, the actress Jennifer Jones. The museum also has one of the better-stocked and reasonably priced bookstores in the city. The Norton Simon Museum is in Pasadena at 411 W. Colorado Boulevard, (818) 449-3730 and is open Thursday through Sunday, noon to 6 P.M. Admission.

Southwest Museum. Sometimes called the "Indian Museum," this has a quite splendiferous collection of Native American objects, art and artifacts, mainly from the southwestern U.S. but also including pieces from as far away as Alaska and southern Mexico. The superb dioramas (in a tunnel leading to the mission-style museum from the street) are augmented inside by a full-sized teepee, a Pomo granary, and a cliff-side petroglyph. The museum towers over the Pasadena Freeway at 234 Museum Drive, (213) 221-2163, and is open Tuesday through Sunday, 11 A.M. to 5 P.M. Admission.

■ OTHER MUSEUMS

Cabrillo Marine Museum. Multimedia shows and recreations of Southern California marine habitats fill this engaging harborfront museum. Located at 3720 Stephen White Drive, off Pacific Avenue in Palos Verdes, (310) 548-7562. Admission.

Children's Museum. Hands-on exhibits let children become firefighters, nurses, or TV newscasters. 310 N. Main Street, downtown, (213) 687-8800. Admission.

Max Factor Beauty Museum. Make-up through the ages. 1666 N. Highland Avenue, Hollywood, (213) 463-6668. Free.

Frederick's of Hollywood Lingerie Museum. Undergarments of the rich and famous. 6608 Hollywood Boulevard, (213) 466-8506. Free.

Hollywood Studio Museum. Small museum focusing on the early, silent days of Hollywood. 2100 N. Highland Avenue, Hollywood, (213) 874-2276. Admission.

Max Factor Museum.

Museum in Black. All manner of art and artifact from African and black America. 4327 Degnan Boulevard, South-Central L.A., (213) 292-9528. Free.

Richard Nixon Library and Birthplace. Extensive exhibits trace the rise and fall of former president Nixon, on the grounds of the house where he was born. 18001 Yorba Linda Boulevard, Yorba Linda, (714) 993-3393. Admission.

Ronald Reagan Presidential Library. Opened in 1992, this repository of Reagan's presidential papers also has a large museum of the "Great Communicator's" life and times. 40 Presidential Drive, Simi Valley, (805) 522-8444. Admission.

Santa Monica Museum of Art. Upstart gallery-cum-museum showing off some of the best emerging L.A. artists. 2435 Main Street, Santa Monica, (310) 399-0433. Free.

Science Fiction Collection. Forrest J. Ackerman's treasure trove of stills, props, magazines, books, art, scripts, and posters. Open Saturdays at his "Ackermansion," 2495 Glendower Avenue, Hollywood, (213) MOON-FAN. Free.

Watts Towers Art Center. Wide variety of exhibitions and events, held at the base of the landmark towers. 1727 E. 107th Street, Watts, (213) 569-8181. Free.

■ COMMERCIAL ART GALLERIES

Ace Gallery. Lodged in a huge space of museum-like proportions, the 30-year-old Ace ranks near the top of L.A.'s gallery scene. 5514 Wilshire Boulevard, (213) 935-4411.

Fahey-Klein Gallery. The premier contemporary photography gallery in Los Angeles. 148 N. La Brea Avenue, West Hollywood, (213) 281-8883.

G. Ray Hawkins. Fine-art photography, displaying both new and vintage prints. 7224 Melrose Avenue, West Hollywood, (213) 550-1504.

Gallery of Functional Art. Furniture-as-art, in a great Frank Gehry-designed space. 2429 Main Street, Santa Monica, (310) 450-2827.

Hunsaker-Schlesinger. Near the Beverly Center, with eclectic exhibitions featuring many California artists. 812 La Cienega Boulevard, West Hollywood, (213) 657-2557.

Iturralde Gallery. L.A.'s best showcase for Latino artists, especially those from Mexico. 154 N. La Brea Avenue, West Hollywood, (213) 937-4267.

James Corcoran Gallery. One of the most important galleries in Los Angeles, showing both international and local artists, and concentrating on abstract expressionist painting. 1327 Fifth Street, Santa Monica, (310) 451-4666.

M. Hanks Gallery. Small space with an all-embracing vision of African-American art. 2669 Main Street, Santa Monica, (310) 392-8820.

Sherry Frumkin Gallery. Specializes in works by emerging artists. 1440 Ninth Street, Santa Monica, (310) 393-1853.

■ STUDIO TOURS

Given the primary focus of this book, I've centered upon those tours and opportunities which allow some insight into the world of the movies, past and present. Unfortunately, there are only two remaining **studio tours** in town, Warner Brothers and KCET; however, both of these are very worthwhile. At the end of this section there is also a short section describing how to go about seeing a movie being made **on location,** or at least getting **tickets** for a taping of a TV show.

■ WARNER BROTHERS STUDIO TOUR

Universal may get all the notice, but the best inside look at Hollywood in action is the Warner Brothers Studios VIP Tour. Over four million people a year go to Universal; under 5,000 see Warners. Small and intimate where Universal is sprawling and impersonal, concerned with the nuts and bolts of moviemaking where Universal is all flash and dazzle, the VIP Tour is probably the truest three-hour look into the film industry that anyone can experience. If Universal is the Great Oz with flashing lights and gusts of multicolored smoke, Warners VIP Tour is Oz after Dorothy has pulled the curtain aside.

Dick Mason, who developed the tour almost 30 years ago, is a film historian whose approach is strictly what-you-see-is-what-you-get. No prepackaged entertainment extravaganzas here. If you get to see live action on the tour, it will be of whatever films are being shot on the lot, or whatever television shows are in production that day. Nothing special is set up, but you'll get to see something perhaps more interesting than staged special effects: the steady quotidian hum of a movie studio at work.

Groups are limited to a dozen but are sometimes smaller. Although the advice is "wear comfortable shoes," much of the time is spent in a golf cart. The guides are usually young interns, with varying degrees of experience, but are well-trained and knowledgeable about what was shot where. They have a wealth of movie history from which to choose: Warner Brothers Studios began in the late teens, and with the success of *The Jazz Singer*, bought the Burbank lot, which they had previously rented from First National. For years the lot was known as First National-Warners, and when Columbia came on board in 1972, it became known as The Burbank Studios, or TBS. In 1990, Warners bought Lorimar Television, which owned the old MGM lot in Culver City, and Columbia and Lorimar switched homes, Columbia going to Culver City, and Lorimar coming onto the Burbank lot.

Warners is one of the busiest studios in Hollywood, much used by Lorimar and as a rental lot by other studios and independent producers. The season for television production runs roughly from July through December, so there is much more action on the lot during those months, but even if you hit the "hiatus" (the period when episodic television is not in production) there are enough films being shot that you are likely to see some action. Nothing is guaranteed, however, and the visit to the studios' New York Street, Hennesy Street (built for the movie *Annie* and named for designer Dale Hennesy), the Jungle (formerly Walton's Flats, after the television show), Laramie Street and Midwestern Street are worthwhile even if they are not dressed and in use. The lot also has the world's biggest sound stage, a massive building enlarged by William Randolph Hearst as per the request of Miss Marion Davies.

The VIP tour also makes quick but fascinating visits to prop departments, sound stages, set constructions workshops—anywhere on the lot where there seems to be activity. These visits, also, are random and not prescheduled. You may see the model shop, where fascinating miniatures like the plane used in *Lost Horizon* are kept. Something as mundane as the prop lighting department, full of lamps and chandeliers, can furnish up treasures like the two huge brass lanterns hung in Rick's Cafe in *Casablanca*. The studio conservatively estimates that the pair are worth $100,000.

Because it is a tour of a working studio, Warners has a minimum age requirement of ten years. Reservations are highly recommended, though sometimes you can squeeze in at last minute. You can also make reservations to have lunch at the

Grave Line Tours *show what Jack Parr meant when he said "the California cemeteries make dying so attractive it's a real effort to keep breathing."*

new Warner Brothers commissary, rebuilt in the fall of 1991. It's a great way to top off a great tour. Warner Brothers Studio is located at 4000 Warner Boulevard in Burbank; call (818) 954-1744 for more information.

■ KCET TOUR

Ever since the NBC Studios in Burbank suspended its guided tour in 1991, KCET, the Los Angeles public broadcasting station, has offered the only tour of a working television studio. The rates of production are vastly different—where NBC has the *Tonight Show,* KCET has the Children's Hospital Telethon—but KCET has one ace-in-the-hole: its history.

The KCET facility is the oldest continuously used studio in Los Angeles, with productions pouring forth since 1912. The guided tour that the station offers on Tuesdays and Thursdays is partially about television production, and partially about the glory days of the lot, when it was home to Monogram and then Allied Artists.

A company called Lubin Manufacturing Corporation first set up shop here, back in the opportunist days of Hollywood, when producers shot anything that was handy. In the neighborhood back then was an alligator farm and an ostrich farm, so sure enough, both were subjects of Lubin movies. When Lubin went under, silent star Charles Ray took over, greatly enlarging the lot. Then it was a rental studio and finally, from around 1940 to 1970 (when PBS took it over) home to one of the great B-movie mills of all time.

Monogram was responsible for such second-bill perennials as *Charlie Chan* (with Sidney Toller), *The East End Kids,* and *The Cisco Kid.* The company changed its name to Allied Artists to escape its B-movie reputation, and made a few great features, too, films like *Love in the Afternoon, Friendly Persuasion,* and *Invasion of the Body Snatchers.* Among the stars to get their start on this lot are Robert Mitchum, Elvis Presley, Bela Lugosi, Errol Flynn, Shelley Winters, Lon Chaney, and Ava Gardner.

The first stop on the tour is a small, one-room, one-plaque museum commemorating KCET's past. Not much smacks of the Monogram years except the Hugh M. Hefner Theater (the *Playboy* publisher paid for its renovation), a charming colonnaded space that used to be the studio screening room. Mostly what you get on the tour is the nuts-and-bolts of broadcasting. KCET tour is an intimate, informal, extremely accessible (and free!) look at the technology of television, limited by the station's purlieu, but enhanced by the lot's history. KCET is located in Silver Lake at 4401 Sunset Boulevard, (213) 666-6500.

■ TICKETS AND TAPINGS

Perhaps the best way to see Hollywood in action is to attend a taping of a show in one of several studio venues around L.A. Some of the more popular shows are difficult to get into—*The Tonight Show* is a notoriously tough ticket—but many syndicated programs are hungry for live bodies. Most programs tape from March through November; game and talk shows tape year-round. Who knows? If you have an especially identifiable laugh, you may hear yourself chuckling on the soundtrack of your favorite TV show soon.

None of the studios will guarantee you a seat for specific shows, but a surefire way to attend a television taping is through a firm called **Audience Associates,** who actively recruit audience-members in front of the Chinese Theater almost every day. They also provide transportation to and from the studio involved.

To get tickets, write or call the following studios, specifying dates, programs (if preferred and you know which studio tapes the show), and the number of tickets desired. Some shows have age limits; usually the cut-off age is 12. Most studios will not send tickets out-of-state, fearing no-shows. They will, however, give you a letter of priority for tickets on the day. Many ask that you include a stamped, self-addressed envelope with your request.

Audience Associates. 6253 Hollywood Boulevard, Hollywood 90068, (213) 467-4697.

ABC Television Center. 4151 Prospect Avenue, Hollywood 90027. There's also a self-service window at 1776 Talmadge Avenue, (213) 520-1222.

CBS Television City. 7800 Beverly Boulevard, Los Angeles 90036, (213) 852-2624.

NBC Broadcast Ticket Division. 3000 W. Alameda Avenue, Burbank 91523, (818) 840-3555. The *Tonight Show* has a limit of four tickets per mail request, with a 16-year-old age requirement.

Paramount Studios. 5451 Marathon Street, Los Angeles, CA 90068, (213) 956-5575. Pick up tickets at Visitors Booth, Monday through Friday, 8 A.M. to 4 P.M. They also offer a very short tour by reservation only.

■ **ON LOCATION**
The **City of Los Angeles Film and Video Permit Office.** 6922 Hollywood Boulevard, Suite 602, across from the Chinese Theatre, is one of the greatest resources for those who want to watch a film set in action. Open to the public, for a nominal charge ($1 plus 10 cents per page), they provide a listing of all films, commercials, and music videos being shot in public locations on that day.

It's called a "Shoot Sheet," and the listings give the address, the hours, and the title of the project, plus the name of producing entity. Some of the listings are very general, giving no more information than "Griffith Park," while some others give specific addresses. While the office cannot guarantee the list's accuracy—some cancellations and last-minute changes might be made—in general this is the perfect way to see moviemaking in action.

"In action," and "inaction," too, since location work is notorious for interminable set-ups, during which nothing much is going on, giving way to a 30-second burst of activity between "action!" and "cut!" For those expecting constant stunts and spectacular dramatics, going on location can be boring and disappointing, but all in all it's an excellent way to catch glimpses of movie stars on the job.

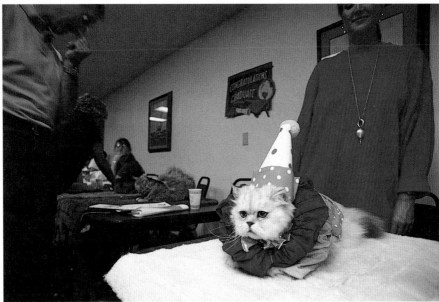

Cat auditions are just as competitive as their human counterparts.

"*To survive in Hollywood, you need the ambition of a Latin American revolutionary, the ego of a grand opera singer, and the physical stamina of a cow pony.*" —*Billie "Wicked Witch of the West" Burke (below) Casting room with extras.*

"It's hard to tell where Hollywood ends and the DTs begin." —W.C. Fields
(Academy of Motion Picture Arts and Sciences)

PRACTICAL INFORMATION

■ CLIMATE

DESPITE WHAT ITS BOOSTERS PROMISE, Los Angeles does not have sunshine 365 days a year, and it does indeed sometimes rain in Southern California. Not often, though: the "rainy" season extends from January through March, and total annual rainfall hovers around 14 inches. That said, do not expect sunshine for the rest of the year. There is the famous "June gloom," with uniformly gray skies until mid-afternoon, when the sun finally burns them off. There are fogs, miasmic smog, the blistering Santa Ana winds—all of which belie the image of Southern California as the land of eternal sunshine.

A recipe for smog: take one mountain-rimmed basin, fill with carbon-fuel burning humans, trap resulting effluvia with a cold air inversion layer from surrounding mountains; cook soup with sunlight; serves 11 million. The word "smog", a portmanteau word combining "smoke" with "fog," was actually imported from Pittsburgh, where the steel smelters put up a smoky veil. The Los Angeles basin had bad air to some degree even before the arrival of the white man and the automobile, but the car took a mild climatological quirk and turned it into a monster. The smog is at its worst during the summer months, when those with respiratory ailments should avoid going outside on days when the air is deemed "unacceptable."

Smog or no, there are enough sunny California days to make them the norm, brilliantly sunny, with Mediterranean blue skies and cooling nights. "The worst climate in the world," writer John Gregory Dunne jokingly called it, and he was perhaps talking metaphysically: all that sunshine is good for tennis, but it may be bad for the soul. The debate about that will rage as long as there is a Los Angeles.

AVERAGE TEMPERATURES AND PRECIPITATION
In Fahrenheit and (Centigrade), inches and (centimeters)

MONTH	HIGH	LOW	RAINFALL
January	65 (18)	46 (8)	3.1 (7.9)
February	66 (19)	47 (8)	3.0 (7.6)
March	67 (19)	48 (9)	2.8 (7.1)
April	70 (21)	50 (10)	1.0 (2.5)
May	72 (22)	53 (12)	0.4 (1.0)
June	76 (24)	56 (13)	0.1 (0.3)
July	81 (27)	60 (16)	0 (0)
August	82 (28)	60 (16)	0 (0)
September	81 (27)	58 (14)	0.2 (0.5)
October	76 (24)	54 (12)	0.6 (1.5)
November	73 (23)	50 (10)	1.2 (3.1)
December	67 (19)	47 (8)	2.6 (6.6)

■ GETTING TO L.A.

The **Los Angeles International Airport,** known universally by the rather dismaying rubric of "LAX" is the world's third largest in terms of volume, handling over 45 million passengers a year. Refurbished as part of a community clean-up for the 1984 Olympics, the airport is the overwhelming choice of travelers flying to Los Angeles.

LAX's terminals are arranged in a horseshoe shape. In the middle of the horseshoe, there is the arcing Theme Building, which looks like a spider and houses a restaurant (California Place), an observation deck, and a bank. At the closed end of the horseshoe is the Bradley Terminal, named after Mayor Tom Bradley and handling most of the international traffic. Airport information is (213) 646-5252.

As clean and well-run as LAX is, most air travelers want to leave it immediately. This has caused a number of transportation services to spring up in support of the need to vamoose. Besides the dozens of car rental companies (see "Getting Around" below for details), there are myriad shuttle van services to and from LAX, including *SuperShuttle* (213) 777-8000, on which you have to share rides with other passengers. The service is door-to-door, but since you may have to detour to accommodate other passengers, it takes longer than by taxi. Shuttles cost around $10–15 depending upon how far you're going; a taxi ride downtown will set you back around $30.

RTD runs a shuttle bus from all LAX terminals to its Lot C bus stop where you can connect to buses serving all areas of the city; call (213) 626-4455, (see "Getting Around" below for more). Long-term parking for $8 per day is also at Lot C, Sepulveda Boulevard at 96th Street, from where there's a free shuttle to the terminals.

Fly with the Stars, on MGM Grand Air. For information call (800) 933-2646.

■ **OTHER L.A. AIRPORTS**

The best-kept secret in L.A. air travel is the existence of domestic flights into three smaller airports, the Burbank Airport in the San Fernando Valley, (818) 840-8847; John Wayne Airport in Orange County, (714) 834-8041; and the Ontario Airport to the east in San Bernardino County (714) 983-8282. Consider them as a low-stress alternative to LAX, especially if you are headed to these areas anyway.

WAITING FOR MR. GOLDMAN

I find Los Angeles a very difficult and potentially dangerous place to work in, and I think anyone seriously contemplating a career as a screenwriter ought to move there as soon as it's humanly or financially possible.

As to its being a difficult and dangerous, that's entirely a personal reaction. I am aware of the number of brilliant writers, painters, and musicians who have thrived in the sunshine. I can't help it that from the very beginning the place has terrified me.

Part of it has to do with money. For the hardcover publication of my first novel, I was paid five thousand dollars. Such was the glory of its reception that, for my second novel, I was paid twenty-five hundred dollars. For *Harper,* my first Hollywood film, I received eighty thousand dollars.

So what's so terrible?

Obviously nothing in a monetary way. It was a fantastic windfall. But—and, remember, we are dealing with *my* neuroses here—there was something unsettling about the discrepancy. If you write a novel, and you get X for your labors, that sets up a value system: You put in a certain amount of effort, you receive a certain amount of reimbursement, just like any other worker. However, if you are lucky or talented enough to become in demand as a screenwriter, the amounts you are paid are so staggering, compared to real writing, that it's bound to make you uneasy.

It was on *Harper* that I first (not counting funerals) rode in a limousine.

Late afternoon. I got off the plane at LAX and started for the baggage claim area. Then I stopped. Dead. A uniformed man was standing by the gate exit, holding a cardboard sign with the name Goldman written on it. It was a paranoid moment for me, because my last name isn't all that uncommon, and I stared at him, wondering what the hell to do. Should I approach him or not? No one had told me I would be met at the airport. What if I pissed him off? The scene might have played like this:

ME: (perspiring lightly) Pardon me, sir, but are you, by any chance, waiting for William Goldman?

HIM: (affronted) No, you fool, who's William Goldman? I'm here to pick up Max Goldman, now get away.

Finally, I went up to him and said, "Pardon me, sir, but are you, by any chance, waiting for William Goldman?" and he smiled and said, "Yes *sir,* Mr. Goldman," and then he took my under-the-seat bag and led me to where the luggage would come belching down the chute. . . .

Eventually, fourth from the end or so, my suitcase came clumping down and he bent for it, my driver did, easily beating me to the task, and then he said, "Just follow me, Mr. Goldman," and I did, hoping nobody I knew would see me.

We trooped out to the sidewalk. He put my stuff down, smiled, and said, "I'm just parked over there, sir, wait right here, I won't be a minute."

I waited until this giant Cadillac appeared. Before I could make a move, he bounced out from the driver's seat, raced around, opened the back door for me. "Watch your head, Mr. Goldman," he advised.

I got in. I sat back. He put my luggage in the trunk. Then he hurried around in front, gave me a little kind of salute, moved in behind the wheel. (It's crazy the things you remember, but believe me, I remember all of this.)

What I remember mostly was sitting in the back of that big car, alone, feeling very close to panic. "What the fuck am I doing back here—I'm not Jackie Kennedy—I shouldn't be here—what does this have to do with writing?"

The motor turned over perfectly, he looked back to see that all was well, and then he skillfully began piloting the car into the stream of airport traffic— and I yelled "Stop!"

He stopped, glanced at me. "Forget something?"

"Can I sit up front with you?" I said.

He looked at me, I thought, kind of weirdly. "Of course, Mr. Goldman. Anything you want."

—William Goldman, *Adventures in the Screen Trade,* 1985

Heaven or Hell's Angels?

■ TRAINS AND BUSES

AMTRAK trains serve the glorious Union Station in downtown Los Angeles (800) 872-7245. The ride along the California coast through Santa Barbara on the Starlighter is one of the glories of modern train travel. There is also a frequent service along the coast from San Diego, and daily trains from the rest of the U.S.

The main **Greyhound bus** station is located in a seedy corner of downtown, at Los Angeles and Sixth streets, (213) 620-1200. There are also stations in Hollywood at 1409 N. Vine Street, (213) 466-6382, and in Santa Monica at 1433 Fifth Street, (310) 394-5433. **Green Tortoise**, (415) 285-2441 or (800) 227-4766, a San Francisco-based hippy holdout is about the only alternative to depression-inducing Greyhound.

■ GETTING AROUND L.A.

Chances are good that a sizeable part of your time in L.A. will be spent getting from place to place—the city sprawls on an unimaginable scale, covering an area larger than any other metropolitan area on earth. Knowing that, it's important to plan ahead, and while having a car won't insure a painless transport experience, it is without doubt the best way to get around. There is a comprehensive bus service, plus an ambitious planned subway system that at present is best counted on for its novelty value. While these are occasionally very useful, there's no substitute for having your own wheels.

■ CAR RENTAL

You're in L.A.; don't argue; you need a car. That's the bad news. The good news is that there is a plethora of car rental agencies, and competition among them has made competition stiff and rates low. Because of the sheer volume, prices are usually lowest at the airport, and the free shuttles which pick you up from the terminals make it the best place to start. Bargain for the lowest rate you can find, and since Los Angeles is so large, demand free mileage whenever possible. All major firms have toll-free 1-800 numbers for making reservations (see their ads in the "Yellow Pages"), and keep in mind that companies will often match their competitors' offers so don't be embarrassed to haggle for a better rate.

If your heart's set on cruising around in a '57 T-Bird or a Rolls-Royce Corniche, firms like *Beverly Hills Car Collection* at (310) 274-9173 and *Luxury Line* at (310) 657-2800 will cater to your whim.

Red, wipe, and blue.

■ THE FREEWAYS

"The rat race of rat races" is what writer Raymond Chandler called them, and they have entered urban mythology as rivers of adrenalin, alienation, and frustration. There are 30 different freeways in greater L.A., 988 miles in all. 13 million people take 18 million vehicle trips on the L.A.'s freeways every day. These facts alone are enough to daunt the most sober-minded native, and for the casual visitor, the freeway is too often a cipher to avoid, not solve.

Somehow, a traffic jam on a Los Angeles freeway has come to symbolize all that is wrong with Southern California, the smog, the congestion, the simple rage with inept urban planning. But the truth is that the L.A. freeway system works brilliantly well when it's not overloaded. You can carp about the curious, non-integrated aspect of the freeway, the tendency to wall them off from communities, as if they were something shameful. But when you're booming down the Santa Monica Freeway late at night, and you cross over the San Diego to feel the first blast of sea air, life is great, and these furious superhighways can seem one of the wonders of the modern world. There is a fluid, almost balletic feel to freeway driving, as you balance your fear of death with your urge to cross four lanes of traffic to get to your exit. It can make you feel transcendent, as if you are plugged into something larger than yourself, however impersonal that something is.

Approach the freeways as you would any mildly exhilarating sport, whitewater rafting, say, or the luge. If you've never experienced freeway driving, it's best to dip only your toe in at first, with a short trip. Simon Hoggart offered these tips for L.A. freeway virgins:

- There are two speeds which apply on the freeways: dangerously fast, and stationary. This is what it's like joining a freeway when the speed is set "fast."

- You drive up a ramp, where there's a small traffic light labeled "One car per green."

- You wait for your light, then advance towards the freeway itself, where there's another sign saying "Merge."

- You merge in the fashion that Belgium merged with Germany in 1914; it is an entirely one-sided process. What you see is six lanes of cars, all driving well above the 55 MPH (88 KPH) speed limit, but bumper-to-bumper nonetheless.

- You are supposed to find a gap in the "slow lane" (i.e. the one in which the traffic is travelling at only 10 MPH [16 KPH] above the limit), and fill it. Except that there are no gaps.
- Over the years of visiting Los Angeles I discovered a sophisticated, foolproof technique for dealing with this problem. I closed my eyes, swung the wheel to the left, and prayed.

One trap for the newcomer is that the freeways are known both by their numbers and by their names, both of which may change mid-stride. The Hollywood Freeway (US-101), for example, flows into the Ventura Freeway (also US-101), or, turning east instead of west, into the Foothill Freeway (I-210). All in the same ribbon of concrete. Getting directions from a native can be dizzying, since they are wont to refer to the freeways both by name and number, interchangeably. Add in the fact that not all freeway exits have both on-ramps and off-ramps, and the system turns really puzzling. "Puzzling," at 55-miles-per-hour translates into "terrifying."

Against the terror you have only two weapons, the knowledge that (A) there is really no way to get around L.A. without the freeways, and (B) freeway driving can be a lot of fun. For tactical support listen to the traffic reports, which are on all stations, even National Public Radio. Angelenos tune in to these like people elsewhere listen to the weather reports, which is just as well, since weather reports in Southern California are uniformly boring.

If you get into trouble, there are the *Road Angels,* a group that helps in emergency situations only (don't call them if you have a flat tire). They also offer sober drivers to substitute for those who have too much to drink. Call (213) 850-9909 for non-emergency info, and (800) 522-6435 in emergencies. There are also emergency "call boxes" placed every mile or so on all freeways.

■ TAXIS AND LIMOUSINES

Though they don't cruise the streets like they do in New York and other cities, there *are* taxis in L.A., and if for whatever reason you don't have a car at your disposal, or simply don't feel like driving, taxis can be very handy. They're not all that expensive, especially for shorter trips, though at $2 plus $1.60 a mile the cost can add up pretty quickly. A few of the larger companies are Checker Cab at (213) 481-2345, United Independent at (213) 653-5050, and Red Top, (213) 395-3201.

Chauffeur-driven **limousines** will set you back around $150 for a three-hour cruise—check the "Yellow Pages" for listings of companies.

■ PUBLIC TRANSIT

The people who run L.A.'s public transit system, known as the RTD, are faced with an impossible task: get half-a-million people to and from countless diffuse places without interrupting the journeys of the many million self-contained commuters who criss-cross the L.A. basin every day. Considering this, they don't do half-bad.

Depending upon where you want to go, riding the bus is a workable option. If you're headed downtown, or to the beach on a summer day, it can even be the preferred mode, not least because it saves the hassle and expense of finding a place to park. Fares are $1.10, with additional amounts for transfers and long-distance express buses which use the freeways. Though the system can seem bewilderingly complex, the RTD's very useful information line will help you find your way. Call (213) 626-4455.

The much eulogized Red Car system, which once linked all of Southern California by tram and inter-urban train, has a modern reincarnation in Metrorail. The first part of this network, the Blue Line, opened in 1990 and runs from Seventh and Flower streets downtown south to Long Beach, terminating within walking distance of the Queen Mary and Spruce Goose. Underground extensions to Hollywood and the San Fernando Valley (the Red Line) are the next sections due to open, with a route to LAX (the Green Line) due in 1996. The entire system is expected to be finished sometime next century; call (213) 620-7245 for the latest information.

■ SIGHTSEEING TOURS

By Bus

Starline/Grayline is the established tour company for Hollywood tours, specializing in the sights and sites of downtown Hollywood, movie-star homes, famous moviemaking landmarks. They can be contacted at the sightseeing kiosk near the Chinese Theater, at the main office at 6451 Hollywood Boulevard, or by calling (213) 856-5900.

Casablanca Tours, which operates out of the Roosevelt Hotel, 7000 Hollywood Boulevard, offers a four-hour tour of Hollywood, and can be reached at (213) 461-0156. For a four-hour nighttime tour of the Sunset Strip and downtown Hollywood, dinner included, contact the Magic Line, 827 N. Fairfax, West Hollywood,

Getting around—L.A. style.

(213) 653-1090. Finally, **Oskar J's** in Sherman Oaks, 13455 Ventura Boulevard, (818) 785-4039, offers a van tour (bus tours have been banned by Beverly Hills) that passes by the homes of over 75 stars.

On Foot

Hollywood Heritage, 1350 N. Highland, offers a program of historical walking tours, (213) 466-6782. The **Los Angeles Conservancy**, 727 Seventh Street, downtown, gives a great walking tour of the Broadway movie palaces, and offers an extensive program of other tours as well. Call (213) 623-2489.

By Hearse

The **Grave Line Tour** is a suitably macabre round-up of the site of famous deaths, graves, murders, and scandals that have happened in Hollywood and environs, most connected to the movie business. Conducted in a retrofitted hearse, complete with taped commentary and driver's patter. Not for everyone, but what other tour comes complete with a photocopy of Marilyn Monroe's death certificate? Contact Grave Line Tours, P.O. Box 931654, Hollywood, reservations and information (213) 876-0920.

By Helicopter

Helinet Aviation Services, 16644 Roscoe Boulevard, Van Nuys, gives the best possible overview tour of Los Angeles, cruising past the Hollywood sign at eye-level before heading on to Beverly Hills and Malibu. Call (818) 902-0229.

■ ACCOMMODATIONS

Because of the flood of visitors to Los Angeles, it has by necessity become a hotel town, belying its history of one-hot-spot-at-a-time sequential favorites. There is today a whole spectrum of style, price range, and location from which to choose a room, a suite, or a bungalow. I've tried to pick out a few favorites and then provide a fairly comprehensive list of the major choices beyond that.

Staying during the off-season or at weekends, or taking advantage of corporate discounts and package rates, can often slice a considerable amount off the standard prices. Call ahead for special deals, and for the most current information be sure to get the free *Lodging Guide* put out by the L.A. Convention and Visitors Bureau (see "Information Sources" below for details). A hotel tax of 12.5 percent will be added to all quoted rates.

I = Inexpensive (under $35)   E = Expensive (under $150)
B = Budget (under $75)   D = Deluxe (over $150)
M = Medium (under $100)

Aztec Hotel. Strange little out-of-the-way hotel most notable for its pseudo-Mayan facade. 311 W. Foothill Boulevard, San Gabriel Valley, (818) 358-3231. M

Beverly Hills Hotel. Landmark luxury hotel, closed for renovation through 1993. 9641 Sunset Boulevard, Beverly Hills, (310) 276-2251. D

Bel Age Hotel. One of a collection of all-suite hotels in the area run by the Ashkenazy family (the others are Le Dufy, Le Parc, and L'Ermitage), all along the same lines: undistinguished exteriors hide luxurious, well-appointed interiors, more like upscale apartments than anything else. 1020 N. San Vicente Road, West Hollywood, (213) 854-1111 or (800) 424-4443. D

Biltmore Hotel. Beautiful throwback to a more luxurious past. The public spaces are the best: exquisitely painted beamed ceilings in the mission style, a lobby that is lush with plants and dark wood furniture. The rooms themselves are a bit small, but very up-to-date and totally refurbished. 506 S. Grand Avenue, downtown, (213) 624-1011 or (800) 421-8000. E

Cadillac Hotel. Newly renovated thirties hotel right on the Venice Boardwalk. 401 Ocean Front Walk, Venice (213) 399-8876. B

Channel Road Inn. Elegant beachfront bed and breakfast. 219 W. Channel Road (310) 459-1920. M

Chateau Marmont Hotel. Not luxurious by any means—"comfortable" is a better modifier for its charming cottage-like bungalows and spacious rooms. 8221 Marmont Lane, West Hollywood, (213) 656-1010 or (800) 242-8328. E

Checkers Hotel. Expense-account luxury and lavish (not garish) taste. The beautifully understated furnishings are backed up by ultra-modern communications systems for the visiting businessman. 535 S. Grand Avenue, downtown, (213) 626-9906 or (800) 628-4900. D

Hollywood Roosevelt Hotel. The elegant charm of this recently renovated Hollywood stalwart is given a boost by its history, symbolized by the archival display on the balcony above the lobby. 7000 Hollywood Boulevard, Hollywood, (213) 466-7000 or (800) 858-2244. E

Holiday Inn (Hollywood). Gives its guests the usual, no surprises. Within striking distance of Hollywood Bowl, Hollywood Studio Museum, and downtown Hollywood. 1755 N. Highland Avenue, Hollywood, (213) 462-7181. B

Hotel Bel-Air. A world unto itself, tucked away in a magnificent 11-acre park. There is no place quite like it, from the swans on the pond to the excellent service. 701 Stone Canyon Road, Bel-Air, (213) 472-1211 or (800) 648-4097. D

Howard Johnson Hotel. Standard chain hotel, well-placed for Disneyland. 1380 S. Harbor Boulevard, Anaheim, (714) 776-6120 or (800) 854-0303. B

New Otani Hotel. A little bit of Japan in downtown L.A. The decorations are spare and minimal, and there are amenities like hot baths and the fabled "Garden in the Sky," a Zen rock garden that is great for tea. 120 S. Los Angeles Street, downtown, (213) 629-1200 or (800) 273-2294. E

Peninsula, Beverly Hills. The newest addition to Beverly Hills's luxury hotels, this makes you feel like you're visiting (very rich) friends—especially if you're fortunate enough to stay in one of the handful of detached villas. 9882 Santa Monica Boulevard, Beverly Hills, (310) 273-4888 or (800) 462-7899. D

Regent Beverly Wilshire Hotel. Lives up to the luxury for which Beverly Hills is known. An antique-filled lobby manages to soothe, not overwhelm, and the rooms, unlike some other upscale hostelries, are huge. Try for the original section, not the new add-on. 9500 Wilshire Boulevard, Beverly Hills, (213) 275-5200 or (800) 421-4354. D

Santa Monica International AYH Hostel. The newest and largest youth hostel on the West Coast, just two blocks from the beach. 1436 Second Street, Santa Monica, (310) 393-9913. I

Shangri-la Hotel. Great homey hostelry near the beach, with wonderful Art Deco charm. 1301 Ocean Avenue, Santa Monica, (310) 394-2791. M

Venice Beach House. Small, eight-room bed-and-breakfast that is very near the beach. 15 30th Avenue, Venice, (310) 823-1966. E

Westin Bonaventure Hotel. Gives the city's skyline a sleek 21st-century look. As with many John Portman-designed hotels, the vast interior space isn't exactly user-friendly, and the rooms tend to be small. Good views, though. 404 S. Figueroa Street, downtown, (213) 624-1000 or (800) 228-3000. D

Westwood Marquis. Gains by its proximity to the happening Village scene. Behind the concrete exterior lurks a hotel of luxury suites. 930 Hilgard Avenue, Westwood, (213) 208-8765 or (800) 421-2317. D

■ OTHER HOTELS AND ACCOMMODATIONS
Amfac Hotel. 8601 Lincoln Boulevard, LAX, (800) 227-4700. M

Barnabey's. 3501 Sepulveda Boulevard, Manhattan Beach, (310) 545-8466 or (800) 562-5285. M

Bel-Air Sands Hotel. 11461 Sunset Boulevard, Bel-Air, (310) 472-2513. E

Beverly House Hotel. 140 S. Lasky Drive, Beverly Hills, (213) 271-2145. M

Beverly Pavilion Hotel. 9360 Wilshire Boulevard, Beverly Hills, (213) 273-1400 or (800) 421-0545. E

Beverly Plaza Hotel. 8384 W. Third Street, Beverly Hills, (310) 658-6600 or (800) 624-6835. M

Carmel Hotel. 201 Broadway, Santa Monica, (310) 451-2469. B

Century Plaza Hotel. 2025 Avenue of the Stars, Century City, (310) 277-2000 or (800) 228-3000. D

Doubletree Hotel. 191 N. Los Robles Avenue, Pasadena, (818) 792-2727 or (800) 528-0444. M

Figueroa Hotel. 939 S. Figueroa Street, downtown, (213) 689-0305 or (800) 421-9092. B

Four Seasons. 300 S. Doheny Drive, Beverly Hills, (310) 273-2222 or (800) 268-6282. D

Guest Quarters Suite Hotel. 1707 Fourth Street, Santa Monica, (310) 395-3332 or (800) 424-2900. E

Hilton Hotel. 5711 W. Century Boulevard, LAX, (800) 445-8667. E

Holiday Inn (Convention Center). 1020 S. Figueroa Street, downtown, (213) 748-1291 or (800) 863-9418. M

Hyatt Hotel. 6225 W. Century Boulevard, LAX, (310) 670-9000 or (800) 325-3535. E

Hyatt Regency Long Beach. 200 S. Pine Avenue, Long Beach, (213) 491-1234 or (800) 228-9000. E

Loews Santa Monica. 1700 Ocean Avenue, Santa Monica, (310) 458-6700 or (800) 223-0888. E

Mayfair Hotel. 1256 W. Seventh Street, downtown, (213) 484-9614 or (800) 821-8682. E

Morrison Hotel. 1246 S. Hope Street, downtown, (213) 748-6442. B

Palos Verdes Inn. 1700 S. Pacific Coast Highway, Redondo Beach, (310) 316-4211 or (800) 421-9241. M

Pasadena Hilton. 150 S. Los Robles Avenue, Pasadena, (800) 445-8667. E

Park Plaza Hotel. 607 S. Park View Street, downtown, (213) 384-5281. B

Queen Mary Hotel. Long Beach Harbor, (310) 435-3511. E

Sheraton Universal. 333 Universal Terrace Parkway, Universal City, (818) 980-1212 or (800) 325-3535. D

Sportsmen's Lodge. 12825 Ventura Boulevard, Studio City, (818) 984-0202 or (800) 821-1625. M

Stillwell Hotel. 838 S Grand Avenue, downtown, (213) 627-1151 or (800) 553-4774. B

Sunset Marquis. 1200 Alta Loma Road, West Hollywood, (213) 657-1333 or (800) 858-9758. E

Westwood Inn. 10820 Wilshire Boulevard, Westwood, (310) 474-1573. M

■ RESTAURANTS

"What kind of food is it?" asks an innocent foreigner of a restaurant featured in Steve Martin's *L.A. Story.* "California!" comes back the chorus. The past two decades have seen a revolution in area dining, as Los Angeles shed its stodgy gustatory image and embarked on the creation of a whole new cuisine. **California cuisine** is marked by creative use of fresh ingredients, artful, visually stimulating presentation, and—perhaps its most famous characteristic—small portions.

The cliché is perhaps overplayed today, but Angelenos do have a distinctive style of eating that has bred a distinctive style of restaurant. **Style** is very casual—no jacket-and-tie required here (except perhaps in the area's country clubs). **Salads** are important, deemed an integral part of the meal. **Drinking** is pared to a minimum —remember those early studio calls!—with white wine still being the drink of choice.

There is another side of Los Angeles dining which is perhaps even more exciting than the well-played development of California cuisine. As the city replaces New York as the entry point for the country's immigrants, with many of them coming from the Pacific Rim, exotic styles of food are flooding the market. Most are inexpensive and delicious, and one style—the sushi bar—has already been adopted as L.A.'s own.

B = Budget (under $10)   E = Expensive ($20-30)
M = Moderate ($10-20 per person)   D = Deluxe ($30 and above)

■ INEXPENSIVE CAFÉS

The Apple Pan. L.A.'s ultimate incarnation of the greasy spoon, serving the best burgers in town. Counter-space only. 10801 W. Pico Boulevard, Westwood, (310) 475-3585.

Authentic Cafe. The benches outside this faintly yuppified in-spot might be the best meat-market in town. Inside, the food is oriented toward Mexico and the Southwest. 7605 Beverly Boulevard, West Hollywood, (213) 939-4626.

Cafe Beverly Hills. Budget eating in Beverly Hills? You bet, and a basic diner atmosphere that's the perfect antidote to too much glitz. 9725 Wilshire Boulevard, Beverly Hills, (213) 273-6397.

Gaucho Grill. The mini-mall atmosphere that you've come to know and love, plus good basic grill food with an exotic Argentine twist. 7980 Sunset Boulevard, West Hollywood, (213) 656-4152.

Gorky's. Pseudo-Soviet fare that plays better now the Evil Empire is dead and gone. Cheap, hearty food, chowed down upon by a young, hip clientele. Two locations: 536 E. Eighth Street, downtown (213) 627-4060 and 1716 N. Cahuenga Boulevard, Hollywood, (213) 463-7576.

Janet's Jerk Chicken. "Jerk" is not a description of the bird's character but a method of cooking, rendering the meat tender and tangy. 1541 Martin Luther King Boulevard, South-Central, (213) 296-4621.

Kokomo. A breakfast tradition for late-breaking screenwriters, as well as other people who crowd the alfresco tables to chow down on chips made from sweet potatoes, grill food, and malts, all made with an inventive twist. In Farmer's Market, Fairfax and Third Street, West Hollywood, (213) 933-0773.

Millie's. Customers come here for the good food and return for the heaping helpings of sarcasm that the help dishes out. Sit-down comedy on Sunset. 3524 Sunset Boulevard, Silver Lake, (213) 661-5292.

Randy's Donuts (opposite), and the Burger that Ate L.A.

Onyx. A coffee shop with a minimal approach to both food and decoration, but a welcome relief after the over-blitzed visual assault of L.A. 1802 N. Vermont Avenue, Los Feliz, (213) 660-5820.

Roscoe's Chicken and Waffles. How's that for a winning combination? They aren't kidding, either: the fluffy waffles and the crispy fried chicken come on the same plate, both to be doused in maple syrup. 1514 N. Gower Street, Hollywood, (213) 466-7453.

Versailles. Also known as the Bay of Pigs, for its heaping portions of Cuban food. The roast chicken is by some accounts better than mom's, and the roast pork is crispy, garlicky, and flavorful. Two locations: 10319 Venice Boulevard, Culver City, (213) 558-3168 and 1415 S. La Cienega Boulevard, West Hollywood, (213) 289-0392.

■ CALIFORNIA CUISINE

Caioti Cafe. Funky canyon mecca with a great California-tinged menu, featuring designer pizzas and reasonable prices. 2100 Laurel Canyon Boulevard, West Hollywood, (213) 650-2988. M

Checkers Restaurant. In the equally trendy Checkers Hotel, this restaurant is a haven for those on an expense account. 535 S. Grand Avenue, downtown, (213) 624-0000. D

Chinois on Main. A brash, expensive collision of East and West, with delicious results. 2709 Main Street, Santa Monica, (310) 392-9025. E

Citrus. Lunch here is for power diners who want the luxury of ignoring the exquisitely styled food. 6703 Melrose Avenue, Hollywood, (213) 857-0034. E

Granita. Wolfgang Puck has brought his deliriously inventive cuisine to where the money and power is, allowing you to enjoy great food and stargaze at the same time. 23725 Malibu Road, Malibu, (310) 456-0488. E

Trumps. An early California cuisine pioneer which features a highly innovative menu, on the expensive side. 8764 Melrose Avenue, West Hollywood, (213) 855-1480. D

■ **ETHNIC AND SPECIALITY FOOD**

ABC Seafood. Southern Chinese seafood in rich, delicious sauces—the lobster Cantonese is ace, as are the dim sum. 708 New High Street, downtown, (213) 680-2887. B

Border Grill. Takes the general Mexican-food idea and runs with it, creating some delicious variations on the theme. 7407 Melrose Avenue, West Hollywood, (213) 658-7495. E

Blue Nile. Ethiopian cuisine that is by turns fiery hot and deliciously flavorful. 1066 S. Fairfax Avenue, West Hollywood, (213) 933-0960. M

Canter's Delicatessen. There are a lot of displaced New Yorkers trying to recreate the deli experience in L.A., but this place beat them all by a couple of decades. 419 Fairfax Avenue, West Hollywood, (213) 651-2030. M

East India Grill. Good, sturdy Indian food, with some standouts like tandoori ribs. So successful that it opened a sister joint across the courtyard. 345 N. La Brea Avenue, West Hollywood, (213) 936-8844. M

Food Nest African Fast Food. Authentic Nigerian cuisine, dished up from a steam table and favored by many a homesick African expatriate. 422 S. San Vicente Boulevard, West Hollywood, (213) 652-6710. B

Inn of the Seventh Ray. Click your crystals together and you're back in the sixties, being served delicious health food next to a babbling brook that is, unfortunately, usually dry. 128 Old Topanga Canyon Road, West L.A., (310) 455-1311. M

Katsu. The best of L.A.'s adopted cuisines is sushi, and here is a brilliant incarnation of it, always superbly fresh. 1972 Hillhurst Avenue, Los Feliz, (213) 665-1891. D

Mi Ranchito. Delicious traditional Mexican food (minus the lard) in a no-man's-land industrial park of a neighborhood. Best *cocido* (Mexican beef stew) in LA. 8694 Washington Boulevard, Culver City, (310) 837-1461. B

Uncle John's Meat Pies. Known for its delicious specialty: *lahmajune,* sometimes called "Armenian pizza." Very cheap and very good. 1108 N. Kenmore Street, Hollywood, (213) 664-8842. B

Saint Estephe. Southwestern food that is a little over-produced, but delicious all the same. Sometimes it's so pretty that you are afraid to eat it. 2640 Sepulveda Boulevard, Manhattan Beach, (310) 545-1334. E

Patout's. Cajun cuisine that lets the good times roll right off the tongue. A long way from blackened redfish. 2260 Westwood Boulevard, Westwood, (310) 475-7100. E

Tommy Tang's. Thai food is a real comer in Los Angeles, but this place has been established as *the* in place, with a clientele that's very Melrose. 7473 Melrose Avenue, West Hollywood, (213) 651-1810. E

■ GREAT FOR VIEWS OR AMBIENCE
Alice's. On Malibu Pier, and great for beach vistas and long leisurely sunsets, with a light, grill-oriented menu. 23000 Pacific Coast Highway, Malibu, (310) 456-6646. M '

Cafe des Artistes. Tucked away in the middle of Hollywood is this marvelous bistro, with a garden court to linger in for hours. 1534 N. McCadden Place, Hollywood, (213) 461-6889. M

"Hollywood ain't dog eat dog; it's man eat man." —*Wilson Mizner*

Castaways. The Valley equivalent of Yamashiro, with superb nighttime panoramas and tiki ambience. 1250 Harvard Road, Burbank, (818) 848-6691. M

Saddle Peak Lodge. Delightful inn tucked away in the mountains above Malibu, perfect for Sunday brunch or a romantic getaway dinner. 419 Cold Canyon Road, Calabasas, (818) 222-3888. E

Yamashiro. It's something of a tourist trap, and the food is negligible, but even natives marvel at the panoramic view. 1999 N. Sycamore Avenue, above Franklin Avenue, Hollywood, (213) 466-5125. M

■ THE L.A. EXPERIENCE

Barney's Beanery. When Hollywood wants to slum, it comes here. The food is good and basic, the range of beers unbeatable, and the help cynical and sassy. 8447 Santa Monica Boulevard, West Hollywood, (213) 654-2287. B

City Restaurant. A favorite of the young hip crowd. 180 S. La Brea Avenue, (213) 938-2155. E

DC-3. Watch the planes take off from the Santa Monica airport as you take in the chic surroundings and sample the eclectic menu. 2800 Donald Douglas Loop South, Santa Monica, (310) 399-2323. E

Duke's. The original hungover, headbanger, don't-call-it-lunch-'coz-I-just-woke-up java joint. A haven for rockers from the nearby Whisky or Sunset Marquis. 8909 Sunset Boulevard, West Hollywood, (213) 652-3100. B

Ed Debevic's. The help here are touted as the most talented around, and are likely to break into song in this popular fifties retro restaurant. 134 N. La Cienega Boulevard, West Hollywood, (213) 659-1952. B

Formosa Cafe. The walls here have eyes—the hundreds of celebrity photos. Strictly for ambience only, as the food is pallid at best. 7156 Santa Monica Boulevard, Hollywood, (213) 850-9050. B

Johnny Rocket's. For Melroids, no shopping paroxysm would be complete without stopping at this retro diner to recharge on burgers, fries, and malts. 7507 Melrose, West Hollywood, (213) 651-3361. B

Los Angeles Police Department Revolver and Athletic Club. The official cop-shop grubhouse, but the public can eat here, too, on the cheap and in the company of uniformed members of the L.A. law. 1880 Academy Road, Echo Park, (213) 221-3101. B

Melrose Bar and Grill. Have lunch with the movers and shakers of L.A.'s interior decorating trade, inside the high-style Pacific Design Center. 8687 Melrose Avenue, West Hollywood, (310) 659-8433. M

Musso and Frank's. Classic Hollywood restaurant, offering everything à la carte—except the flavor of history which permeates the place. 6667 Hollywood Boulevard, (213) 467-7788. M

Palm Restaurant. Great food, on the expensive side, and you'll have fun picking out the faces of the celebrity portraits on the walls. 9001 Santa Monica Boulevard, Hollywood, (213) 550-8811. E

Polo Lounge. In the Beverly Hills Hotel, the one, the original. 9641 Sunset Boulevard, Beverly Hills, (213) 276-2251. E

Pink's. Downscale dogstand favored by bleary-eyed late-night revelers. 711 N. La Brea Avenue, West Hollywood, (213) 931-4223. B

Rex II Ristorante. L.A.'s best restaurant, installed in wood-paneled Art Deco plushness of the Oviatt Building. 617 S. Olive Street, downtown, (213) 627-2300. D

Spago. Some say Wolfgang Puck's eatery is the best restaurant in the world, and the stars treat it like their very own living room. 1114 Horn Avenue, West Hollywood, (213) 652-4025. E

Tail-o'-the-Pup. You've seen it in photos, you've seen it in movies—it's a hot dog stand shaped, yes, like a hot dog! 329 San Vicente Boulevard, West Hollywood, (213) 652-4517. B

■ **STARGAZING**
Broadway Deli. A trendy eatery that has little in common with a real New York deli. The Westside stars like Sunday brunch here. 1457 Third Street, Santa Monica, (310) 451-0616. M

Chasen's. An institution, with the most expensive chili anywhere—but so good Liz had it flown to her on the *Cleopatra* set. 9039 Beverly Boulevard, West Hollywood, (213) 271-2168. E

Columbia Bar & Grill. Actually on the old Columbia lot, with many of the industry types coming here for lunch. 1448 N. Gower Street, Hollywood, (213) 461-8800. E

Hugo's. An industry hang-out par excellance. The fresh pasta is extremely good. 8401 Santa Monica Boulevard, West Hollywood, (213) 654-3993. M

Imperial Gardens. In Preston Sturges's old Player's Club, and retaining some of its starry appeal. 8225 Sunset Boulevard, West Hollywood, (213) 656-1750. E

Jimmy's. An old-style watering hole favored by a celebrity clientele. 201 Moreno Drive, Beverly Hills, (310) 879-2394. E

La Loggia. The Valley version of an industry hangout. 11814 Ventura Boulevard, Studio City, (818) 980-1122. M

Le Dome. Cooly elegant upscale power boutique. 8720 Sunset, West Hollywood, (213) 659-6919. E

Malibu Adobe. Where the Colony types feel at home. 23410 Civic Center Way, Malibu, (310) 456-2021. E

Maple Drive. Dudley Moore fronts this trendy eatery, but he is not an absentee owner, and tends to bring his friends along when he comes. 345 Maple Drive, Beverly Hills, (213) 274-9800. E

Matteo's. Sunday night this becomes an extension of Hollywood's home dining rooms, with the stars so thick there should be a staff chiropractor to deal with all the strained necks. 2321 Westwood Boulevard, West L.A., (310) 475-4521. E

Morton's. There's a reason why the rich and powerful frequent this place: good food and great service. The Byzantine social ranking by seating is gravy. 8800 Melrose Avenue, West Hollywood, (213) 276-1253. E

Nicky Blair's. Strip glitz, and doesn't care who knows it. Lifestyles of the riche and famous. 8730 Sunset Boulevard, West Hollywood, (213) 659-0929. E

Orso's. An Italian trattoria which brings the stars in just like its predecessor at the same spot, Joe Allen's. 8706 W. Third Street, Beverly Hills, (213) 274-7144. E

Patrick's Roadhouse. For the new Harley crowd, Sunday breakfast here is a tradition. Right off Pacific Coast Highway at 106 Entrada Drive, Santa Monica, (310) 459-4544. M

72 Market Street. Producer Tony Bill opened this immensely popular eatery with Dudley Moore and other celebs as partners. 72 Market Street, Venice, (310) 392-8720. E

Trader Vic's. In the Beverly Hilton, and a haven of funkiness you wouldn't imagine stars would cotton to. But they do. 9876 Wilshire Boulevard, Beverly Hills, (213) 276-6345. E

L.A. POWER DINING

The rites and rituals associated with getting a good table in some of L.A.'s trendier eating establishment would be equally well applied in getting a position close to the throne in the court of Louis XIV, say, or the ear of the Byzantine emperor.

For those not in know, it matters little getting relegated to "Siberia"—that part of the restaurant given over to the tourists and plebes. But if you are plugged into the Hollywood hierarchy, being placed at a bad table at Morton's, say, can lead to rumors of a downturn in your career. Conversely, if you are seated at a window table at Spago, you can rest assured your place in the pecking order is secure.

There are weekly gatherings of that endogamous tribe called Hollywood that serve as communal ceremonies: part business, part tail-sniffing, part parade. Sunday night at Matteo's, for example, or Monday night at Morton's, the film community engages in table-hopping that is as elaborately coded as a minuet.

How to break into this hermetic society? A hit film helps. More importantly, you must be recognized as belonging by a host of Hollywood insiders. How about if you just want to observe—just want to see Jack say hello to David, or Cher nod cooly to Barbra? That, too, is difficult, since the keepers of this kingdom recognize the prime urge of the royalty is to be uncontaminated by the peasantry.

Wolfgang Puck and his wife Barbara are the doyens of L.A.'s finest eateries.

But there are ways. Knowing the name of the maitre d' (to give you a headstart, we listed a few of them below), or coming at a time when you can be slipped into a table with the minimum of problems for the management, are two surefire tips. It's always best to reserve far in advance, at least a week and sometimes more; if you still get shut out, remember that all this is transitory, and that the Spago of today will become the footnote of tomorrow. For further information, see the "Stargazing" section of the restaurants listings. (For addresses see "Restaurants" in this section.)

Chasen's: The old stand-by, favored by many generations of Hollywood heavies. Scott McKay is maitre d' for lunch, Julius Reh for dinner. (213) 271-2168.

Citrus: Try it for lunch, and go for the food as well as the Hollywood scene. The maitre d' is manager Jean-Jacque Retourne. (213) 857-0034.

Hugo's: West Hollywood hotspot, especially for weekend brunching. Maitre d's are Brian Kelly and Jasmine. (213) 654-3993.

Morton's: The toughest nut to crack, but you can try an early dinner and linger. Maitre d's: Rick Cicetti and Doug Murch. West Hollywood, (213) 276-1253.

72 Market Street: Try to distinguish yourself from the hordes of tourists who descend on this place in the hopes of seeing Dudley (as in Dudley Moore, one of the owners). Robert Schwan and Tony Bamin are the maitre d's. Venice, (310) 392-8720.

Spago: Reservations are taken only between 3 P.M. and 8 P.M., and it helps to have an automatic redialer, because the line is always busy. The maitre d's name is Bernard Erpicum. Downtown, (213) 627-2300.

■ NIGHTLIFE

If New York is the city that never sleeps, Los Angeles is the city that puts the cat out and is in bed by 10:30. It wasn't a great night-time town right from the start. Some say it was the movie industry which set the pace for L.A.'s early-to-bed evenings. All those morning calls to be on the set at 6 A.M., taking full advantage of daylight. But the town's basically conservative beginnings are not all that far removed in time, and they may explain its roll-up-the-sidewalks reputation. For whatever reason, the nightlife of Los Angeles was for quite some time relegated to that truncated amphetamine artery, the Sunset Strip

But if it never was a great late-night city, Los Angeles has always been a music town nonpareil, since along with the movies the music industry has made L.A. its capital. During World War II, dozens of acclaimed musicians and composers fled to L.A from war-torn Europe, while at the same time the concentrated brilliance of the Central Avenue jazz and blues clubs saw the emergence of Charles Mingus, Dexter Gordon, and many others. Those with memories extending only to the sixties remember the Beach Boys and the Doors, the raging innovations of the South Bay punk scene in seventies, and the mega-success of heavy metal bands like Van Halen and Guns 'N Roses. More recently, rap groups like nwa have come to national prominence out of L.A.'s multi-ethnic ghettos.

Perhaps the oddest characteristic of Los Angeles nightlife is the curious duality of movie-going. While the city does feature great theater venues and the occasional lavish Hollywood premiere, it can't be said to be a particularly great movie-going town. Commercial movies are given widespread exhibition, but the art film, the foreign film is given curiously short shrift. This is understandable, considering the home-town bias, but is partially made up for by numerous revival and retrospective programs, as well as screenings at the city's film schools.

Another, more recent, surprise has been the emergence of an extremely healthy regional **theater** scene in Los Angeles. Away from the often claustrophobic confines of New York City, theaters like the Mark Taper Forum engendered a well-supported and fiercely independent "Off-Broadway" scene. Drawing on a huge pool of acting talent, playwrights found willing collaborators for new works, even as producers on the East Coast stuck with established repertory. Comedy, also, counts L.A. as a prime breeding ground. Proximity to the show business of Hollywood only partially explains this; appreciative audiences count for a lot, too.

Groups like the Groundlings, and venues like the Comedy Store, fostered a comedy explosion that shows no sign of abating.

For the most current listings of what's on and where, check the "Calendar" section of the *L.A. Times* or any of the many free newspapers available around the city (see "Information Sources" below for more). **Tickets** are generally available at box offices, or through Ticketmaster at (213) 480-3232.

■ MOVIE THEATERS

Bruin Theatre. Gorgeous moderne masterpiece by L.A.'s premiere movie designer, S. Charles Lee. 948 Broxton Avenue, Westwood, (310) 289-6266.

Chinese Theatre. The one and only. 6925 Hollywood Boulevard, Hollywood, (213) 464-6111.

Cineplex Beverly Center. The archetypical L.A. experience: going to a movie in a mall. 8522 Beverly Boulevard, West Hollywood, (213) 652-7760.

Cineplex Odeon Universal City Cinemas. Billed as the world's largest multiplex, weighing in with 18 screens. Universal City, (818) 508-0588.

The L.A. party scene never stops.
"I'm always afraid I'll wake up at 12 o'clock and find the place turned back into a pumpkin."
—Fred Allen

Pacific Cinerama Dome. Geodesic exterior, and lush reclining seats inside. 6360 Sunset Boulevard, Hollywood, (213) 466-3401.

El Capitan Theatre. Legit house gorgeously converted by Disney into a prime movie palace in 1991. 6834 Hollywood Boulevard, Hollywood, (213) 467-7674.

Fox Village Theatre. The oldest in Westwood, opened in 1931 and retaining the area's original Spanish Mission-themed architecture. 961 Broxton Avenue, Westwood, (310) 289-6266.

Melnitz Hall. Superb, constantly changing schedule of retrospectives, classics, contemporary discoveries, and little-known gems, many of them free. Circle Drive southwest of Hilgard and Sunset Boulevard, UCLA, (310) 206-3456.

South Gate Drive-In. One of the last alfresco movie venues in L.A. 5131 Firestone Boulevard, South Bay, (213) 564-1137.

Silent Movie. Billed as a museum, not a theater (the better to outrun the zoning code), but offering a great lineup of originals with organ music accompaniment. Regular shows are at 8 P.M. on Fridays and Saturdays, with many special events. 611 N. Fairfax Avenue, West Hollywood, (213) 653-2389.

"Ever since they found out that Lassie was a boy, the public has believed the worst about Hollywood." —Groucho Marx

Vagabond Theatre. One of L.A.'s best revival houses. 2509 Wilshire Boulevard, downtown, (213) 387-2171.

Vista Theater. Crazed, cryptic-Egyptoid theater showing a superb lineup of classic revivals. 4473 Sunset Boulevard, Hollywood, (213) 660-6639.

■ **LIVE THEATER**

Ahmanson Theater. Middle of the three Music Center theaters, hosting touring Broadway productions. 135 N. Grand Avenue, downtown, (213) 972-7211.

James A. Doolittle Theater. Used primarily by UCLA's always strong performing arts department, with a few visiting shows. 1615 N. Vine Street, Hollywood, (213) 365-3500.

The Mark Taper Forum. Most intimate and innovative of the Music Center theaters. 135 N. Grand Avenue, downtown, (213) 972-7211.

Pantages Theater. Elegant Art Deco house presenting musicals and plays. 6233 Hollywood Boulevard, Hollywood, (213) 410-1062.

Pasadena Playhouse. Intimate Mission-style theater featuring a highly-rated summer season. 39 S. El Molino Avenue, Pasadena, (818) 356-7529.

Shubert Theater. Large modern theater hosting touring productions of Broadway hits. 2020 Avenue of the Stars, Century City, (310) 201-1500.

■ **CLASSICAL MUSIC, OPERA, AND BALLET**

Ambassador Auditorium. Superb acoustics attract big name performers. 300 W. Green Street, Pasadena, (818) 304-6161.

Dorothy Chandler Pavilion. The largest hall in the Music Center complex, hosting the L.A. Philharmonic, the Joffrey Ballet, and numerous touring groups. 135 N. Grand Avenue, downtown, (213) 972-7211.

Greek Theatre. Lovely outdoor amphitheater, holding a wide variety of summer concerts in the foothills of Griffith Park. 2700 N. Vermont Avenue, (213) 410-1062.

Royce Hall. Large hall on UCLA campus holding a diverse range of events. (310) 825-9261.

■ ROCK, JAZZ AND COUNTRY

Al's Bar. Artsy, offbeat beer bar featuring live bands, poetry, and performance art. 305 S. Hewitt Street, downtown, (213) 687-3558.

The Baked Potato. The Valley's oldest jazz venue. 3787 Cahuenga Boulevard, North Hollywood, (818) 980-1615.

Bebop Records. Record store-cum-music showcase favored by a young, eclectic crowd. 18433 Sherman Way, San Fernando Valley, (818) 881-1654.

Club Lingerie. Name acts from vanguard art-rock and college music favorites. 6507 Sunset Boulevard, Hollywood, (213) 466-8557.

Coconut Teaszer. Anchors one end of the Strip with raucous rock'n'roll. 8117 Sunset Boulevard, West Hollywood, (213) 654-4773.

Comeback Inn. Venerable Venice jazz venue. 1633 W. Washington Boulevard, Venice, (310) 396-7255.

The Dresden. Showcase piano lounge adopted by a hip, kitsch-hungry crowd. 1760 Vermont Avenue, Los Feliz, (213) 665-4294.

Foothill Club. South Bay club with a country slant. 1922 Cherry Avenue, Signal Hill, (310) 494-5196.

Gazarri's. Dishes up punk, speed, thrash, etc. on the Strip. 9039 Sunset Boulevard, West Hollywood, (213) 273-6606.

Lighthouse Cafe. South Bay jazz and world music venue. 30 Pier Avenue, Hermosa Beach, (310) 540-2274.

McCabe's Guitar Shop. Strange hybrid of instrument store and folk, blues, and rock venue. 3101 W. Pico Boulevard, Santa Monica, (310) 828-4403.

Music Machine. Wide variety of music, concentrating on reggae and blues. 12220 W. Pico Boulevard, West L.A., (213) 820-5150.

The Palomino. L.A.'s standout country venue. 6907 Lankershim Boulevard, North Hollywood, (818) 764-4010.

The Roxy. The showcase Strip institution, giving tone to a whole rock'n'roll streetscape. 9009 Sunset Boulevard, West Hollywood, (213) 276-2222.

(following pages) Santa Monica beach on a hot summer day is the Coney Island of California.

St. Mark's. Beachfront jazz club. 23 Windward Avenue, Venice, (310) 452-2222.

Trancas. Old-style nightclub with live music and comedy acts. 30765 Pacific Coast Highway, Malibu, (310) 457-5516.

Whisky-a-Go-Go. With the Roxy, the twin devil of Strip rock'n'roll. 8901 Sunset Boulevard, West Hollywood, (310) 652-4202.

■ COMEDY AND CABARET

The Cabaret Comedy Club. 17271 Ventura Boulevard, San Fernando Valley, (818) 501-3737.

Cafe Largo. 432 Fairfax Avenue, West Hollywood, (213) 852-1073.

The Comedy and Magic Club. 1018 Hermosa Avenue, Hermosa Beach, (310) 372-1193.

The Comedy Store. 8433 Sunset Boulevard, West Hollywood, (213) 656-6225.

Groundlings Theater. 7007 Melrose Avenue, West Hollywood, (213) 934-9700.

The Ice House. 24 N. Mentor Boulevard, Pasadena, (818) 577-1894.

Improvisation. 8162 Melrose Avenue, West Hollywood, (213) 651-2583.

The Magic Castle. 7001 Franklin Avenue, Hollywood, (213) 851-3314.

Second City. 214 Santa Monica Boulevard, Santa Monica, (310) 451-0621.

■ BEACHES

The beaches of Los Angeles stretch for over 75 miles, from Malibu to Orange County, and each has a slightly different flavor. Malibu, with its mansions of the rich and famous, and the equally star-studded ocean fronts of Venice and Santa Monica, are but the best known of L.A.'s many beaches. There are many more to the south, through the South Bay trio of Manhattan, Hermosa, and Redondo, around Palos Verdes to the hardcore surf capitals of Huntington and Newport. The cliff-hugging shoreline of Palos Verdes itself is too rocky to admit many beaches, but James Dean fans might like to know that it was on the bluffs here

that the "chicken" scene in *Rebel Without a Cause* was filmed—the loser driving off the cliff and crashing into the surf below.
A dozen of the more popular and character-full L.A. beaches are listed below, from north to south.

Leo Carrillo State Beach. Named for the man who played Pancho on TV's *The Cisco Kid*, this is one of the most spectacular L.A. beaches, featuring a natural tunnel, a campground, and one of the city's only clothing-optional sites. 36000 Pacific Coast Highway, Malibu, (818) 706-1310.

Zuma Beach County Park. The only beach sung about by both Neil Young and Mick Jagger, and populated by various constituencies—families, volleyballers, Valley Girls, and surfers. 30000 Pacific Coast Highway, Malibu, (310) 457-9891.

Malibu Surfrider State Beach. Very popular surfing beach adjacent to picturesque Malibu Pier. 23200 Pacific Coast Highway, Malibu, (818) 706-1310.

Will Rogers State Beach. Wide, uncrowded two-mile long beach bequeathed to the state by the wily Depression-era comic. 16000 Pacific Coast Highway, Pacific Palisades, (310) 394-3266.

Santa Monica State Beach. Wide, sandy beach stretching to either side of the Santa Monica Pier, with volleyball courts and quiet surf. Pacific Coast Highway at Colorado Boulevard, Santa Monica, (310) 451-2906.

Venice Beach. Surprisingly uncrowded, palm-tree-lined beach fronting the lively Venice Boardwalk. 1531 Ocean Front Walk, Venice, (310) 394-3266.

Dockweiler State Beach. Very wide and often rowdy beach beneath the runways of the L.A. airport and bordered by an oil refinery and a sewage treatment plant. Facilities include barbecue pits, volleyball courts, and a campground. Vista del Mar Boulevard, Playa del Rey, (310) 322-5008.

Manhattan State Beach. Prototypic South Bay beach—surfers, cyclists, and volleyball players share space with families and fishermen. Highland and Manhattan Beach boulevards, Manhattan Beach, (310) 372-2166.

Redondo State Beach. Wide, sandy beach stretching south from the King Harbor sportfishing pier. Esplanade at Knobhill Avenue, Redondo Beach, (310) 372-2166.

Malaga Cove. The only sandy beach on the Palos Verdes peninsula, accessible via a paved path down from the bluffs. Paseo del Mar at Via Arroyo, Palos Verdes, (310) 372-2166.

Abalone Cove County Beach. A great little hideaway, gazing out at Catalina Island. Excellent tidepools, and as an added treat you can climb the bluffs to the magical stone and glass Wayfarer's Chapel. 5755 Palos Verdes Drive South, (310) 372-2166.

Huntington State Beach. Wide, three-mile-long (5 km) beach with volleyball courts, bike paths, showers, and food stands. Pacific Coast Highway at Beach Boulevard, Huntington Beach, (714) 536-1454.

Newport Beach. Upmarket Orange County beach famed for clean sands, beautiful bodies, and "The Wedge" bodysurfing area, near the breakwater at the southern tip. Balboa Boulevard, Newport Beach.

Even on a calm day, Malibu's surfers take to the beach.

■ ANNUAL EVENTS

JANUARY

Tournament of Roses Parade. New Year's Day along Colorado Boulevard, Pasadena, (818) 449-7673.

Japanese New Year, "Oshogatsu". Japanese-American Cultural and Community Center, Little Tokyo, (213) 628-2725.

FEBRUARY

Black History Month Celebration and Exhibits. Watts Towers Community Arts Center, (213) 569-8181, and William Grant Still Community Arts Center, (213) 734-1164.

Chinese New Year Celebration. Chinatown arts and crafts festival, plus a dragon parade. Chinatown, (213) 617-0396.

Mexican Mardi Gras. El Pueblo de Los Angeles State Historic Park, (213) 625-5045.

MARCH

Los Angeles Marathon. Memorial Coliseum, Exposition Park, (213) 444-5444.

St. Patrick's Day Parade. March 17 through downtown Los Angeles, (213) 413-1273.

Academy Awards. Music Center, downtown, (310) 278-8990.

APRIL

American Film Institute Film Festival. (213) 856-7707.

Blessing of the Animals. El Pueblo de Los Angeles, (213) 625-5045.

Cherry Blossom Festival. Little Tokyo, (213) 680-8861.

Easter Sunrise Service. Hollywood Bowl, (213) 666-9555.

MAY

Cinco de Mayo Celebration. May 5th at El Pueblo de Los Angeles, (213) 625-5045.

City Roots Festival. Celebration of L.A.'s diverse ethnic heritage. Griffith Park, (213) 485-6759.

"In Hollywood a girl's virtue is much less important than her hairdo." —Marilyn Monroe.
Below, the Briefcase Brigade marches forward during Pasadena's annual Doo Dah Parade.

This exclusive photograph (below) captures His Holiness, the Pope, and Desert Storm hero General Schwarzkopf together at the Doo Dah Parade. Neither, however, is likely to approve of the wild goings-on of West Hollywood's annual Gay Pride Parade and Festival (top).

JUNE

Playboy Jazz Festival. (213) 854-7471.

Festival of Folk Art. Natural History Museum, (213) 744-3466.

Gay Pride Parade and Festival. West Hollywood Park, (310) 656-1227.

JULY

African Marketplace. William Grant Still Community Arts Center, (213) 734-1164.

4th of July fireworks. Queen Mary, Long Beach, (310) 435-3511.

Hawaiian Festival. Alondra Park, Lawndale, (213) 329-9794.

Watts Towers Music and Arts Festival. Free concerts at the Watts Towers Community Arts Center, (213) 485-2433.

Kaleidoscope Dance Festival. (213) 343-5120.

AUGUST

Hollywood Summer Fair. (213) 467-6847.

Nisei Week. Little Tokyo, Japanese-American Cultural and Community Center, (213) 687-7193.

International Surf Festival. South Bay beaches, (310) 545-4502.

Multi-Cultural Film Festival. William Grant Still Community Arts Center, (213) 734-1164.

SEPTEMBER

Korean Festival. Koreatown, (213) 730-1495.

Los Angeles County Fair. Pomona Fairgrounds, (714) 623-3111.

Mexican Independence Day—16th de Septiembre Celebration. El Pueblo de Los Angeles State Historic Park, (213) 625-5045.

OCTOBER

Halloween Carnival. Barnes Park, Monterey Park, (818) 307-1391.

American Film Institute Video Festival. (213) 856-7787.

NOVEMBER

Dia de los Muertos. El Pueblo de Los Angeles, (213) 625-5045.

Doo Dah Parade. Wacky alternative to the Rose Parade. Pasadena, (818) 796-2591.

Hollywood Christmas Parade. Celebrity parade down Hollywood Boulevard, (213) 469-2337.

DECEMBER
Las Posadas Christmas Procession. El Pueblo de Los Angeles, (213) 625-5045.

■ INFORMATION SOURCES

Things change very quickly in L.A., and for the most up-to-the-minute information it's a good idea to check in with local sources. The great variety of newspapers, many of them free, means it's easy to find out what's on where, and there are a few visitors bureaus offering timely advice.

■ PERIODICALS

The morning *Los Angeles Times* is the main L.A. daily newspaper, and has the largest circulation by far of any West Coast paper. The *Times's* "Calendar" section, focusing on arts and entertainment, is required reading for all those who want to know what's going on culture-wise, especially the tabloid-sized edition published every Sunday. The city's two widely distributed free weekly newspapers, the *L.A. Reader* and the *L.A. Weekly*, offer alternative views and even more extensive coverage of art, music, and movies. For news of home, try *Universal News Agency*, 1655 N. Las Palmas Avenue, (213) 467-3850; or the 24-hour *World Book and News*, 1652 N. Cahuenga Boulevard, (213) 465-4352. Both are just off Hollywood Boulevard and carry out-of-town and foreign newspapers as well as "the trades."

■ BOOKSTORES

Birns and Sawyer. The tekkie's choice for books on lighting, camera operation, etc. A fascinating glimpse at the nuts-and-bolts matters of below-the-line moviemaking. 1028 N. Highland Avenue, Hollywood, (213) 466-8211

Bodhi Tree. Shirley MacLaine's favorite bookstore, a haven for mysticism and the New Age where you can pick up a crystal along with your book. 8585 Melrose Avenue, West Hollywood, (213) 659-1550.

Book Soup. Without peer as a bookseller, meeting-place and cultural touchstone. A good place for star-gazing, too. 8818 Sunset Boulevard, West Hollywood, (213) 659-3310.

Collectors Book Store. Books, publicity stills, posters, production scripts, even a small memorabilia section. 1708 Vine Street, Hollywood, (213) 467-3296.

Edie Brandt's Saturday Matinee. A real L.A. find, a video store that specializes in vintage black-and-white classics, and sells books, publicity stills, and movie posters as well. A must-visit for every true cinemaphile. 6310 Colfax Avenue, North Hollywood, (818) 506-4242.

Elliot Katt Bookseller. Jam-packed with books on film, television, and theater, all housed in a cozy second-story shop. 8570 Melrose Avenue, West Hollywood, (213) 659-1733.

Larry Edmunds. Great selection of film books as well as a great location, across from Musso and Frank's. 6644 Hollywood Boulevard, Hollywood, (213) 463-3273.

■ **VISITOR CENTERS**

The **Los Angeles Visitors and Convention Bureau**, 695 S. Figueroa Street, (213) 624-7300 or (213) 689-8822, is the main source of tourist information for people planning to visit L.A. Smaller cities around the metropolitan area also provide maps and basic information on their locality. These include:

Beverly Hills Visitors Bureau, 239 S. Beverly Drive, (310) 271-8174 or (800) 345-2210.

Hollywood Visitors Bureau—Janes House, 6541 Hollywood Boulevard, (213) 461-4213.

Long Beach Convention and Visitors Council, 180 E. Ocean Boulevard, Long Beach, (310) 436-3645.

Orange County Convention and Visitors Bureau, 800 W. Katella Avenue, Anaheim, (714) 999-8999.

RECOMMENDED READING

■ BIOGRAPHIES

Barlett, Donald L. and James B. Steele. *Empire: The Life, Legend and Madness of Howard Hughes.* New York: Norton, 1979. The definitive work about Hughes, and the best about his Hollywood years, when his workmanlike competency fought with his egomania to create an empire.

Beardsley, Charles. *Hollywood's Master Showman: The Legendary Sid Grauman.* New York: Cornwall Books, 1983. A rollicking tour of the rollicking world of the greatest impresario of the movies. Grauman is remembered for having created the press agent's dream memorial in front of his Chinese Theatre, but he was a man who worked the distribution end of the movies with the same brilliance and verve as the great moguls.

Berg, A. Scott. *Goldwyn.* New York: Knopf, 1989. An eminently readable, warm, and sympathetic portrait of a very complicated mini-mogul, Sam Goldwyn, who after stormy relationships with UA and Fox endured to become the greatest

A helping hand lends support to Beach Boy Brian Wilson during a recent book-signing at Waldenbooks in West L.A.

independent producer Hollywood has ever known. Berg is particularly good on verifying or debunking "Goldwynisms," the mythic malapropisms ("Include me out") that Goldwyn coined.

Brady, Frank. *Citizen Welles.* New York: Scribner, 1989. An eminently readable life of Orson Welles, with Chaplin and perhaps a handful of others, the only geniuses Hollywood has seen fit to accept within its fold. As this book reveals, the industry's acceptance of Welles was uneven at best.

Chaplin, Charles. *My Autobiography.* New York: Simon and Schuster, 1964. Should be read with John McCabe's *Charlie Chaplin* (1978) as a reality check, but it remains a fascinating look into the mind of early Hollywood's greatest comic.

Dalton, David. *James Dean: The Mutant King.* San Francisco: Straight Arrow Books, 1974. A pulpy but readable biography of the doomed young actor whose cult has only grown in the years since his death.

Guiles, Fred Lawrence. *Norma Jean: The Life of Marilyn Monroe.* New York: Mc-Graw-Hill, 1969. Along with the same author's *Legend: The Life and Death of Marilyn Monroe,* a fairly complete portrait of Hollywood's ultimate creation.

■ FICTION

Bukowski, Charles. *Post Office.* Santa Barbara: Black Sparrow Press, 1971. The laureate of L.A. low-lifes, Bukowski is justly celebrated for his view of the city as seen through the bottom of the bottle. This book is only one of Bukowski's countless stories, poems, and novels in which L.A. figures big, and upon which the movie *Barfly* was based.

Cain, James. *Three Novels.* New York: Knopf, 1941. A fine noir portrait of the pains and humiliations of upward mobility, L.A.-style. In *Mildred Pierce,* Cain's heroine (immediately memorable from Joan Crawford's definitive portrayal in the 1945 film) manipulates her way up the ladder of Los Angeles society, finally to find the emptiness beyond the last rung. The other two novels are *The Postman Always Rings Twice* and *Double Indemnity.*

Chandler, Raymond. *Farewell, My Lovely.* New York: Vintage Books, 1976. You can take your pick of Chandler's other Philip Marlowe novels: *The Big Sleep* (1939), *The High Window* (1942), *The Little Sister* (1949), and *The Long Goodbye* (1953) for some of the best writing on Los Angeles in any genre. Chandler's dark, elegant style fits perfectly the shadow side of sunny L.A..

Didion, Joan. *Play It as It Lays.* New York: Farrar, Straus & Giroux, 1970. It reads almost like a parody of itself now, taking world-weariness much too seriously, but back then it was a revelation: a smart portrait of Angelenos, with a wit as dry as a brushfire in the Hollywood Hills.

Ellis, Bret Easton. *Less Than Zero.* New York: Simon and Schuster, 1985. A glib foray through the world of L.A.'s disaffected youth, zombified by too many drugs, too much sex, too much choice.

Fante, John. *Dreams from Bunker Hill.* Santa Barbara: Black Sparrow Press, 1982. A visceral portrait of ethnic L.A. as seen through the eyes of Arturo Bandini, Fante's alter ego, and a man struggling to become a writer in 1930s L.A. The author's *Ask the Dust* covers some of the same territory.

Fitzgerald, F. Scott. *The Last Tycoon.* New York: Charles Scribner's Sons, 1940. Line-for-line some of most perfect writing America has ever produced. Even in its unfinished state—perhaps *because* of its unfinished state—one of the best books about ever-evolving Hollywood. Fitzgerald tells us the thinly disguised story of Irving Thalberg, boy genius of MGM. Along the way, he gets at the best, and the worst, of the town some say killed him.

Hansen, Joseph. *Death Claims.* New York: Harper and Row, 1973. Follow gay insurance claims investigator Dave Brandstetter on his rounds. In this and other Brandstetter books (*Fade Out, Gravedigger, Skinflick*), Hansen makes expert use of the broad L.A. canvas.

Huxley, Aldous. *After Many a Summer Dies the Swan.* London: Chatto and Windus, 1939. Huxley focuses his refined, expatriate sensibilities on the subject of Southern California and finds it severely wanting in aesthetic honesty. With *Citizen Kane*, this is one of two great works of art based on the life of William Randolph Hearst, and proof once again that Los Angeles is an ironist's playground of the first order.

(following pages) "The year you win the Oscar is the fastest year in a Hollywood actor's life. Twelve months later, they ask, 'Who won the Oscar last year?'" —*Cliff Robertson*

Lambert, Gavin. *The Slide Area.* New York: Viking Press, 1959. A brittle account of Venice, California, in the days when it was turning into a counter-cultural free-fire zone. Beatniks and beach bunnies share the same turf, with uneasy results.

Leonard, Elmore. *Get Shorty.* New York: Delacourte Press, 1990. The dean of contemporary crime fiction spins a tale of Tinseltown, about a Miami loan shark who finds that his sensibility meshes perfectly with Hollywood's. One of the best punchline titles ever.

Lurie, Alison. *The Nowhere City.* New York: Coward-McGann, 1965. Why are the best contemporary writers on Los Angeles all women? Lurie joins Didion at the top of the heap, with Eve Babitz (see below), Paula Fox's *The Western Coast* (1972), Cynthia Buchanan's *Maiden* (1970), and Carolyn See's *Mother, Daughter* (1977), indicating that there may be some kind of trend here.

MacDonald, Ross. *The Moving Target.* New York: Knopf, 1967. MacDonald's Lew Archer is a classic hardboiled private eye, and he is put through his paces here by a lineup of the city's most entertaining criminals. *The Way Some People Die* and *The Barbarous Coast* are two more of his many L.A.-based tales.

Rayner, Richard. *Los Angeles Without a Map.* New York: Weidenfeld & Nicholson, 1988. He doesn't drive. That's what makes L.A. different for Rayner's English protagonist, who comes to live out his Hollywood fantasies and winds up weirding out on the city itself.

Santiago, Danny. *Famous All Over Town.* New York: New American Library, 1983. Is it live or is it Memorex? This book became problematic when it was revealed its author was a writing student not intimately connected with the *barrio.* But it still packs a wallop.

Schulberg, Budd. *What Makes Sammy Run?* Garden City, New York: Sun Dial Press, 1941. A title character as craven and manipulative as any in the Hollywood canon—or in the Hollywood boardroom. Grasping, clawing and empty, Sammy Glick scrabbles his way to the top. Schulberg, born and bred in the bosom of Hollywood (Paramount producer Ben Schulberg was his father), turns the snake back upon itself.

Sinclair, Upton. *Oil!* Cambridge, Massachusetts: R. Bentley, 1980 (reprint of 1927 edition). Little-remembered is the fact that the muckracker Sinclair ran for governor of California and almost won, but his socialist politics were too threatening to the powers-that-be. This book is him at his vintage best, beginning in the Signal Hill oil fields of Long Beach and spiraling out to include the scandals of the Teapot Dome.

Vasquez, Richard. *Chicano.* Garden City, New York: Doubleday, 1970. A brilliant but uneven picture of the East L.A. *barrio,* with a tortured hero who matches steps with the author. Good for its pictures of nascent L.A. street gangs, who came of age during the seventies.

Waugh, Evelyn. *The Loved One.* Boston: Little, Brown, 1948. Another argument for the idea you must be an outsider—preferably a brilliantly acerbic Englishman—to really see Los Angeles. Waugh does Forest Lawn, pet cemeteries, and the whole Southern California cult of death in a perfectly turned—and curiously life-affirming—way.

Wambaugh, Joseph. *The New Centurions.* Boston: Little, Brown, 1970. L.A. cops, and a good portrait of the community they come out of, as well as the East L.A. streets they patrol. Written by a long-time veteran of the LAPD's Hollenbeck Division.

West, Nathanael. *The Day of the Locust.* New York: New Directions, 1962. Some would argue this is the prototypic Hollywood book, but it's not really about the movies. West takes as his subject the human detritus left behind in the big whoosh of movie hoopla—unemployed actors, failed starlets, aging hucksters, alienated extras—who form a raw army in this terrifying vision of the L.A. apocalypse.

■ MOVIETOWN, USA

Anger, Kenneth. *Hollywood Babylon.* San Francisco: Straight Arrow Books, 1975. This and its sequel are the bibles of the underbelly of Hollywood. Anger, a former child actor, knows where all the bodies are buried, and he digs up the kind of deliciously salacious gossip that never makes it to the august columns of the

Los Angeles Times. "If you don't have anything nice to say, come sit next to me," as it were.

Behlmer, Rudy. *Behind the Scenes.* Hollywood: Samuel French, 1989. From *The Maltese Falcon* to *Frankenstein, Lost Horizon* to *Stagecoach,* this book gives you the inside dope, the memos, the setbacks, the triumphs-against-all-odds of some of the best movies of all time.

Brownlow, Kevin. *Hollywood: The Pioneers.* New York: Knopf, 1979. The early days, De Mille, Griffith, Ince, and the rest. Brownlow is the pre-eminent film historian on the early silent era, and this is the textbook on the early Hollywood. See his trilogy: *The Parade's Gone By* (1969), *The War, the West and the Wilderness* (1978), and *Behind the Mask of Innocence* for a complete guide to the pre-talkie days.

Carey, Gary. *All the Stars in Heaven.* New York: E.P. Dutton, 1981. The story of MGM, the Cadillac of studios, with a never-equalled collection of hits and stars. The classic account of the classic studio of Hollywood's Golden Age.

Friedrich, Otto. *City of Nets: A Portrait of Hollywood in the 1940s.* New York: Harper and Row, 1986. A year-by-year treatment of one of the most important times for Hollywood and for filmmaking. Friedrich wisely begins in that watershed year of 1939, when the town was filled with European expatriates like Bertolt Brecht and Arnold Schoenberg, who was very nearly harnessed for soundtrack work. A trenchant, superbly readable book, one of the best ever written on Hollywood.

Gabler, Neil. *An Empire of Their Own: How the Jews Invented Hollywood.* New York: Crown Publishers, 1988. An important sociological treatise masquerading as lively, approachable popular history. Gabler (of PBS's *Sneak Previews*) justifies his faintly unsavory subtitle with hard analysis, well-researched insights, and superb portraits of the great studio moguls of the Golden Age—all of them Jewish.

Goldman, William. *Adventures in the Screen Trade.* New York: Warner Books, 1985. The screenwriter of such hits as *Butch Cassidy and the Sundance Kid* and *All the President's Men* presents a writer's eye-view of Hollywood, warts and all.

Marching band warms up at the Hollywood Christmas Parade (top). "To Protect and to Serve"—cadets at the real Police Academy.

Hadley-Garcia, George. *Hispanic Hollywood: The Latins in Motion Pictures.* New York: Citadel Press, 1990. An illustrated overview of the lengthy, troubled, rewarding alliance between L. A.'s most celebrated industry and its largest ethnic group. From the silents through Rita Hayworth up to today's stars, Hadley-Garcia is even-handed about the down side and the up side of Hispanics in Hollywood.

Kanin, Garson. *Hollywood: Stars and Starlets, Tycoons and Flesh-Peddlers, Moviemakers and Moneymakers, Frauds and Geniuses, Hopefuls and Has-Beens, Great Lovers and Sex Symbols.* New York: Bantam Books, 1976. With a subtitle like that, how can you resist?

Phillips, Julia. *You'll Never Eat Lunch in this Town Again.* New York: Random House, 1991. Hollywood tell-all by one-time hot-shot producer.

Powdermaker, Hortense. *Hollywood: The Dream Factory.* Boston: Little, Brown, 1950. A classic study by an anthropologist, which reads a bit breathy today, but is adept at placing moviemaking in a larger social context.

Salamon, Julie, *The Devil's Candy.* Boston: Houghton Mifflin Company, 1991. The making of an H-bomb, in which the "H" stands for Hollywood. Salamon was allowed total access to Brian de Palma's *Bonfire of the Vanities,* and her portrait of the Dream Machine at work is worthwhile even though the movie turned into a nightmare.

Skolsky, Sidney. *Don't Get me Wrong—I Love Hollywood.* New York: Putnam, 1975. Skolsky was a troll-like man who hid under the bridge—or on a stool at Schwab's—and recorded the comings and going of the Tinseltown elite. As gossip columnist, Skolsky pioneered a style of celebrity reportage that went beyond the press release and into the bars and boudoirs.

Schatz, Thomas. *The Genius of the System: Hollywood Filmmaking in the Studio Era.* New York: Pantheon Books, 1988. A brilliant survey on what made Hollywood work during the Golden Age of movies. Schatz gets into the guts of the studios, reprinting memos, unearthing organizational structures, sketching out the in-house social apparatus.

Stein, Ben. *Hollywood Days, Hollywood Nights.* New York: Bantam Books, 1988. A little sleeper of a journal that is one of the best books ever written about the frame of mind that is Hollywood. Stein is a former Nixon speechwriter, but don't hold that against him—he's also a screenwriter, an actor, an idea man, a master of the elegiac feelings of middle age.

■ HISTORY

Blumenthal, John. *Hollywood High: The History of America's Most Famous Public School.* New York: Ballantine Books, 1988. A sort of microcosmic look at Los Angeles through the alma mater of some its most celebrated native sons and daughters.

Caughey, John and LaRess, eds. *Los Angeles: Biography of a City.* Berkeley: U.C. Press, 1976. A good, sturdy selection of essays about the history of L.A., taken from a wide range of writers.

Dash, Norman. *Yesterday's Los Angeles.* Miami: E.A. Seamann Publishers, 1976. A survey of pre-boom L.A. that places you in the hands of a fine historian for a leisurely, interesting tour. What's astounding is how little the issues of the past differ from the issues of today.

Heizer, Robert F. and Albert B. Elsasser. *The Natural World of the California Indians.* Berkeley: U.C. Press, 1980. Locates the state's aboriginal people—including the original inhabitants of Los Angeles—within the context of their environment. Good on the brief tragic history of their demise, also.

Henstell, Bruce. *Los Angeles.* New York: Knopf, 1980. There are almost as many books in print on the history of the Los Angeles Dodgers (20) as there are about Los Angeles itself (26), an indication as to how seriously the city takes its past. This lively and lavishly illustrated book is one of the best.

Hart, James D. *A Companion to California.* Berkeley: U.C. Press, 1987. An encyclopedic reference work, with short, pithy entries and an all-embracing approach to the state's history, events, and personages.

Longstreet, Stephen. *All-Star Cast: An Anecdotal History of the City of Los Angeles.* New York: Crowell, 1977. Lively but limited, this book thinks nothing of leaving out whole gobbets of the city's past. What's there is quite entertaining and informative, however.

McWilliams, Carey. *Southern California Country: An Island Upon the Land.* New York: Duell, Sloan & Pierce, 1946. Written as description, it remains the best history of pre-war Los Angeles, a vital document in understanding the whole area. What McWilliams does best is place things in context: L.A.'s cult-mentality within the context of the town's booster-engineered reputation for health, the city's rootlessness in the context of wide-ranging migrations from the rest of the U.S. and other countries. Fifty years on, this book still informs much that is written about Los Angeles.

Nadeau, Remi. *City-Makers.* Garden City, New York: Doubleday, 1948. Here it is, the inside story of how a loose cabal of promoters, boosters, and downright crooks created the modern metropolis of Los Angeles. A sobering account of origins, detailing the seeds of problems still germinating today.

Starr, Kevin. *Inventing the Dream.* New York: Oxford University Press, 1985. This book, along with Starr's other masterworks, *Americans and the California Dream* (1973) and *Material Dreams* (1990), are among the finest cultural histories anywhere, and they just happen to take California and Los Angeles as their

Young hopefuls in Hollywood High drama class.

subjects. Starr has a learned, discursive, wildly intelligent grasp of his subject. *Americans* focuses in on San Francisco and the north, while the other two paint a fine, incisive picture of L.A..

Weaver, John D. *Los Angeles: The Enormous Village.* Santa Barbara: Capra Press, 1981. A thesis-based book which dissects the enormity of L.A. in bite-sized chunks. Weaver is a recognized expert who was selected to write the *Encyclopedia Britannica*'s section on the city.

■ TRAVEL BOOKS AND GUIDES

Babitz, Eve. *Eve's Hollywood.* New York: Delacourte Press, 1989. With *L.A. Woman* and *Slow Days, Fast Company* is part of a fast, snappy informal trilogy on Los Angeles. Sometimes Babitz is too smart for her own good, but then, goodness has nothing to do with it.

Banham, Reyner. *Los Angeles: The Architecture of Four Ecologies.* New York: Harper and Row, 1971. An outsider's cerebral analysis of the city as divided into four spheres: mountains, plains, beaches, and freeways.

Baudrillard, Jean. *America.* New York: Verso, 1987. A lot of hyperextended writing on L.A. by the terminally trendy philosopher-king of post-structuralism. Flashes of insight alternate with tremendous gusts of flatulence.

Begoun, Paula and Deborah Brada. *The Best Places to Kiss in Southern California: A Romantic Travel Guide.* Seattle: Beginning Press, 1990. A little too cutesy for its own good (the ratings are lipstick marks), but worthwhile nonetheless—the authors have found a whole array of secluded coves, candle-lit restaurants, etc.

The California Coastal Commission. *California Coastal Access Guide.* Berkeley: U.C. Press, 1991. Your key to the sea. Replete with maps, lists of entry points, facts and statistics.

Cameron, Robert. *Above Los Angeles.* San Francisco: Cameron, 1976. One of the only ways to truly understand Los Angeles is from the air, and Cameron gives us an amazing collection of photographic documents by which to do so. Best thing about the book is the older photos, which indicate the explosive growth of the region.

Culbertson, Judi, and Tom Randall. *Permanent Californians: An Illustrated Guide to the Cemeteries of California.* Chelsea, Vermont: Chelsea Green, 1989. Just what it sounds like, and a handy reference to a lot of people who really *aren't* going anywhere.

Davis, Mike. *City of Quartz: Excavating the Future in Los Angeles.* New York: Verso, 1990. The city as a deconstructionist adventure waiting to happen. Davis's smoothly cerebral, mild-mannered Marxist approach to L.A. makes him one of the most-mentioned, though perhaps least-read, authors writing about the city.

Gagnon, Dennis. *Hike Los Angeles.* Santa Cruz, California: Western Tanager Press, 1985. In the middle of Los Angeles, the Santa Monica Mountains furnish some superb hiking opportunities, some of it through surprisingly untrammeled territory. This book and its sequel volume give you access to what some would say is a contradiction: L.A. on foot.

Gebhard, David and Robert Winter. *Architecture in Los Angeles.* Santa Barbara: Peregrine Smith, 1977. This at times spotty but generally incisive handbook will do as the starting point for an investigation of the city's marvelously diverse architecture.

Gill, Brendan. *The Dream Come True: Great Houses of Los Angeles.* New York: Lippincott & Crowell, 1980. A leisurely tour by one of the elegant masters, a man most often associated with the skyline of New York, but here doing serviceable work as a docent of L.A..

Immler, Robert. *Mountain Bicycling Around Los Angeles.* Berkeley: Wilderness Press, 1991. If you want to get deep into the outback but can't bear to give up the thought of wheels, mountain biking is the newest craze for you. This book clues you into how and where.

Morino, Marianne. *The Hollywood Walk of Fame.* Berkeley: Ten Speed Press, 1987. A gushy, fan's tribute to the Hollywood Chamber of Commerce and its work preserving the Hollywood landmark. The meat of the book is a complete listing, complete with short bios, of every star (up to 1986) enshrined in the walk.

Pearlestone, Zena. *Ethnic L.A.* Beverly Hills: Hillcrest Press, 1990. A worthwhile guide to the dizzying mosaic of modern L.A. Although this book will not tell you where the nearest Thai restaurant is, it will clue you in on L.A.'s vast and variegated ethnic neighborhoods, from the *barrios* of East L.A. to the English enclaves of Pacific Palisades.

Riegert, Ray. *Hidden Southern California.* Berkeley: Ulysses Press, 1990. Does not quite deliver on its promise, but a bountiful offering anyway. Particularly good on the outlaying regions, for day-hikes, short automobile jaunts, excursions into the desert.

Roberts, Brian and Richard Schwadel. *L.A. Shortcuts: The Guidebook for Drivers Who Hate to Wait.* Los Angeles: Red Car Press, 1989. Required equipment for the rigors of the road—but is there really any way around L.A.'s asphalt Sargasso? These boys do their best, although some of their shortcuts are really long-cuts. Would you rather drive extra miles and be moving, or sit and stew in traffic? This book lets you decide.

Shindler, Merrill and Karen Berk, eds. *Zagat Los Angeles and Southern California Restaurant Survey.* New York: Zagat Survey, 1992. Questionnaires collected from foodies result in an uneven but always interesting compendium of opinion on L.A. eating places.

(following pages) "You can make a case for hating it. Or loving it. L.A. is not something you have to have an opinion about, you know." —Steve Martin

YESTERDAY
THEY WERE BUSINESSMEN.
TODAY THEY'RE COWBOYS.
TOMORROW
THEY'LL BE WALKING FUNNY.
CITY SLICKERS
BRINGING IN THE HERD JUNE 7.
NOW PLAYING
Chateau
FOR SALE
(213) 851-6666
JOSEPH D'AMORE

I N D E X

PHOTO BY JONATHAN E. PITE

■ ABOUT THE AUTHOR

GIL REAVILL IS A JOURNALIST, screenwriter, playwright and novelist. His screenplay *The Fingerman*, written with director Sandy Smolan, was recently optioned for a feature film, as was his crime novel, *Shang*. He has had five plays produced, including *Oneida/ . . . coming into awareness* (1986) and *The Autobiography of Enola Gay* (1987). He currently divides his time between Los Angeles and New York with his wife Jean and his daughter Maud.

PHOTO BY STEVE CRISE

■ ABOUT THE PHOTOGRAPHER

MARK WEXLER'S FASCINATION WITH unusual sub-cultures has taken him on assignments from Siberia to sub-Saharan Africa to Hollywood. Mark grew up in Los Angeles and later attended U.C. Santa Cruz, where studies in cultural anthropology sparked an interest in photojournalism. His photographs have appeared in *Time, Life, National Geographic, Geo, The New York Times* and the *Los Angeles Times*, as well as in seven of the *A Day in the Life of . . .* books. His work has been recognized with three World Press Awards, and has been exhibited at the International Center for Photography.